More Praise for
Empowering Your Sober Self

"We badly need more roads to recovery. Nicolaus' book details one such road: positive, empathetic, down to earth – and a great read."
— Lonny Shavelson MD, author, *Hooked*

"Offers a sensible and doable discipline for anyone serious about getting free of drugs and alcohol, regardless of personal beliefs."
— Doug Althauser MEd., LCDC-II, MAC, CRC, author,
You Can Free Yourself From Alcohol & Drugs

"I could not put it down. The book is engaging, touching, and at the same time quite informative – a must read for the addict and non-addict alike."
— Asma Asyyed MD, Berkeley, California

"An excellent tool for recovery, particularly for those put off by the concepts of 'powerlessness' and 'higher power.'"
— Ralph Cantor, coordinator of Drug Prevention
at the Alameda County Office of Education, Hayward, California

"The book chronicles the emergence of LifeRing – a promising alternative to AA but without powerlessness, insanity, the supernatural, and other elements of AA that have deterred millions from participating in self-help groups. . . . Masterfully done."
— William Cloud PhD, MSW, professor, Graduate School of Social Work,
University of Denver, Colorado

"In a field where most treatment is driven by myth, politics, and ideological dogma, Nicolaus' book is a breath of fresh air. It is well written, contemporary, research based and client centered; it will without a doubt help people find recovery who would otherwise become lost."
— Dr. B. J. Davis, clinical director, Strategies for Change,
Sacramento, California

"Using the best thinking and best science, *Empowering Your Sober Self* examines what works and what doesn't, and provides new hope and new solutions for anyone who craves a sober life, but can't make a go of it in the 12-step world. The book is well-written to boot, full of smart prose, great good humor, sparkling analogies, and fascinating nuggets of history and science."
— Matt Dean, LifeRing convenor, Charleston, South Carolina

"'Reducing the addict self by itself has no effect unless the sober self grows and fills the gap.' Martin Nicolaus' new book, a compilation of stories and principles to assist recovery, fills the gap for those who wish to avoid 12-step programs and the mythos of disempowerment."
— David A. Kaiser PhD, editor, *Journal of Neurotherapy*

"Provides a compelling analysis of the philosophy of LifeRing and how it compares to Alcoholics Anonymous. Readers will learn a great deal about the implications of the disease concept of alcoholism (to the alcohol industry, to coverage for treatment, and to the social stigma of addiction), of powerlessness (versus a healthy respect for addiction), and of the genetics of addiction."
— Lee Ann Kaskutas PhD, senior scientist, Alcohol Research Group, Emeryville, California

"Reinforces the view that the brain's reward systems are usurped by drug addiction and is a strong argument for linking mechanisms of recovery with the concept that addiction is a disease of the brain."
— George F. Koob Ph.D., The Scripps Research Institute, La Jolla, California

"An excellent, well-written work, appropriate for all audiences — treatment providers, clients, as well as the general public. Its uniqueness consists in the fact that it presents an alternative to many other treatment approaches to substance abuse. Especially valuable is its explication of the non-religious, neutral approach which is so sorely lacking in the field of substance abuse treatment, research, and prevention. An excellent and interesting read.
— John Langrod Ph.D., ACSW, APA Chair, Governing Board, South Bronx Mental Health Council, Inc. Bronx, New York

"Many people in recovery who are searching for an alternative to the disease model of addiction and the 12-Step program will find the LifeRing approach to be an interesting path to follow."
— G. Alan Marlatt PhD., Director, Addictive Behaviors Research Center, University of Washington, Seattle

"Finally an author who understands that an individual's success in recovery starts with the option of choice. There is no wrong way to sobriety, just one that is wrong for me."
— Garry Mehlhorn, Ontario, Canada (sober 3 years)

"Introduces a new, rational approach to addiction recovery, grounded in secularity, and informed by modern science. The LifeRing program mobilizes the power of caring and connection to liberate the sober self that lives inside everyone who struggles with addiction."
— Tom Moon MFT; columnist, *San Francisco Bay Times*

EMPOWERING
Your SOBER Self

The LifeRing Approach
To Addiction Recovery

Second Edition

Martin Nicolaus

Foreword by
William L. White

LifeRing Press
www.lifering.com

Library of Congress Cataloging-in-Publication Data

Nicolaus, Martin, date

      Empowering your sober self: the LifeRing approach to addiction recovery / Martin Nicolaus – 2nd ed.

p. cm.

Includes bibliographical references and index.

ISBN 978-0-9659429-6-6 (pbk.)

1. Addicts - Rehabilitation 2. Self-help techniques 3. Substance abuse - treatment I. Title

HV4998.N53 2014

616.86-dc22

SECOND EDITION

PB Printing 10 9 8 7 6 5 4

To Fred and Jack

CONTENTS

FOREWORD

There are many pathways to and many styles of addiction recovery. That proposition is a central finding of modern addiction science and a foundational premise of the new addiction recovery advocacy movement. Yet these pathways and styles have not been fully mapped out; their existence and diversity have not been broadly communicated to service professionals and the American public.

The 12-step program of Alcoholics Anonymous (AA) is the best known of such recovery frameworks due to its historical longevity, membership size, widespread accessibility, and influence on American models of addiction treatment, as well as to its adaptation to address a multitude of other human problems. AA's dominance as a spiritual framework of recovery has been challenged in recent decades by an ever-growing menu of both secular and explicitly religious support groups, all of which differ significantly from AA in their organizational structures, philosophies, meeting rituals, and recovery support tools.

The growing variety of recovery experience in America underscores the need for people concerned about alcohol and other drug problems to become serious students of these divergent recovery strategies. More specifically, it suggests the need for addiction treatment programs and allied helping institutions to forge formal linkages with these new recovery support groups and for professional helpers to become intimately familiar with the operation of such groups. All recovery support groups have individuals who optimally respond, partially respond, and fail to respond to the group's particular approach to recovery initiation and maintenance. Optimal responses could be increased through better matches between individuals and particular support groups. This would require greater professional and public knowledge of recovery support alternatives and encouragement of a philosophy of choice related to recovery pathways. Acquiring such knowledge and adopting such a philosophy have been limited in part by the sparseness of professional and lay literature on alternatives to AA. Martin Nicolaus has added to this needed literature with the publication of *Empowering Your Sober Self: The LifeRing Approach to Addiction Recovery*.

Nicolaus offers us a clear window into the basic approach of LifeRing Secular Recovery, one of the major secular alternatives to AA. LifeRing was founded in the San Francisco Bay Area in 1999 and became a national organization at a founding conference in Florida in 2001. LifeRing hosts face-to-face recovery support meetings. It also has e-mail lists for member-to-member communication, online support and information (*www.lifering.org*), chat rooms, an Internet forum (bulletin board), an online social network (*lifering.ning.com*), LifeRing social events, and the annual LifeRing Congress.

In *Empowering Your Sober Self*, Nicolaus has created an engaging text for individuals seeking recovery and for service professionals wanting a greater understanding of LifeRing's core ideas and recovery support strategies. *Empowering Your Sober Self* includes the voices of many LifeRing members, whose personal stories illustrate key points in the book.

The discussions in this book include some of the more controversial issues in the addictions field. Nicolaus outlines positions on these issues clearly and forcefully and in ways that help distinguish LifeRing Secular Recovery from 12-step programs. This book is intended to inform rather than to convert. Not everyone will agree with the ideas and approaches set forth here, but for the past decade, individuals and families have used LifeRing Secular Recovery as an effective framework to initiate and maintain long-term recovery from life-impairing addictions. Those recoveries are cause for celebration, and this book details how they did it. Those seeking a solution to alcohol and other drug problems and professionals assisting people with such problems will find great value in these pages.

William L. White
Author, *Slaying the Dragon: The History of Addiction Treatment and Recovery in America*

ACKNOWLEDGEMENTS

"Dad, you're a drunkard, aren't you?" These words from the lips of a ten-year-old boy started the chain of events in my life that resulted in – among other things – this book. All other debts that I need to acknowledge pale beside that one. When the poet wrote, "The child is father to the man," he meant something else, but the words hold truth and power in this instance as well.

Love also means forbearance. To my wife, Sheila Jordan, I owe thanks not only for her forbearance from alcohol – a small gift, because she never liked it anyway – but also for her much greater forbearance from tasking me with many of the duties of a partner and housemate during the writing of this book. I am grateful to her for her unfailing encouragement and support.

A work of advocacy such as this is a composite of a multitude of voices. What I have done is to listen to hundreds of people on countless occasions, to reflect on what I heard, and to try to formulate those scattered expressions in a concentrated, systematic form and with enough clarity so that I will be understood by those who taught me. To name all of those who, in thousands of LifeRing sessions, face-to-face and online, contributed ideas for this book is more than anyone could do. Among the LifeRing conversations that shine most brightly in my memory are those with Al R., Alicia B., Andrée G., Andy R., Annalisa S., Bettye D., Bill C., Bill S., Carola Z., Chet G., Craig O., Craig W., Dan V., David F., Deanna H., Dru B., Geoff G., Gillian E., Jacquie J., Jay C., Jim R., John B., John D., Karen I., Kathleen G., Laura L., Linda L., Lisa E., Lorraine R., Lou Anthony G., Marjorie J., Mark C., Mark L., Marylou B., Michael W., Mona H., Nanita B., Owen P., Patty V., Paula B., Richard H., Robbin L., Syl S., Robert B., Shauna W., and Tom S. Apart from a few personal paragraphs in the introduction, there is very little in the book that is original with me. I am mainly channeling a movement.

It is a movement, however, that seeks to walk on the paths of science. Therefore, I have held the received ideas of the recovery subculture against the evidentiary yardstick of research whenever possible. I have important debts to acknowledge to individuals whose scientific credentials are greater than mine. Sarah Zemore Ph.D. and Lee Kaskutas Ph.D., both of the Alcohol Research Group in Emeryville California, shared their expertise with me, took time to discuss my concerns, and opened the facility's excellent library to me. Lorraine Midanik Ph.D., Dean of the School of Social Work at the University of California at Berkeley, took time to meet with me to discuss the public health perspective. Antonello Bonci Ph.D., of the Ernest Gallo Clinic and Research Center in Emeryville, met with me at his laboratory to discuss his cutting-edge work on the long-term effect of single doses of addictive substances on the brain. Howard L. Fields M.D., Ph.D., also of the Gallo Center, was kind enough to answer my questions via e-mail. Ulrike Heberlein Ph.D., of the Gallo Center and the University of San Francisco, showed me around her laboratory and explained her research on alcohol addiction in fruit flies. George Koob Ph.D., of the Scripps Research Institute in San

Diego, took time to answer my questions, steer me toward key literature, and discuss my concerns by telephone. Marc Schuckit M.D., at the Veterans Administration in San Diego, probably the leading researcher in the genetics of alcoholism in humans, took time out from his sabbatical to respond to my questions via e-mail. Ron Roizen Ph.D., formerly of the Alcohol Research Group in Berkeley, California, was kind enough to discuss my concerns and share his extensive knowledge of the literature with me via e-mail. B. J. Davis Psy.D., of Strategies for Change in Sacramento, shared his research and insights with me and offered encouragement. The historian and mentor to thousands of treatment professionals, William L. White M.A., is present in these pages not only through my numerous citations to his work but also through his personal encouragement and his shining embodiment of the ideal of the scholar-advocate. The historian Ernest Kurtz Ph.D. (*Not-God*) has been helpful and supportive of the LifeRing effort from the beginning, and I am grateful for that. Professors Reid Hester and William R. Miller's *Handbook of Alcoholism Treatment Approaches: Effective Alternatives* is a path-breaking work that has powerfully influenced my thinking, and I share their desire to see Motivational Interviewing and other evidence-based treatment modalities made available as an option throughout the chemical dependency treatment industry.

Special acknowledgement as contributing authors is due to the following, who provided short personal testimonials of their experience with LifeRing. They are Alceon, Berin H., Bettye D., Cathy K., Craig W., Dan H., Dan K., David F., Dru B., Gail C., Gal, Gillian E., Ginger S., J. Jones, James G., Jim R., Jo R., John B., John D., Kat, Lee H., Mark H., Mary B., Michael W., Robert B., Sam H., Sharon B., Shauna W., Shawn B., Trish M., and Troy B. I regret that due to editorial constraints, not all of their contributions appear in print in this edition.

Alan Rinzler, the legendary editor, is the godfather of this book. For reasons that are in his province to explain, he approached me to get this book written. He then mercilessly slashed and flamed my creation until it was good. I thank him for both prongs of his effort.

LifeRing is famously nonauthoritarian. The only writing that represents the official position of LifeRing is its Bylaws, including the LifeRing meeting charter, which sets out the Three "S" philosophy – Sobriety, Secularity, Self-Help – in a few words. Everything else, including this book, is the personal opinion of its author.

Martin Nicolaus
Berkeley, California
February 2009

PREFACE
TO THE SECOND EDITION

The text of this second edition corrects several typographical errors. The worst of these was the inexcusable misspelling of the last name of Jean Kirkpatrick, founder of Women for Sobriety. Neither I nor the publisher's otherwise eagle-eyed copy editor caught the mistake in time. It is rectified here, with apologies.

A new Supplement for this edition touches on several recent publications that deal with the addiction rehab industry and with research developments in genetics.

The recent publications underline and reinforce the message of Chapter 6 that addiction rehab is ripe for thoroughgoing reform.

Already in 2009, decades of belief in the existence of an "alcoholism gene" had been severely shaken. In its place stood guarded generalities about multiple genes and gene-environment interactions, as I point out in Chapter 7. Since then, a series of genome-wide association studies has all but pulverized the "alcoholism gene" theory. Scientists can now say with confidence that there is no significant difference between the DNA of alcoholics and non-alcoholics. The Supplement provides details and references.

I want to express my deep appreciation to Lesley Iura of Jossey-Bass, the publisher of the first edition, and to Jennifer Peters of its parent company John Wiley & Sons, for their gracious agreement to revert the rights to the book after the publisher's print run was exhausted. It seems entirely appropriate that this book, which is dedicated to the LifeRing network, should from now on be published by LifeRing Press.

This new edition also updates references to the LifeRing web site; it is now *www.lifering.org*. There are also some changes in layout and typography, and there is a new Index.

A gratifying number of people have told me that the first edition has been a force for good in their lives. There is no greater reward for an author than this.

Martin Nicolaus
Berkeley, California
October 2014

EMPOWERING
Your SOBER Self

INTRODUCTION

Most alcoholics and addicts lead two lives. In their public lives, they have jobs, homes, friends, families, or not, like anyone else. But in their private, often secret, lives, they are alcoholics and addicts.

If you knew who they were, you might be surprised. Alcoholics and addicts are active at all levels of the economy, the political order, the military, as well as the educational, religious, and cultural establishments. Chances are that among the people you know, there are alcoholics and drug addicts, and you have no idea.

The alcoholics and addicts that you can easily identify are only the tip of the iceberg. For every down-and-outer in the gutter, there are ten more who walk briskly, dress well, pay the mortgage, meet the payroll, and coach the soccer team. I know. I was one of them.

Most alcoholics and addicts keep their second lives secret. Then, inevitably, at some point the facade of their normalcy normality falls away, and they turn into different people. Everything they valued in normal life – job, home, friends, family members – no longer matters. All that drives them now is the drink, the drug. They become as if possessed by demons. They may lapse into paralysis, or they may do unspeakable acts. Then they pass out, and come to again as normal people, ready once again to walk in the world as if nothing had happened.

Managing these two opposite lives takes skill and effort. Early on, there may be romance in it – the thrills of the cat burglar, the con man, the high high-wire artist. Over time, it becomes tedious and boring work. It may become torture. Eventually, depending on circumstances, the balancing act breaks down. The pillars of normality crumble. The person tumbles down the stairway of losses and abandonments. There is great danger then. Every study of recovery tells us that the chances of survival depend on reaching people while they still have something left to lose. By the time they land in the gutter, only a miracle can save them.

In this book, I want to share with you an approach that saved me and is saving many others who are torn between these two lives. It is an approach that makes use of resources and powers that you already have. It will show you the power for good within yourself, not from an external or supernatural higher power. It suggests ways of connecting with other people that you will quickly be able to do.

It is an approach that will not shame you or blame you, force a label on you, or require you to declare yourself diseased. It is a wholly positive approach that makes use of the most effective psychological methods known for bringing about deep emotional and behavioral change. It can work for you regardless of your religious beliefs or lack of them. You will always be in charge of the changes you make. It will help you recover your life, or find a new life of your choosing, before your situation becomes unmanageable.

Its name is LifeRing.

But before I tell you details about the LifeRing approach, let me tell you how I got here.

My Story

In the summer before my eighteenth birthday, my mother, who had raised me as a single parent, took me aside and told me, "You're going to be a man soon. You need to drink and smoke."

This was in Wisconsin in 1959. She started me on diluted Scotch whiskey, the kind with a couple of dogs on the label. I gagged and ran to the kitchen sink. Wine was a little easier to get down, but I hated the way it made my head spin. My mother smoked Pall Malls, and I lit one up. I retched and had to lie down. Becoming a man was more of an ordeal than I had thought.

If I had listened to the messages my body was sending me, loud and clear, I would have quit right there. But I couldn't turn my back on manhood. I persevered. Before I went away to college in the fall, I could get modest amounts of alcohol and tobacco into my system without obvious distress.

On the campus of Wesleyan University at that time, most students lived in fraternity houses after their freshman year. The houses competed for incoming freshmen the way the British Navy recruited sailors: by getting them drunk. The frats set out kegs of beer, jugs of wine, and every kind of hard liquor that could be bought in the State of Connecticut. It was all free.

I dived right in. If drinking a little bit made me a man, drinking a huge amount would make me a superman, right? Before the evening was very far advanced, superman was crawling on hands and knees back to his dormitory. In the morning, I woke up covered in my own vomit. It's a lucky thing I didn't inhale some of it and choke to death, as many other drinkers have. I'd shower and wash the bedding, and get ready to do it again. Before very long, I acquired tolerance.

I discovered that I could drink a lot and still talk and walk. Wasn't I a man, now?

I also discovered, uneasily, that I couldn't put down and walk away from half a glass of anything alcoholic. Well, I could, I told myself, but why would I want to?

Professor Coopersmith, who taught freshman psychology, did a unit on deviance, including alcoholism. I discovered that the college library had a complete set of scholarly journals on alcoholism, published by an institute at nearby Yale. I sat down and leafed through the whole musty set, reading whatever struck my eye, and picked up various bits of information. It never occurred to me to reflect on why I was so interested in this topic.

Although the campus was swimming in alcohol, there was no alcohol counseling or prevention effort of any kind. The doctor and nurses in the campus infirmary never inquired about my drinking, or anyone else's, to my knowledge. I saw no pamphlets or handouts about the issue. Alcohol-free, drug-free, and smoke-free college housing was still thirty years in the future.

Experimenters in laboratories routinely convert healthy rats into alcoholic rats or drug addict rats for research into addictive behavior. It's done by dripping alcohol or another addictive drug into their systems via IV, or by keeping them in a vapor chamber where the air is saturated with the substance. Fraternity rush was like one of those laboratories, and we freshmen were the rats.

I became a binge drinker. I drank nothing during the week, but on weekends and other special party days I would get drunk. Sometimes party days came strung together like boxcars in a freight train. Nevertheless, I did well in school. I graduated with honors, Phi Beta Kappa, and a Woodrow Wilson fellowship to graduate school at Brandeis University.

After I completed a master's in sociology at Brandeis, I moved to Vancouver B.C., working on a Ph.D. and lecturing in sociology at Simon Fraser University just outside the city. *Sgt. Pepper's Lonely Hearts Club Band* came out that summer. Outwardly, things were good. I was popular. My lectures and seminars were full. People were friendly. There were interesting battles, wonderful colleagues. But inwardly I felt like a refugee, stranded and alone. I needed to belong to something.

Smoking marijuana looked like the ticket to belonging to the subculture. I applied myself energetically to qualifying. There were periods when I smoked on waking, between lectures, at lunch, in the afternoon, and into the night. Some friends and I bought marijuana by the kilo and spent hours dividing it up and cleaning it. I scattered the seeds in the National Forest. We played the Beatles and Dylan, the Doors and the Airplane and Leonard Cohen, until the needle wore out.

In 1969, I said good-bye to academic life, packed my belongings into my VW bug and headed south to San Francisco. I had a contract to translate a nine hundred–page manuscript, Karl Marx's *Grundrisse*, from German to English.

After a time, I met someone. When we were dating, getting serious, and I proposed to move in together, she said, "I'd love to, but I couldn't live with a cigarette smoker. You have a choice to make." I enrolled in a stop-smoking class of the American Lung Association in Oakland. It worked for me. I'll always be grateful. Quitting that nasty, filthy, deadly addiction was a great liberation. I can still see the brown water running off the windows and woodwork when I sponged them down.

We got married and had a son. I entered Boalt Hall School of Law in Berkeley, graduated, and passed the California Bar. Another son arrived. I had a busy law practice. I coached and refereed youth soccer.

I tapered off the marijuana on my own. There was nobody left to smoke with. It made me paranoid. As a lawyer, I had too much to lose if I got caught. It was next to impossible to hide the smoke from the kids. I concentrated harder on drinking instead. I was now drinking almost every night to the point of passing out.

When he was eighteen months, as I was tucking him in after sneaking a toke, my son said, "Daddy, are you funny?"

He didn't know the right word but he could tell I was in an altered state.

I Get the Wake-Up Call

One day – it might have been after the evening I hit on one of her girlfriends during a blackout – my wife took me aside and asked, tentatively, whether I'd considered the possibility that I might be an alcoholic.

My defensive shields snapped into position instantly. Oh, no! Alcoholics lie in the gutter and piss on themselves. Alcoholics get drunk in bars. Alcoholics don't have law practices and wives and children and don't run marathons and ride centuries. You're trying to set me up for a divorce settlement. Blah, blah, blah. After that talk, I switched to wine or beer in most of my weeknight drunks. Now I had to drink more to get to the same place.

Another day, my wife showed me a newspaper ad offering 10 percent off if you bought bottles by the case: "Why don't you buy a case?" I made no reply. In my mind, I answered, "Because if I bought a case, I would drink it all and kill myself." My next thought was, "She knows that."

Each morning, I would look at myself in the mirror and talk to myself. "You don't look so hot. Your eyes are baggy. Your skin is dry and puffy. Your gut is out of control. You don't feel good. You're going downhill. You isolated again last night. You hid from your wife. You hid from your kids. You don't have any friends. What happened to the dreams you had for your life? Do you even remember your dreams, asshole? If this keeps up, there's going to be a funeral soon, yours, and there won't be a lot of people crying. You need to stop drinking. It's a monkey on your back. A ball and chain. Get free of it!"

Braced, I would launch into my busy day, get the kids breakfast, drive them to school, go to the office, and step into the roles of Buttoned-Down Lawyer, Go to Guy, Computer Whiz, Valued Colleague, Managing Associate, Pit Bull Litigator, Wise Counselor, Soccer Coach, and the rest.

At the end of the day, I would head home filled with good intentions. But there was something wrong with my car. I'd be driving past the Jay-Vee Liquors or the Safeway and some remote power would take control and turn the wheel into the parking lot. Wires from a spaceship seized my limbs and paraded me like a puppet into the market. I'd check out with some bread, eggs, milk, or other groceries and-oh, yes, almost forgot!-a supply of alcohol.

At home, I'd lift the eggs, bread, or milk like stage props out of the paper bag and put them away with broad public gestures, as if on camera. I'd unobtrusively elbow the bag with the alcohol remaining in it off to the side until no one was looking.

Getting started drinking each night was a performance. The kids must not suspect. First, Dad was a Hardworking Tired Lawyer, who deserved a glass or two to unwind. Then, Dad was a Gourmet Cook, who carefully selected an appropriate alcoholic beverage or two or three to go with the dinner. Then, Dad became a Jolly Fellow who tossed back a few quick ones to warm up for reading the kids their bedtime stories. Good night, darlings! Then the real drinking began and continued until I passed out.

Next morning, same monologue in front of the mirror. Same day. Same night. Wash, rinse, repeat. Whoever said alcoholism serves the pleasure instinct hasn't been there. I've had boring assembly line jobs. Boring clerical jobs. I've lived in boring towns, read boring books, seen boring movies, taken boring classes, been in boring relationships. Nothing in my experience has come even close to the Boredom Quotient of addiction to alcohol.

But, as Heraclitus said, you never step into the same river twice. I was stuck in my deadly cycle. But my kids were growing up and staying up longer. Seeing more. Seeing more of Dad later at night.

One Saturday afternoon, my elder boy, then ten, came into the living room holding a chapter book they were reading in middle school. *The Great Horned Spoon*, it was; about the California gold rush days. One chapter features a brawl in a saloon. With the air of a boy looking for help with homework, wanting a vocabulary word explained, he spoke to me:

"Dad, you're a 'drunkard,' aren't you?"

I had no shields for that word, coming from him. The missile went straight into my heart. I was blowing the Daddy act.

I grew up without a dad. My father, Fritz Nicolaus, was a young pastor in the Protestant church in Germany in the 1930s. Germany did not have separation of church and state. The government bankrolled the two major churches. Taxpayers could check a box on their return to dedicate their money either to the Protestants or the Catholics. When the Nazis took over the government, they had an easy job taking control of the churches. Priests and pastors had to put a portrait of Der Führer on the altar, lead the congregation in prayer for victory in war, denounce the Jews, and so on, or they'd lose their jobs.

A section of the Protestant church rebelled. Pastor Martin Niemöller was the spiritual leader of this movement, which took the name *Bekennende Kirche* (loosely, authentic church). They had to meet clandestinely in restaurants, warehouses, basements, and private homes. They listened to BBC and put out leaflets. My father and his friends were almost caught one time transferring a mimeograph machine from one hideout to another. They set up an underground railroad to smuggle Jews across the borders. My mother was part of it. She had met my father while both were studying with the liberal theologian Karl Barth in Basel, Switzerland. Years later, some of the people who escaped helped my mother when we arrived in the United States.

My father never made it here. In 1940, the SS arrested and held him for months without charges. He was let go without explanation on Christmas Day, but a month later he was drafted into the Wehrmacht. As a pastor, he was given a choice: serve as a chaplain for Hitler, with a chance at an easy assignment in France, or serve as infantry on the Eastern Front. The Eastern Front was tantamount to a death sentence. In July, 1941, my mother received the dreaded telegram that announced his death somewhere in Russia. I was born in September.

Lots of good people have grown up without fathers. But I wanted my kids to have it better. Now I was blowing it. I pondered whether a kid who has a drunkard for a dad is worse off than a kid who has no dad at all. Instead of making a better life for my kids than I had, maybe I was making it worse.

That brief conversation with my eldest boy left me changed inside, at least temporarily. The balance between the "me" that wanted to get free of drinking, and the "me" that wanted to die drunk, had tipped. Within a few days, while the impact of my son's one-child, one-word intervention still burned inside of me, I telephoned the Alcohol and Drug Abuse Program of the Kaiser Permanente HMO, to which the family belonged. It seemed like hours before someone answered the ring. My hands shaking, voice straining to sound casual, I made an appointment.

Beginning Treatment

Dr. Bryer, the medical director of the Kaiser program in Oakland, took me through the intake interview. He looked at the form I filled out, asked me a series of questions, and outlined the program. Among other things, he wanted to know, did I recognize any powers greater than myself?

"Yes. Of course. Gravity. The weather. Laws of nature. Earthquakes ..."

"OK, but what about more personal powers?"

"Definitely. The U.S. Army. General Motors. The IRS ..."

Was that an annoyed look on the doctor's face?

Drawing the session to a close, Dr. Bryer advised me that as part of the program, I would be required to attend support groups.

"What are support groups?" I asked.

"You'll see. Don't worry about it. Here are your choices."

He held up, in one hand, a booklet containing the schedule of local AA meetings, and in the other, a crumpled single sheet with the address of the local alternative meetings. In a few questions, I found out that the AA meetings revolved around a "higher power" or "God as you understand Him," whereas the alternative groups were secular.

"We don't care which ones you go to. Your choice. But do at least two a week."

I ran the choices through my mind. I was raised religious. My father was a pastor, and my mother studied theology, planning to enter the ministry. (The rise to power of the Nazis cut that off; they barred women from the ministry.) As a "rug rat" in our postwar apartment in Frankfurt (then West

Germany), my nose had bumped into the collected works of Luther, Calvin, Augustine, Thomas Aquinas, among others.

My mother and I went to church regularly and I got a child's grounding in the Bible and in Protestant doctrine. I remember at one time wanting to become a missionary. When we emigrated from Germany and moved to Brooklyn in 1953, I was confirmed in an Episcopalian church on Avenue M. My mother felt most comfortable in the mainstream Episcopalian church.

One summer, not long after arriving in the United States, I was sent to a religious summer camp run by a fundamentalist group. It was all my mother could afford. We spent endless hours playing Bible games. The group leader would read a passage and we would have to identify the chapter and verse, or vice versa. John 3:16 was often the right answer, so we guessed that one if we didn't know. Revival meetings where we were "saved" were staged nightly.

When my mother took a job in Kansas City, Kansas, I became an altar boy in the local Episcopalian church. I probably could still perform the ritual handling of the cruets of wine and water today. After the service, I saw the priest drink off the leftover communion wine, and thought nothing of it. My mother became involved in church activities. We got to know the church behind the scenes – not a good place to be if you intend to keep your religious faith. I began to see the church as a kind of business.

When I got my first pair of eyeglasses, I was amazed. Trees had been solid blobs of green on smooth stems of brown, like a child's drawing. Suddenly, I saw a complex, stirring mass of leaves and an intricate pattern of bark. The world became clearer and more complicated at the same time. Losing my religious faith as a high school student in Kansas was like that. I didn't have a crisis of conscience. There was no agony, no bitterness, no regrets. I just saw the world differently now. Nothing in my life since high school had changed my perspective.

So when Dr. Bryer gave me a choice of support groups, I went first to the secular one.

First Encounters

I entered my first meeting apprehensive but determined. I was motivated to make it work for me.

My motivation almost died in that initial meeting. The first person to speak began, "Hi, I'm Joe, I'm an alcoholic." My defensive shields snapped into position. I glanced around the room to see if anyone knew me. I didn't want my friends to see me associating with alcoholics. I knew that I had to stop drinking, but that was a very different thing than labeling myself an alcoholic. OK, maybe I was a drunkard, but not an alcoholic. It seemed like an important difference at the time.

I was puzzled when Joe-the-alcoholic said he hadn't touched alcohol for years. Why would he call himself an alcoholic?

It got weirder immediately.

The next person introduced herself, "I'm Jane, heroin addict." An electric shock went through me. I'd known heroin addicts, but I'd never known anyone who admitted out loud to being one. I fought the impulse to bolt. She looked really healthy, even photogenic. If this is what heroin addicts looked like, the thought crossed my mind, maybe I'd like to try it.

By the end of the meeting, I was still confused, but more at ease. I could handle this. These people weren't going to hurt me.

I went to my second meeting of the same group later that week. In the meetings, I met and liked other people who were enrolled in the Kaiser program. Gradually, I got accustomed to the strange jargon of some people who labeled themselves alcoholics and addicts when they hadn't touched a drop or picked up a needle in years. (Some used the label, others didn't.) We clustered together.

In our Kaiser treatment program sessions in those years, counselors used to ask everyone how many 12-step meetings they had attended during the past week. We would say, "None." The counselor would frown and begin to lecture us on the program requirements. Then we would add that we had been to two meetings of the secular group.

"Oh."

Our little informal caucus grew, and most of us stayed resolutely sober. Meanwhile patients who were attending 12-step groups were dropping like flies all around us. Today, the Kaiser counselors ask, "How many *outside support groups* have you attended this week?"

The path I was on was working for me. I kept going to the secular meetings. I never did go to an AA meeting, get a sponsor, or work the steps. As I write this, I'm fifteen years clean and sober.

In February 2001, two dozen sober activists met at a rustic Unitarian-Universalist retreat in Brooksville, Florida. We debated and adopted a set of bylaws, and constituted LifeRing as a national organization.

> We the members of LifeRing Secular Recovery, in order to establish a free-standing, democratic recovery support network based on abstinence, secularity, and self-help, adopt the following Bylaws.

Like the makers of the Declaration of Independence, we all signed the document.

The twenty-four of us at the Brooksville Congress on Feb. 17, 2001 are the founders of LifeRing. Some of us, including me, had been members of an earlier group, Secular Organizations for Sobriety. Others came from 12-step groups or were new. With our distinctly egalitarian philosophy, we would have preferred to have no leadership positions at all, but corporation law requires officers. I became the CEO.

Today those twenty-four have turned into thousands. We don't issue membership cards, and because of confidentiality we can only estimate our numbers, but we know from a sample of meeting sign-up sheets and meeting facilitator reports that we currently serve somewhere between five thousand and twelve thousand people a year in face-to-face meetings. We're spreading from our original base in Northern California into other states and other countries.

Many hundreds more visit our online chat rooms, forums, social network, and e-mail lists. Our main Web site, *www. lifering.org*, registered 38,852 unique visitors and more than 2,444,000 hits in the month of March 2007 alone. I hear more and more people saying that in the world of addiction recovery support groups, your basic options are 12-step and LifeRing.

The LifeRing Philosophy

Clearly, something about what we do is attractive to more and more people. Almost every day, we get calls or e-mails from people saying, "I'm so glad I found you." "Where were you when I tried to get sober ten years ago?" "This is so exactly what I was looking for." I'm going to spell out the LifeRing philosophy and practice in more detail in the later chapters of this book. Here is a thumbnail view for purposes of orientation. We subscribe to the Three "S" philosophy – Sobriety, Secularity, and Self-Help. Here's how it works:

1. Sobriety means that the purpose of participating in our process is to achieve and maintain complete abstinence from alcohol and "drugs." If that is also your objective, you can belong. Surveys of people who have decided to

break their dependence on alcohol show that more than 90 percent choose to abstain completely, as we do, rather than try to drink moderately or in controlled amounts.

2. Secularity means that you take responsibility for your recovery into your own human hands. Your belief or disbelief in a God or other higher power remains your private business and does not matter in LifeRing. Inside our meetings, much like in meetings of WeightWatchers®, religious as well as atheistic and agnostic discussion is off topic. As a matter of statistics, about 40 percent of our members (in a 2005 poll) attended church or another house of worship during the past year, which is about the national average.

3. Our third "S," self-help, means that LifeRing is a supportive environment for you to build the life recovery program that fits you and works for you – a personal recovery program (PRP). We do not have and do not want a standard, one-size-fits-all program that we "suggest" you and everyone else adopt.

Our position is in line with the best research on treatment effectiveness, which shows that the secret to success is matching the treatment to the individual. This also means that decisions such as whether to label yourself as alcoholic or addict, and decisions about whether to frame your condition as a disease or not, are up to you, and LifeRing takes no organizational position on them.

Our simple basic philosophy finds expression in our meeting format. At most LifeRing meetings, we sit in a circle facing one another. The meeting facilitator – we call them convenors – reads, or asks a volunteer to read, a very short opening statement, taking a minute or less. Then the convenor asks, "How was your week?" Each person narrates the highlights and heartaches of their the past week, and looks ahead to their next week.

After each person has given this personal news summary, the floor is open for questions and feedback from other participants. Then we move on to the next person. The atmosphere is relaxed and conversational. At the end of the meeting, we give ourselves and one another a round of applause for our efforts in sober living. There are variations on this format in different settings.

Some Similarities and Differences with 12-Step

If you are familiar with the recovery universe, you will know that the dominant force in this sphere for the past fifty years or more has been the 12-step approach of Alcoholics Anonymous (AA). The first "S" of the LifeRing philosophy – Sobriety – is the same as the approach of AA. Like AA, LifeRing firmly, exclusively, and unambiguously supports abstinence.

People whose objective is not to stop but to cut down on their drinking/using, to drink/use in moderation, or to drink/ use at a controlled level, will not find support in LifeRing, any more than in AA. They need to find other groups.

There are some subtle differences: LifeRing groups integrate people struggling with alcohol as well as with drugs other than alcohol, whereas AA refers individuals with drug issues other than alcohol out to separate drug-specific groups, such as Narcotics Anonymous, and Marijuana Anonymous.

LifeRing does not require but actively encourages smoking cessation, whereas AA is silent at best.[1]

We support people taking prescribed psycho-active medications, whereas the prevailing attitude in AA tends to oppose pharmacological tools.

Our great and fundamental agreement on abstinence is the reason why about a third of the people who participate in LifeRing also participate in 12-step organizations. It is also the reason why the philosophical and practical differences between LifeRing and AA on other issues never rise to the level of enmity. Although we may travel on widely divergent roads, we are on the same journey with the same objective.

On philosophical issues other than abstinence, however, we tend to see many things differently from AA and other 12-step groups.

We have different attitudes toward the etiology (causes) of addiction.

The notion that we are quite powerless over alcohol, fundamental to AA, resonates within LifeRing only as applied to the second drink. We do possess, or we can through effort develop, the power to abstain from the first.

Consequently, we do not join in the recommendation, urgently made in the 12 steps, to hang our recovery program on belief in a higher power, or "God as you understand Him." We believe that such a belief is not necessary for recovery and may even be counterproductive.

We also do not see good evidence to pin the cause of alcoholism on defects of character, as the 12 steps imply.

LifeRing also has a different vision of many issues that are not core doctrinal beliefs of AA, as the 12 steps are, but nevertheless have come to define the organization. There is more about these issues in later chapters.

The discussion of our differences with AA should never obscure the fact that the brave band of people who hang in with the 12-step organizations are our brothers and sisters in recovery. Something about what they do works for them. We would not wish their organization to go away or to fall down. All that we are asking is that people in recovery everywhere have a choice.

I was a very lucky patient. My case manager at Kaiser gave me a choice of recovery support group options from Day One of my recovery journey. What I advocate here is the replication of that model of choice.

The Majority of Recoveries Happen Outside AA

At least 60 percent of alcoholics who achieve successful recoveries – defined as five years or more of continuous abstinence – get there without using AA.[2] This finding is not just one man's opinion. It is based on a very extensive forty-year study conducted under the auspices of Harvard Medical School, and headed by George Vaillant M.D., a member of the AA Board of Trustees. It was republished in the *AA Grapevine*.

I quote Dr. Vaillant on this point because he cannot be accused of having an anti-AA bias; on the contrary, he is an AA insider and a vigorous advocate.

Other studies put the percentage of non-AA recoveries as higher. Deborah Dawson, then of the National Institute on Alcohol Abuse and Alcoholism, analyzed a broad population survey and found that approximately 75 percent of people who had at some point in their lives met the definition of *alcohol dependent* became free of symptoms of dependence or abuse without participating in treatment.[3]

Professors Robert Granfield and William Cloud of the University of Denver cite a series of studies in the United States and Canada showing that recovery without AA (or treatment) is at least as common as recovery with.[4] A recent large-scale sample study of alcoholics in Germany similarly concluded that the majority of recoveries occur without organized assistance.[5]

These findings are not news and they are not attacks on AA or on treatment. These findings have been reported in the addiction research literature for decades and are not seriously disputed. AA's own leadership is or was well aware of the approximate numbers. AA co-founder Bill Wilson already asked at AA's thirtieth anniversary in 1965: "What happened to the six hundred thousand who approached AA and left?"[6] He estimated that AA "reached less than 10 percent of those who might have been willing to approach us."[7]

The point of these findings is to give heart to the legions whom AA does not attract or who have tried AA and left. Seeking help by approaching AA can be a huge effort and a psychological milestone for many vulnerable, hesitant people early in recovery. Coming to see that AA is not the answer for them can be a demoralizing experience. It can discourage them from ever seeking organized help again. It can reinforce their addictive side and drive them toward relapse. This danger may be especially high if they have been told that AA is the only way.

One of the purposes of this book is to encourage people to persist in their struggle to free themselves from alcohol and other addictive substances regardless of their negative experiences with the 12-step approach. You *can* find freedom from alcohol outside AA. Independent sobrietists, those who succeed at freeing themselves from alcohol outside AA, are not an aberration or an exception. We are the majority.

Calling for Help on the Front Lines

Nobody knows the trouble with the 12-step approach better than front-line addiction counselors. Well over 70 percent of them are employed in treatment programs that use the 12-step approach. Because treatment is short and addiction recovery may be long, one of the counselor's prime directives in this type of program is to persuade the client to connect with 12-step support groups. Getting clients to buy in to step 1 (and sometimes steps 2 and 3) is the heart of the counselor's work in this type of institution.

My first glimpse of the problem from the counselor's side came one Christmas holiday season. I had just finished convening a LifeRing meeting at a 12-step treatment program and was putting the literature box away in the reception desk area. One of the staff counselors put his head on the table and sobbed, "I don't know why we even bother." He continued, "The 12 steps, the 12 traditions, the 12 promises, it just doesn't work. We promise them all this shit and it doesn't happen and they go out on us."

Chad D. Emrick, a researcher strongly sympathetic to AA, who surveyed the body of literature regarding its effectiveness, writes:

> We are as yet unable to predict with any certainty who will affiliate with AA and who will be helped by participation in the organization. Also, AA's relative effectiveness as treatment has not been demonstrated....Treatment providers are cautioned against insisting that all alcohol-troubled individuals become intensely involved with AA.[8]

Emrick's research found that only a small minority of alcohol-dependent individuals – perhaps 5 percent – become AA members.[9] This is consistent with the 95 percent walk-away rate from AA, documented later in this section.

Prof. Vaillant's own reviews of the studies, as well as his own research, led him to admit that "direct evidence for the efficacy of AA ... remains as elusive as ever."[10]

The *Substance Abuse Factbook*, prepared for the Robert Wood Johnson Foundation, concludes that accurate information about the efficacy of 12-step groups is "not available."[11]

A recent comprehensive review of studies about the effectiveness of AA and similar 12-step approaches, published in the authoritative *Cochrane Database of Systematic Reviews*, concluded that "the available experimental studies did not demonstrate the effectiveness of AA or other 12-step approaches in reducing alcohol use and achieving abstinence compared with other treatments."[12]

In other words, there was a scientific foundation for the emotional pain that the sobbing counselor felt. What research has shown over and over is that the 12-step approach works for some people, but the expectation that it's a magic pill and that everyone will benefit from it is bound to lead to professional frustration.

Voices from the Field

During the past year, I attended three conferences, where I met hundreds of addiction treatment professionals. Standing in front of the LifeRing table, I asked each person, "Do you have clients who are willing to give recovery a shot, but they tell you that 12-step is not their cup of tea?" Here is a small sample of what I heard:

- A counselor from a small Midwestern town said, "Twelve-step has too many walls." There is the "powerlessness wall," which is the biggest one, the "God wall," and a series of others. He said that the 12-step approach was "a hard sell" with his clients. He had had more than a hundred clients in his town and only three of them had formed a stable attachment with a 12-step group. "People need to find a group that fits who they are. The important thing is social support for recovery."

- A counselor from a federal prison in Arkansas said that her clients find God when they arrive, and leave him when they go.

- A counselor for an Army treatment center in Hawaii said she's been in the counseling profession long enough to know that 12-step doesn't work for everybody. They'll go, and they'll come back to her and say there must be another way.

- A counselor from Birmingham, Alabama, said "for sure" there are people who do want to do recovery but don't want to do it the 12-step way.

- A young counselor from Metro Public Health in Nashville said that patients who object to the 12-step approach are "very common" but the only alternatives available are church-affiliated.

- A counselor from Vermont said that the issue of clients wanting to do recovery but not 12-step "comes up a lot" in her practice.

- A counselor from a very small town in Iowa, when I asked her whether she had clients who said yes to recovery but no to 12-steps, replied, "Yes, most of them."

- A senior counselor from Helena, Montana, said he "absolutely" has clients who are interested in recovery but not in 12-step. He said, "We need something, we need something."

- A counselor from Seattle said, "I'm open to whatever works. As counselors, we can't just send people to AA or tell them not to use medications. 'Whatever works' is the motto."

- A physician from La Crosse, Wisconsin, said, "Anything that is an alternative to AA is useful and of interest." He has "tons of people" that won't do AA.

- A counselor from Jonesboro, Arkansas, said "AA has so many people court-ordered attending that it's been diluted. Nobody's serious about recovery in those meetings. The serious people don't go to AA anymore."

- A counselor from a university in New Jersey who is finishing her doctorate and has worked in substance abuse in the past – she is an older student – says "a lot" of her patients were deeply troubled by "the God thing" in AA and got no benefit from it.

- A clinician at a university health center in Sacramento, California, said that AA works for some people but turns a lot of other people away and an alternative is necessary.

- A counselor doing addictions counseling in Glendale, California, says she has clients that go in and out of 12-step inpatient programs – "Hello, something isn't working there."

- A counselor at a VA facility in Pittsburgh, Pennsylvania, said, "Being in combat cuts two ways. Some people get more religious. For other people, the whole religion thing drops away. They want nothing more to do with it." He said that when they send those veterans to 12-step groups, they just don't relate to it at all.

- A private practitioner from San Diego who has addiction clients said, "I have group members who go to AA or NA, and they come back to me and say it is not working for them. I want them to keep going and try something new."

- A psychologist from Manchester, New Hampshire, said that 12-step works for some people, but some people have to sink pretty low before they are willing to go there, and other people want to approach abstinence from a different perspective. "I've had a lot of clients that go to 12-step programs and the sponsors that are available may still have their own mental health issues that they are still working on, so it is not helpful for my clients and it turns them off prematurely."

- A psychologist and professor at a medical school in Miami, Florida, said, "We have a clinic in the middle of the ghetto. We have nine thousand patients. And the few who we can get to go to AA will come back to us and will say, 'Yeah, I gave it to God, and it didn't do anything,' and they'll get angry at us, 'Why did you send me to them, I thought you liked me.' And we're their primary care physician."

- A top administrator from a psychiatric hospital affiliated with the University of California said that she has a lot of substance abuse clients who don't benefit from the 12-step approach, or don't want to do it, and she hasn't known where to send them.

- A counselor from Warrensburg, Missouri, said that even in this small town she constantly runs into people wanting a secular alternative to AA.

- A Ph.D. from Raleigh, North Carolina, works with teenagers. Some of them did not relate to the 12-step programs at all.

- A counselor from Orofino, Idaho, leads a program with twelve clients and says quite a few of them have trouble with the 12-step approach, particularly the "higher power thing."

- A social worker from San Diego says she has people "all the time" who can't or won't do the 12 steps and are looking for alternatives.

- A counselor who retired from a position heading up drug addiction programs in Davenport, Iowa, said that without question there are a lot of people who do not get anything from the 12 steps and need an alternative.

Over and over, these treatment professionals spoke about the need for more options, choices, and alternatives, in order to serve their clients. Virtually all of these voices were 12-step practitioners, who work day after day to achieve client buy-in to the first step. Not a single counselor felt that the 12-step approach worked for all of their clients. The only differences were ones of degree.

AA Retains 5 Percent
of Those Who Approach It

The same problem is evident from the other side of the treatment relation: the population of clients or potential clients. In the course of this book, you will hear a number of individual voices describing their search for a meaningful support group and treatment approach, and walking away from their encounters with 12-step groups. Statistically, the walkaways hugely outnumber those who stay.

Over a period of nearly thirty years, AA's own triennial membership surveys show the pattern. A staunch partisan of AA, Don McIntire, analyzed AA's membership survey numbers in the *Alcoholism Treatment Quarterly*, and found that out of a hundred newcomers who attend their first AA meeting, only five are left at the end of a year.[13] See Figure 1, next page.

McIntyre cites the following:

- More than 80 percent of first-time attendees walk away within the first month.

- At the three-month mark, 90 percent have walked out; only 10 percent remain.

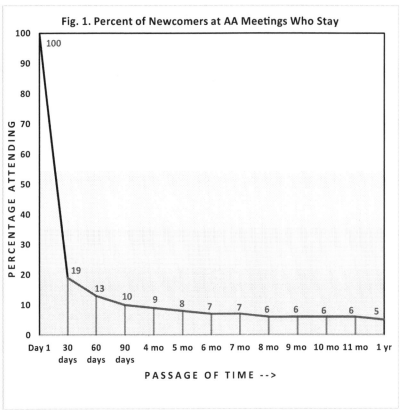

Fig. 1. Percent of Newcomers at AA Meetings Who Stay

Source: Adapted from Figure C-1 in Don McIntyre, "How Well Does A.A. Work? An Analysis of Published A.A. surveys (1968-1996) and Related Analyses/Comments," *Alcoholism Treatment Quarterly,* 18, no. 4, 2000.

- By the end of the year, half of that 10 percent are gone. Five percent are left.

Unfortunately, as McIntire concludes, "There seems to be no way in which the reasons for departure can be determined."[14] There is considerable speculation, but apparently no one has ever tried to follow the walkaways and ask them.

Similar numbers operate in the area of treatment. Because most addiction treatment in the United States is 12-step based, this should not be surprising. Every survey of the issue has concluded that the vast majority of people who meet diagnostic criteria for substance dependence do not seek out the existing treatment system.[15]

Mark Willenbring, the director of the Division of Treatment and Recovery Research at the National Institute on Alcohol Abuse and Alcoholism, wrote, "The treatment system we currently have ... was devised in 1975, when all we had for treatment was basically group counseling and AA." A primary problem with this system, says Willenbring, is that "most people don't want it; they have to be forced into it."[16]

In short, both on the professional side and on the client-patient side, there is a strongly felt need for additional choices. In a later chapter, I will explore some of the reasons for the mismatch between client and professional that leads to so much lost opportunity and so much frustration on both sides.

The LifeRing approach is one response to this frustration. Clients are demanding something more. Professionals are demanding something more. Maybe LifeRing is the answer for both sides.

My Client-Side Perspective

Most of the analytical literature on addiction is written from the professional perspective, as distinct from the client side. A notable exception is the "Big Book" of Alcoholics Anonymous, a work of client-side literature *par excellence*, whose first 164 analytical pages have achieved an enormous influence, including influence over professionals. The sole empirical basis of that work was the personal experience of its author after four years of sobriety, together with the experiences of some of the early members of the organization. Most of the modern client-side literature is autobiographical, anecdotal, or devotional.

Most of what I know to be true about addiction and recovery comes from what I have heard and seen in the course of my personal participation in more than fifteen hundred face-to-face LifeRing meetings, plus uncounted hours – perhaps five thousand hours or more – communicating with other LifeRing participants online. The lectures and readings to which I was exposed in my treatment program have also contributed. I have supplemented this knowledge base with active reading, not only of the recovery genre of literature, but also of technical scientific research in addiction, and readings in some related fields. These will be found in the References section.

At times, my voice in this book is strongly partisan on the side of the recovering person, particularly when I believe that specific attitudes and approaches used by certain professionals are counterproductive to the client's progress and wellbeing. On the whole, my experience with treatment professionals has been and continues to be a positive one. In the field of substance addiction treatment, perhaps more than in any other field, there is everything to be gained from an empathetic, collaborative relationship, and everything to be lost from confrontation and attack.

This book has some obvious implications for treatment, but it does not contain a treatment protocol, and is not meant to displace any of the treatment protocols currently in use or coming into use. The treatment professional will notice philosophical affinities with Motivational Interviewing, Solution-Focused Therapy, and other strength-based approaches. But the LifeRing approach is compatible with any abstinence-based professional treatment modality. The fundamental message for the professional here is one of general attitude toward the client, and has been well stated by William L. White:

> What [the professional is] responsible for is creating a milieu of opportunity, choice, and hope. What happens with that opportunity is up to the addict and his or her god. We can own neither the addiction nor the recovery, only the clarity of the presented choice, the best clinical

technology we can muster, and our faith in the potential for human rebirth.[17]

The main burden of this book is to show that a real basis for a collaborative relationship between professional and client exists, that the presentation of choices is an effective recovery strategy, and that faith in the potential for human rebirth has a solid foundation within the person suffering from substance addiction.

Notes

1. See http://newrecovery.blogspot.com/2007/09/why-some-alcoholics-find-it-hard-to.html, http://newrecovery.blogspot.com/2006/12/bar-owners-aa-club-unite-to-fight.html, http://newrecovery.blogspot.com/2006/10/aa-group-wants-exemption-from-smoking.html, http://newrecovery.blogspot.com/2006/09/settings-with-highest-smoking-rates.html.
2. George E. Vaillant, "Interview: A Doctor Speaks," AA Grapevine, May 2001.
3. Deborah A Dawson, "Correlates of Past-Year Status Among Treated and Untreated Persons with Former Alcohol Dependence: United States, 1992," Alcoholism: Clinical and Experimental Research 20, no. 4 (1996): 771-779.
4. Robert Granfield and William Cloud, Coming Clean: Overcoming Addiction Without Treatment (New York University Press, 1999), pp. 13 –15.
5. Gallus Bischof et al., "Stability of Subtypes of Natural Recovery from Alcohol Dependence After Two Years," Addiction (Abingdon, England) 102, no. 6 (June 2007): 904 – 908.
6. William White, Slaying the Dragon: The History of Addiction Treatment and Recovery in America (Chicago: Chestnut Health Systems, 1998), p. 139.
7. Bill Wilson, "What Happened to Those Who Left?" 1965, http://www.silkworth.net/aahistory/billw2/gsc1965.html.
8. Chad Emrick, "Alcoholics Anonymous: Emerging Concepts. Overview," in Marc Galanter, Recent Developments in Alcoholism: Treatment Research, vol. 7, (New York: Springer, 1989), p. 4.
9. Ibid., p. 8.
10. George E. Vaillant, The Natural History of Alcoholism Revisited (Harvard University Press, 1995), p. 265.
11. Constance Horgan, Substance Abuse: A Comprehensive Factbook (Princeton, N.J.: Robert Wood Johnson Foundation, 2001), p. 106.
12. M. Ferri, L. Amato, and M. Davoli, "Alcoholics Anonymous and Other 12-step Programmes for Alcohol Dependence," Cochrane Database of Systematic Reviews (Online) 2006, no. 3, doi:doi: 10.1002/14651858.

CD005032.pub2., http://www. mrw.interscience.wiley.com/cochrane/clsys-rev/articles/CD005032/frame.html.

13. Don McIntire, "How Well Does A.A. Work? An Analysis of Published A.A. surveys (1968 – 1996) and Related Analyses/Comments," Alcoholism Treatment Quarterly 18, no. 4 (2000): 1– 18.

14. Ibid., p. 17

15. Diana M. Doumas, Christine M. Blasey, and Cory L. Thacker, "Attrition from Alcohol and Drug Outpatient Treatment Psychological Distress and Interpersonal Problems as Indicators," Alcoholism Treatment Quarterly 23, no. 4 (June 9, 2005): 55 – 67; R. C. Kessler et al., "Lifetime and 12-Month Prevalence of DSM-III-R Psychiatric Disorders in the United States. Results from the National Comorbidity Survey," Archives of General Psychiatry 51, no. 1 (January 1994): 8 – 19.

16. Quoted in: Emily Singer, "Technology Review: More Effective Alcoholism Treatment," Technology Review Published by MIT, October 27, 2006, http://www.technologyreview.com/read_article.aspx?id=17669&ch=biotech.

17. White, Slaying the Dragon, p. 342.

▼

Chapter One

A PERSON ADDICTED
IS A PERSON IN CONFLICT

Every patient carries his or her own doctor inside.
— Albert Schweitzer

Alan strode toward the exit with his head down and his hands making fists in his pocket. It's all over now, he thought. As a front-line supervisor, he was responsible for his unit's performance, and his numbers had been lagging. Some of his best people were taking long weekends, coming in late and leaving early to make up for it. Today he had it out with Simon about his absenteeism. But instead of playing humble, Simon had thrown it back in Alan's face, and Alan had lost it. "But I was really sick, you asshole!" Alan had shouted. Simon had got a sarcastic grin on his face and left Alan's cubby. Later that day, Alan was called in to the front office. Lowell, the HR boss, read him the riot act about losing his temper at direct reports.

When I first met Alan, we were both in an outpatient program, and the shouting incident in his cubbyhole was only a few weeks behind him. His angry outburst had shocked him more than it shocked his subordinate. As he was driving home, stuck in traffic as usual, his head was a war zone.

Part of him said, "Fuck it! The hell with them! I'll find another job!" Another part said, "Like heck you will. Simon was right. You missed as much work as he has. And you weren't sick, you were drunk and hung over. And he knew it. They all know it."

Alan didn't sleep much that night. The next morning, he had made up his mind. Alan went back to Lowell, the HR boss, and asked for a referral to the Employee Assistance Program. He entered and completed outpatient treatment. Alan became a regular at LifeRing meetings. There, he met and married a sober woman.

Alan is now a vice-president of the company, with responsibility for two hundred employees. His name is in the papers from time to time when his firm launches a new development. His main job problem is whether to stay with the firm until retirement, or to take a tempting offer from a different company that has been recruiting him.

Yolanda looked up from her glass as the band stopped playing. She hoped they would play another slow one. Then she would have enough courage to get up and ask the guy at the far end of the bar to dance with her. Her eyes lingered over the table to her left. A young woman in a white blouse and a loose blue skirt was laughing and flirting with her male companion. A cocktail sat before her. Yolanda had been watching. The woman had hardly touched her drink. I used to be like that, Yolanda thought. Damn. I hate that bitch, she thought. She got up, unsteadily, found her feet, walked slowly to the bar for a refill, and turned toward the guy at the far end. But when he saw her, he got up and left.

I met Yolanda online in a LifeRing e-mail group. After that evening in the bar, something changed inside her. She felt something like a pinpoint of light amidst the gloom in her mind. That evening, she paced her studio apartment restlessly. She opened her closet. Her eyes came to rest on a battered black case with a handle, and on a pile of papers under it. Trembling, she took the case into her hands. Her flute. She hadn't played it in twelve drunken years. Her brain flooded with memories. She opened the case and assembled the instrument. She shuffled through the stack of sheet music and chose one.

Taking a deep breath, hesitantly, she began to play. She felt the pinpoint of light inside her growing brighter.

Today, Yolanda has eighteen years clean and sober. She plays flute in an amateur group that meets in one another's living rooms. She has a steady job. She's not serious about anybody, but she's at the center of several extensive networks of friends, face-to-face and online, all of whom come to her for advice and empathy. She counts herself a happy woman.

Sandy heard the sirens far, far away. The next thing he knew, the air on his face was cold and he was being bumped and shaken. Then the air got warm again. He opened his eyes a slit and saw neon lights moving from his head toward his feet. He felt suddenly heavier, then lighter. More neon lights. Then he was pushed into a bed and things got quiet. He slept. When he woke up, a nurse was asking him questions. She explained that he was in a safe place and would be staying here for about seventy-two hours. Sandy groaned. Oh, no, he thought. I got 51-50'd. Again.

I happened to be present, waiting to lead a LifeRing meeting, when Sandy was brought into the intensive care psychiatric lockup on a gurney. Sandy's face looked white, almost blue. He had tried to slash his boyfriend's face with a pizza cutter and then locked himself up in the bathroom and shot up with heroin. The boyfriend called 9-1-1.

A couple of weeks later, Sandy looked like a new man. He had good color, his face was animated, he made jokes and laughed. He radiated love for life. His doctor, who prescribed buprenorphine for Sandy's detox, also referred him to LifeRing. Today, Sandy has four years clean and sober. He belongs to a gay comedy group. He has a "normie" boyfriend, who does not drink or use drugs. He is a legal assistant at a law firm and is studying for a teaching certificate.

Alan, Yolanda, and Sandy are three of the hundreds of people I've met during my involvement with LifeRing. Not everyone I've met has been as successful as these three. I tell their stories here because they embody the great mystery of recovery. Every day, wherever people use addictive substances, a certain number of them turn around and stop.

At first, you see them enraged, stupefied, intoxicated, passed out, or otherwise in the grip of their addiction. They're isolated and alone, or they're at war with those around them.

At a later time, they are lively, intelligent, warm, sympathetic human beings leading sober, fulfilling lives. You see them in a recovery group or another social setting, laughing heartily at themselves and one another, enjoying the company, sober and having a good time. You might ask yourself the following questions:

- What happened to bring about this transformation?
- How is it possible that these are the same people?
- Where did these bright, warm, lively, sober folks come from?
- Where had they been hiding during their active addiction?
- How can we make this miracle happen more often?

That's the great mystery of recovery from chemical dependency.

The Divided Self

The person in the grip of dependency on an addictive substance is a person in conflict, with a personality that has split into two antagonistic camps.

There is the old, original person, the person that existed before addictive substances became a priority. And there is the more recent person, the addict, who lives in the person's mind and body like a parasite, sucking up more and more resources, and driving the person toward premature death.

The inner struggle between these two personalities inhabiting the same person is the central psychological reality of life as an addict. So typical is this inner split that "Dr. Jekyll and Mr. Hyde" is hands down the favorite modern metaphor for the condition.

In Robert Louis Stevenson's *The Strange Case of Dr. Jekyll and Mr. Hyde*, Hyde was the addict who committed unspeakable crimes while under the influence. Dr. Jekyll was the rational physician, a pillar of the community, always helping and doing good. The great hair-raising thrill of the story to this day is the audience's gradual dawning that they were in fact one and the same person.

In this chapter, I will show that this inner division is characteristic of addicted persons and that a number of leading authorities recognize it as such. In so doing, my intent is to show that the inner conflict within a person suffering from addiction, although it is often uncomfortable and even painful to the point of torture, actually carries great hope and is the basis for positive change.

The Divided Self Is a Clinical Reality

The addict's divided self is more than a literary metaphor. It is a clinical reality. A number of writers with long clinical experience and with the empathy of nonjudgmental observers have seen this conflict and characterized it as a defining experience of addiction.

The historian William L. White, whose book on the two hundred-year history of recovery from addictions in America has opened many eyes, and who is himself a veteran clinician and trainer of counselors, makes this profound generalization:

> Addicts simultaneously want – more than anything – both to maintain an uninterrupted relationship with their drug of choice and to break free of the drug. Behaviorally, this paradox is evidenced both in the incredible lengths to which the addict will go to sustain a relationship with the drug and in his or her repeated efforts to exert control over the drug and sever his or her relationship with it.[1]

The physician/journalist/photographer Lonny Shavelson, author of a portrait of five addicts in San Francisco (*Hooked*), expresses the same insight in fewer words:

> [T]he fierce power of an addict's obsession with drugs is matched, when the timing is right, by an equally vigorous drive to be free of them.[2]

The senior researcher Professor Edward Senay of the University of Chicago, speaking from decades of clinical experience, approaches the issue via a critique of the notion that addicts are always in denial and therefore blind to the downside of their situation. That may be true of some, he says, but he also says the following:

> The majority of substance abusers . . . are intensely ambivalent, which means that there is another psychological pole, separate from and opposite to denial, that is in delicate, frequently changing balance with denial and that is a pole of healthy striving.[3]

Professor George Vaillant of Harvard, a psychiatrist with a long experience in treating and studying alcoholics, says:

> Alcohol abuse must always create dissonance in the mind of the abuser; alcohol is both ambrosia and poison.[4]

Dr. George Koob of the Scripps Institute in San Diego, an eminent neurobiologist, writes that addictive substances set off an "opponent process" – part pleasurable, part antipleasurable.[5] In other words, there is a neurochemical foundation for the feeling of being torn that is at the core of addiction.

Recognition that the inner world of the addicted person is in conflict is also embedded in the *Diagnostic and Statistical Manual* (DSM-IV), the book that defines what symptoms psychiatrists and psychologists must find in order to make a diagnosis and submit a bill for insurance payment.

Among the DSM criteria for substance dependence is "a persistent desire or unsuccessful effort to cut down or control substance use" or the "knowledge of having a persistent or recurrent physical or psychological problem that is likely to have been caused or exacerbated by the substance."[6] In other words, a dependent person can be recognized not only by his use of substances but also by his recognition that the substances are causing his problems and by his desire to cut down or control his use. In other words, by inner conflict.

No wonder, then, that I get a strongly positive reaction whenever I speak to recovery audiences about my own Dr. Jekyll and Mr. Hyde experiences. I turn to my listeners and ask, "Am I the only weird one who has two people living in one head?" Nearly all the hands go up. "Me, too." "Yes, that's me exactly!" Inner conflict centered on using or not using the substances is a core psychological reality for everyone in the room.

Addictive Substances Hijack the Brain

In this book, I use the term *addictive substances* or just substances to refer to nicotine (the addictive ingredient in tobacco), ethanol or ethyl alcohol (the addictive ingredient in alcoholic drinks), cocaine (powder and crack), opiates (such as heroin, morphine, Vicodin®, Oxycontin®, and the like), methamphetamine and similar stimulants, THC (the addictive ingredient in marijuana), and a miscellany of other harmful habit-forming drugs, such as club drugs and benzodiaz-epines (tranquilizers). Whether caffeine should be included here is a matter of debate in the literature, and I leave the issue for another time.

Altogether, out of the millions of known chemical com-pounds, only this small handful of substances has the prop-erty of causing human beings to digress from whatever other pursuits they were following, including the quest for food, shelter, social esteem, and sex, and of engendering the pat-tern of repetitive use despite the negative consequence that is called *addiction*.[8] For this reason, these substances have been called *addictogenic* substances.[9]

Lumping the legal substances (ethanol, nicotine) together with the illegal may surprise some readers. Many of us are ac-customed to seeing the legal substances as less harmful than the illegal. The numbers tell just the opposite story. Each year in the United States, more than half a million people die as a result of putting the legal substances nicotine (four hundred thousand plus) and ethanol (one hundred thousand plus) into their bodies. The number of deaths attributable to all of the illegal substances combined is fewer than thirty thousand.[10]

Alcohol, in particular, tends to get put in a special mental category, separate from the other addictive substances. Phras-es such as *alcohol and drugs* rest on this artificial separation. There is no scientific basis for such a distinction. Ethanol (eth-yl alcohol) is the addictive ingredient in alcoholic beverages in the same way that nicotine is the addictive ingredient in ciga-rettes. As Dr. Avram Goldstein says quite rightly, alcohol is a dangerous addictive drug.[12] An alcoholic is simply a person who has become addicted to the addictive substance ethanol.

To understand how the repeated use of these substances drives a wedge into the human personality and splits it into two antagonistic personas, it's helpful to know some basic brain chemistry. Scientists discovered in the 1980s that the healthy brain contained its own built-in opiates, together with microscopic areas known as vesicles and receptors, which transmitted and received molecules of these native substances.[13] The discovery of endogenous equivalents to nicotine, cannabis, cocaine, methamphetamine, and other drugs followed.

Ethanol is special in one sense: it not only mimics the action of opiates and enters dedicated opioid receptors, it also bypasses receptors altogether and penetrates directly through the membranes of brain cells in numerous locations of the brain.[14] It is in that sense the dirtiest, most polluting among the addictive substances.[15]

Wherever they go, these external substances combine and interfere with chemistry that is already present in the normal brain. They travel along brain pathways that have evolved over millions of years and serve useful survival purposes. Despite their different immediate effects – uppers, downers, and sidewinders – the addictive drugs all appear to affect the level and distribution of the neurotransmitter dopamine, a versatile chemical workhorse that is found in many areas of the brain. Like oil in a mechanism, it facilitates a wide range of important functions, including learning, memory, movement, and emotion.[16]

It would be different if there were a specific "addiction gland" in the brain, not serving any other function but just sitting there waiting for addictive substances to come activate it. Suffering from addiction might then be something like having swollen tonsils or an infected appendix. If the surgeon's endoscope could reach the offending organ deep within the folds of the brain, the end of addiction would be just a snip away.[17]

But the biology and neuroscience of alcohol and drugs don't work like that. Because addictive substances seize on active mainstream brain circuits that do a great deal of necessary and useful work, their entry into the brain is often compared with a hijacking. The normal operation of the brain is en route to *x*. Along comes the outside drug and redirects it to *y*.

Thanks to modern chemistry, the outside drug is much more powerful than the internal equivalent. Eating food, for example, increases brain dopamine levels by 45 percent. A dose of methamphetamine or cocaine registers at 500 percent.[18] When the outside drug dissipates, the inside drugs have to try to pick up the pieces and resume their normal course. The conflict between the priorities of the brain's natural chemistry and those of the external chemicals is one dimension of the psychic split arising from substance use.

The Impact on Our Lives

Addictive substances also have a way of splitting personal priorities, schedules, and other resources. A graduate student phoned me from a Western state last week. He was supposedly working on a Ph.D., he said, but he was actually spending a lot of time drinking.

I know a young father who was trying to be a good dad to his daughters, but he was spending their new-shoes money on drugs.

A mother was trying to help her youngster with asthma but having a hard time quitting smoking.

An athlete dreamed of a career as a professional race car driver, but his marijuana habit got in the way of serious training.

Practically every substance user has a similar "but" story to tell. Using substances, after all, takes time and money and energy away from other priorities.

Some people fool themselves with the argument that the substance use fits in with or advances their other goals. Creative types are especially liable to buy into this dodge. But this illusion breaks down over the long run, as harmful consequences pile up. Eventually, the contradiction between the dream and the drug flashes in neon.

The split between the person's positive self and substance-using self is so characteristic that one effective school of counseling – Motivational Interviewing – trains its practitioners to look for it and help the client see it and articulate it, as a way of bootstrapping recovery.[19]

"A" (Addicted Self) Versus "S" (Sober Self)

If you are trying to clarify who is who and what is what in the inner landscape of a substance-using person, perhaps you yourself, you may encounter frustrations in reading the expert literature. If you read deeply enough, you will find that the mavens in the field disagree about basic issues of definition.[20]

Should we call it *addiction* or *dependence*? Are either of them basically different from *abuse*, or is it a matter of degrees? Is there really such a thing as *alcoholism*, and if so, is there one kind of alcoholism or several? Are tolerance and withdrawal essential to defining addiction or not? Is addiction even a scientific term? What do we really mean by *craving*? Is it or are they *diseases* or something else, and if so, what? What do we really mean when we say *recovery*? And so on.

The disjointed definition of substance dependence in the DSM-IV, where any three hits on a laundry list of seven criteria make the diagnosis, is symptomatic of the underlying discord in the field about basic concepts. This is a definition-by-committee, and it is still evolving.[21]

A Radical Simplification

To move past this pit of definitional and political quicksand, so that we can get on with the project of change, I propose that you and I adopt a radical simplification.

Everything that speaks for, promotes, or defends the use of addictive substances, I will call "A" for *Addicted Self.*

Everything that speaks for, promotes, or defends living life free of addictive substances, I will call "S" for *Sober Self.*

Do you hear an inner voice that suggests a cocktail? That obviously comes from your "A." What about the voice that suggests a bike ride in the hills? That probably comes from your "S," unless your drug connection happens to live on your usual hillside bike route, in which case the idea probably came from your "A." You can eavesdrop on your inner message traffic and with a little practice learn to distinguish the voices of the "A" and the "S" on an ongoing basis.[22] You can spot the "A" and the "S" messages in movies and all around the culture. You can survey your friends and acquaintances and group them into mainly-A or mainly-S types. The A-and-S metaphor is a general tool for making sense of the inner and outer world of addiction.

Feel free to use any other abbreviations that make sense to you. For example, if you feel comfortable with the disease concept of addiction, you might substitute "D" for disease in place of the A, and "I" for immune system in place of the S. If other concepts and abbreviations work better for you, go for it.

Similarly, if the Jekyll v Hyde or Sober Self v Addict Self metaphor veers too closely to schizophrenia or multiple personality disorder for your comfort, then by all means substitute a less-threatening metaphor, such as perhaps Jiminy Cricket on one shoulder and Foulfellow the Fox on the other, as in the movie *Pinocchio* (which is, however, plenty scary to small children).

My point is not to propose a new nomenclature or to insist on an anthropomorphic metaphor but rather to create a functional basis for thinking about and working productively with the inner conflict that arises from addictive substances. Any labels and any metaphors that help you understand, accept, and work with these contradictory inner drives are fine. The essence is not in the label, but in the contradiction.

In Conflict Lies Hope

Inner conflict is no fun. Ambivalence is like standing on the fulcrum of a teeter-totter, constantly fighting for and losing balance. Some people react to the stress by using even more substances –"hair of the dog." No wonder that many feel powerfully seduced by the promise of a conflict-free mental state – enlightenment, serenity, satori, nirvana, or the ultimate great quiet, death.

Yet, without this pain, there is no gain. Imagine a substance-using person whose inner experience is entirely like the rational, sober Dr. Jekyll. This person is highly successful in school, career, and social life. The pattern of substance using is present, but it makes no negative impact on the person's consciousness. This person is not conflicted. There is no psychic discomfort. So long as that remains the case, the person is not going to change.

Now imagine the opposite: a person whose psychic reality is entirely that of the drug-demented Mr. Hyde. This person has no career or social life other than in pursuit of the substance. There is no tug to realize any higher goals in life. No ambivalence, dissonance, or pain related to substance use. This person revels in the substance, identifies with it completely. This person is not going to change. This person is going to die.

Our brains seem to be hardwired to favor simple, one-sided beliefs.[23] Perhaps this explains why both outsiders and insiders to the reality of substance use have so much difficulty wrapping their minds around the painful yin-yang that defines the condition. Users themselves tend to flip-flop between two irreconcilable absolutes:

"I don't have a problem. I can quit any time I want to."

But "I can't help myself. I'm powerless to change."

Both are phrased in absolute terms, and both are wrong. The oft-quoted metaphor that the addicted person's self-image is a "baby at the center of the universe" expresses the same abstract dualism. You're either an absolutely helpless baby, or you're the power that rules the world.

Outsiders have the same trouble. Much of the time, outsiders are blind to substance use. They see the tightly wound, competent performer and never guess at the flipside of substance dependence. Then, when they do come face-to-face with addiction, they flip into seeing only the addiction and nothing else. "The addict" becomes a comic-book monster, a chemically determined robot with but a single focus – the destruction of self and everyone within range.

It took decades before scientists understood that electricity has both a negative and a positive pole and that you cannot make any practical sense of it before you grasp this inner opposition. It took even longer to decide whether light is a wave or a particle and to realize that it is both.[24] Part of my purpose in writing this book about LifeRing is to nudge the understanding of addiction away from one-sided flip-flop stereotypes and toward the recognition and embrace of the inner conflict that substance use creates in the self.

Absolutist approaches are neither true nor useful in bringing about change. If we don't see the power of the addiction in ourselves or in others, nothing will change. If we don't see the power to get free of the addiction, nothing can change. Absolutist approaches look at the phenomenon with one eye shut. To see it in its three-dimensional reality, we have to open both eyes and see both the A and the S inside the addicted person at the same time. So long as there is this inner conflict, there is hope.

The great virtue of understanding the addicted person as a person in conflict is to recognize that the force Dr. Senay called "the pole of healthy striving" is always in there, so long as the person is alive.

As Albert Schweitzer said, "Every patient carries his or her own doctor inside." The S inside the addicted person is that physician.

Archimedes said, "Give me a place to stand on, and I can move the earth." The S inside the addicted person is that place to stand.

This chapter has focused on learning to recognize that the use of addictive substances tends to split a person's "self" into two antagonistic camps. For simplicity's sake, I've labeled these as the "S" or sober self, and the "A" for addict self.

If you have been using the substances long enough and heavily enough for them to have had an impact on your life and on your sense of who you are, you will find yourself pulled in these two different directions. You will have not only two selves but also two lives in which these selves play the leading roles.

If you have this experience, you are not alone. A divided self is a natural consequence of using addictive substances in our society, or in any society, and this phenomenon has biochemical as well as psychological causes. Leading clinical scholars have seen this dualism and described its main features. It is recognized in the official diagnostic manual.

Most approaches to the person who suffers from addiction see mainly (or only) the A and launch one or another therapeutic attack on it from outside. In later chapters, I will show why those approaches are often counterproductive. The Life-Ring approach, while keeping the A in clear focus, operates instead by lending support to the person's inner S. Instead of hammering on the A, LifeRing pumps up the S. The S then does the job of taking the A down to size.

In the next chapters, I will suggest some methods for reinforcing the addicted person's own inner recovery powers. First, we'll discuss some ways to boost one's confidence for making the decision to put addictive substances aside. Then we'll talk about how the LifeRing meeting process works to empower the sober self.

Notes

1. William L. White, Slaying the Dragon (Chicago: Chestnut Health Systems/ Lighthouse Institute, 1998), p. 335.
2. Lonny Shavelson, Hooked: Five Addicts Challenge Our Misguided Drug Rehab System (New York: New Press, 2001), p. 36.
3. Edward C. Senay, "Diagnostic Interview and Mental Status Examination," in Joyce H. Lowinson (ed.), Substance Abuse: A Comprehensive Textbook, 3rd ed. (Philadelphia: Lippincott, 1997), p. 364.
4. George E. Vaillant, The Natural History of Alcoholism Revisited, p. 298.
5. George Koob and Michel Le Moal, Neurobiology of Addiction (Orlando: Academic Press, 2006), Ch. 1.
6. American Psychiatric Association, American Psychiatric Association. Diagnostic and Statistical Manual of Mental Disorders, 4th ed. (Washington, D.C.: American Psychiatric Press, 1994).
7. A good introduction is in Avram Goldstein, Addiction: From Biology to Drug Policy, 2nd ed. (New York: Oxford University Press, 2001), Ch. 13.
8. Eliot Gardner, "Brain-Reward Mechanisms," in Joyce H. Lowinson (ed.), Substance Abuse: A Comprehensive Textbook, 3rd ed. (Philadelphia: Lippincott, 1997).
9. For example: Y. Khazaal, E. Frésard, and D. Zullino, "[Exposure to Addictogenic Substances, Conditioned Response and Treatment of the Exposure

with Response Prevention]," L'Encéphale 33, no. 3, pt 1: 346-351, doi: MDOI-ENC-6-2007-33-3-0013-7006-101019-200730038.

10. Horgan, Substance Abuse: A Comprehensive Factbook.

11. Robin Room, "Sociology and the Disease Concept of Alcoholism," in Research Advances in Alcohol and Drug Problems, vol. 7 (New York and London: Plenum Press, 1983), pp. 47-91, http://www.robinroom.net/sociolog.pdf.

12. Goldstein, Addiction: From Biology to Drug Policy, pp. 4, 319. The supposedly exceptional character of alcohol among the addictive drugs – the only one whose addictive properties are believed to lie in the man rather than in the substances – is a relatively recent historical belief, cultivated by the alcohol industry. See, for example, R. Roizen, "The American Discovery of Alcoholism, 1933-1939," (Doctoral dissertation, sociology, University of California, Berkeley, 1991), Ch. 1, http://www.roizen.com/ron/dissch8.htm.

13. For a fascinating account of these discoveries, see Candace B. Pert, Molecules of Emotion: The Science Behind Mind-Body Medicine, 1st ed. (New York: Simon & Schuster, 1999).

14. Traute Flatscher-Bader, et al., "Alcohol-Responsive Genes in the Frontal Cortex and Nucleus Accumbens of Human Alcoholics," Journal of Neurochemistry 93, no. 2 (April 2005): 359-370.

15. Goldstein, Addiction: From Biology to Drug Policy; Asma Asyyed, Daniel Storm, and Ivan Diamond, "Ethanol Activates cAMP Response Element-Mediated Gene Expression in Select Regions of the Mouse Brain," Brain Research 1106, no. 1 (August 23, 2006): 63-71, doi:S0006-8993(06)01647-7; Koob and Le Moal, Neurobiology of Addiction (Orlando: Academic Press, 2006) p. 183, p. 191, p. 211, p. 221. David M. Lovinger and John C. Crabbe, "Laboratory Models of Alcoholism: Treatment Target Identification and Insight into Mechanisms," Nature Neuroscience 8, no. 11 (November 2005): 1471 discuss the ongoing search to pin down alcohol's exact molecular targets in the brain.

16. A committee-like summary of the neurobiology of addiction is available in the World Health Organization report Neuroscience of Psychoactive Substance Use and Dependence (World Health Organization, 2004); Koob and Le Moal, Neurobiology of Addiction p. 447; Roy A. Wise, "Addiction Becomes a Brain Disease," Neuron 26, no. 1 (April 2000): 27-33, doi:10.1016/S0896-6273(00)81134-4.

17. For the theory that surgery (prefrontal lobotomy) could cure addiction, see White, Slaying the Dragon, p. 94. A tantalizing hint that a single spot in the brain held the key to at least one addiction – nicotine – appeared in 2007 with a study showing that heavy smokers with lesions in the insula "forgot" to smoke. Carl T. Hall, "Smokers, your addiction is all in your head, study finds," San Francisco Chronicle, January 25, 2007, http://www.sfgate.com/cgi-bin/article.cgi?f=/c/a/2007/01/25/BAG89NOCVN9.DTL& feed=rss.news.

18. World Health Organization, Neuroscience of Psychoactive Substance Use and Dependence, p. 51.

19. Motivational Interviewing calls this "enhancing discrepancy." See Reid K. Hester and William R. Miller, Handbook of Alcoholism Treatment Approaches: Effective Alternatives, 2nd ed. (Boston: Allyn & Bacon, 1995).

20. John F. Kelly, "Toward an Addiction-ary: A Proposal for More Precise Terminology," Alcoholism Treatment Quarterly 22, no. 2 (June 21, 2004): 79-87; Gail Gleason Milgram, "The Need for Clarity of Terminology," Alcoholism Treatment Quarterly 22, no. 2 (June 12, 2004): 89-95; Robert D. Sparks, "Watch Your Language!" Alcoholism Treatment Quarterly 22, no. 2 (June 21, 2004): 97-100.

21. See, for example, Marc Schuckit, Drug and Alcohol Abuse: A Clinical Guide to Diagnosis and Treatment (New York: Springer, 2000), p. 56.

22. Jack Trimpey, in Rational Recovery: The New Cure for Substance Addiction (New York: Pocket Books, 1996), proposes a set of techniques for recognizing the inner addictive voice.

23. Michael Schermer, "Adam's Maxim and Spinoza's Conjecture," Scientific American, March 2008.

24. See, for example, "Wave-particle duality" Wikipedia, the free encyclopedia. http://en.wikipedia.org/wiki/Wave%E2%80%93particle_duality .

Chapter Two

PREPARE YOUR SOBER SELF
FOR ACTION

Glenda, one of the leading characters in Lonny Shavelson's book *Hooked*, was Number One on San Francisco's list of homeless alcoholics most likely to die on the street. A Lakota off the reservation, she was the picture of alcoholic depression and negative self-esteem. A city rescue team basically kidnapped her off the streets and put her into Friendship House, a Native American recovery center, in the care of counselor Evelyn.

> My counselor, Evelyn, tells me, "Glenda, you're a strong, wise lady." She says all kinds of things about me that make me feel really good.[1]

The counselor, Evelyn, is a strong, wise lady herself, and she knows that focusing on Glenda's many deficiencies and shortcomings would be a pointless and abusive therapeutic exercise. Glenda has been beaten up enough. Healing cannot come by reopening her wounds; it must begin with recognizing and reinforcing her positive, sober side.

Reinforcing Your Sober Self

There's a Glenda inside most people who have put too many addictive substances into the body. We may not be part of a beaten-up minority; we may not be far from our people;

My Turnaround

I'm a bookseller, with a small-town store that sells both new and used books. As my drinking presented more and more problems in my life, I tried to convince myself to call AA. But I'd seen used copies of the "Big Book" come through the store and was totally turned off by its tone. The whole approach seemed phony and lacking in any sort of intellectual underpinning. There was no way I was going to buy into it and I couldn't imagine benefiting from being in a room filled with people who did.

I began to search the Internet, looking for some hope. It took many tries but eventually I found the LifeRing web site. As soon as I began to read, I felt a surge of hope. There was a choice! There was a group offering help for people like me! I wasn't alone!

Never in my life had I experienced such a climate of openness, honesty, and support. People whose lives had been turned into a complete mess by their addiction, people who were financially ruined, had health problems, had torturous relationship issues to deal with, had the energy to offer kind words to me and others. More than kind words, there was real friendship.

It was LifeRing that gave me what I needed to become a former drinker. I've never been to an AA meeting. I've never even been to a face-to-face LifeRing recovery meeting! But my life was saved by the Internet and by the men and women who learned how to use it to help people like me.

– Craig W., Port Townsend, Washington

we may not be jobless, homeless, and in rags. But we often do a good job beating ourselves up, giving ourselves reason to be depressed, and pushing other people away. If we are in that negative frame of mind, we will have a hard time gathering our forces to make a change for the better in our lives.

In this chapter, I will introduce some methods for breaking through initial paralysis. These concepts and practices may help you feel more courage, so that you can not only think about getting free of substance use, but you can actually do it.

Stop Beating Yourself Up

People who use addictive substances are notoriously hard on themselves. The reason is partly that the world is hard on people whose substance use has become too obvious, and we internalize those value judgments. There are elements in the traditional recovery protocol that reinforce these negative judgments, as we'll see in later chapters of this book. But there's an internally generated reason as well.

The previous chapter showed how there's an A and an S inside of the addicted person. The A is the voice that tells you to drink and use. It does more than that. It tries to keep you in the appropriate state of mind so that you will keep feeding it. That state of mind is miserable and stressed.

The A does not want you to feel good about yourself, to feel confident, to feel capable, except perhaps in an exaggerated, grandiose way that makes you seem foolish and that deepens your despair when your tall schemes come to nothing. If you begin to see your strengths realistically and to make small but real gains that give you confidence, you may no longer want or need to keep using the substances. So, when you beat yourself up, what's really happening is that your A is beating up your S.

When people come back from a relapse, the most common thing is to hear them beat themselves up. I'm no good, I'm a very sick puppy, I'm just a worthless so-and-so, I'll never get it, and so on. Mentally, they're still in the relapse. Their A is hammering away at their sense of self-worth, hoping to break them down so they'll drink again right away or at least lay the psychological foundations for the next slip down the road.

The response they get from LifeRing people, online and face-to-face, almost universally, is "Stop beating yourself up! You deserve credit for coming out of your relapse and getting back into recovery! That's not easy! Give yourself a pat on the back for doing that!" We try to be the wise counselor Evelyn for one another.

If we don't happen to have an Evelyn in our lives, to tell us that we're strong and wise people, what are we to do? There's no other solution. We simply have to become our own Evelyn. We have to stop beating ourselves up and start seeing our strengths.

No S Is Too Small to Start

Meth addict and schizophrenic Darlene, in her first interview with Dr. Pablo Stewart, a wise addiction-certified psychiatrist, is telling him that if an addict doesn't want to get off drugs, "You can just talk at them until your eyes turn blue, and they'll just tell you to fuck off."

This is not news to Dr. Stewart, and he has an answer. Holding up his thumb and forefinger pinched together, he says, "Just possibly, that person who you're speaking about may have the teeniest of desires" to deal with her drug problem.

Darlene joins in the game, holding up her fingers and pinching them together harder. "Well, what if that person has only the teeniest, teeeniest, tiniest wanting to be off drugs?"

"Then," says Dr. Stewart, standing up and offering her his hand, "I would think that such a person would do very well."[2]

And Darlene does very well. Dr. Shavelson, who followed Darlene (in *Hooked*), witnessed her metamorphosis. If you have a copy of Shavelson's book, you can see two photographs of Darlene. In the first, she is pushing a shopping cart at a homeless camp that's just been wrecked by the Public Works Department. Her hair is a wild bush, her clothes are in rags, and she looks insane. In the second photo, Darlene wears a tidy hat, her eyes are clear, she's smiling a little, and she looks the picture of togetherness.

Even though she had "only the teeniest, teeeniest, tiniest wanting to be off drugs," that was enough of a starting point for the transformation of her life.

You don't have to wait until your desire to stop putting those substances into your body becomes overwhelming. It won't become overwhelming until you start working to make it stronger. Great trees grow out of tiny acorns. Start small. But start.

People who were forced into treatment and into recovery support groups also often have a very small S, as Darlene did. Their S may be buried under heavy layers of A-serving ideas, habits, and emotions. If you want to help such a person, you may need a magnifying glass. But if you can connect with that almost microscopic S and facilitate its expression and growth, you may become the midwife to miracles.

Listen for Your Wake-Up Call

In some of us, the S is big but asleep. We may have a great sober potential, but we're not acting on it.

The great Romantic poet Percy Bysshe Shelley penned these lines in a memorable poem of outrage against a British atrocity in 1819:

> *Rise like lions after slumber*
> *In unvanquishable number,*
> *Shake your chains to earth like dew*
> *Which in sleep had fallen on you —*
> *Ye are many — they are few.*[3]

Take all the years of your life before you started heavy substance use. Add any other periods when you were clean and sober. Give yourself points for anything you achieved in life despite using substances. (You couldn't have climbed those mountains with that monkey on your back if you didn't have strong legs.) Add in your sober relationships, your good qualities, your insight and understanding. That's your sober base.

To use an economic metaphor, it's your sober capital.[4] The poet would call it your lion. But you're still using substances. Why? Your lion is asleep.

There can be all kinds of wake-up calls. For some people, it's a sudden catastrophic event. Looking at the face of death can sometimes have a very stimulating effect on the drive to survive. Sometimes a crisis can resolve a person's ambivalence decisively in the S direction.

The wake-up call needn't come with crashing drums and cymbals. A few quiet words can do it. My ten-year-old son's question, "You're a drunkard, Dad, aren't you?" was my wake-up call. I've heard many similar stories where children stirred the S in their father or mother out of slumber and into action.[5]

A few pointed words from a doctor or dentist have poked the sober power in many a man and woman into wakefulness. Sometimes people get the wake-up call just by looking in the mirror, literally or figuratively. If they are able to see and to feel their S – the better person that they could be and that they are deep down inside – then they can change.

In some people I have met, the wake-up call didn't come from a bad happening, but from a good turn of fortune. They got a job, or a better job; they got into a school; they met someone they cared for; they got interested in a sport, a hobby, or volunteer work; they met new friends. Their improved circumstance brought out the sober self in them and gave them the situational strength to leave the substances behind.

Whatever helps to grow the sober self leads toward recovery. Just reducing the addict self by itself has no effect unless the sober self grows and fills the gap. Programs that focus on trying to confront, attack, and destroy the program client's A will generally fail, because they do not recognize, honor, and support the S.[6]

Some people believe that an addict's situation has to get worse before it can get better. Their advice is to keep using the substances until the person "hits bottom." This is very risky advice. With each passing day of using substances, the A tends to grow larger and more powerful at the expense of the S. The typical outcome of "searching for the bottom" is that the person loses more and more of the resources that are needed for recovery.

In the exceptional case where a person does turn around after having sunk very low, it's because the inner S, with its back to the wall, has finally awakened and begun to fight. These are remarkable stories, but they are exceptional. On the whole and on the average, those with the best chance of recovery still have a job, a family, a home, and other resources.[7]

As the poet said, "Shake your chains to earth like dew, Which in sleep had fallen on you." How true that is. In the addiction, the habit of drinking and using feels like a set of heavy chains, impossible to cast off. This appearance, too, is the work of the A. Just as the A minimizes the S, it magnifies its own power. But when you stand up and shake yourself, the chains fall off like dewdrops. How many times have I seen people newly sober, amazed that they can do it! They look surprised. They thought it would be impossible to stop or at least much more difficult.

Actually, stopping is relatively easy. With competent medical help, even nightmare withdrawals from alcohol and opi-

This Isn't Me

In 1978 I was in a major car accident and was not expected to live. Alcohol became the tool I used to cope, but what began as a tool slowly became a physical need. I began sneaking drinks whenever I could: sneaking downstairs late at night to quickly drink a tumbler of wine then sneaking back to bed; sneaking extra drinks at parties when no one was looking; sneaking wine in the house and breaking my right hand tripping on a coffee table; sneaking extra booze in drinks I poured; sneaking drinks at a friend's house and breaking my arm and shoulder when I fell down a landing I didn't see. Sneaking, sneaking, sneaking. I knew my drinking was out of control but had no idea what to do about it.

The fact is, I didn't think there was anything I could do about it – as far as I knew the only way to cure alcoholism was to go to AA and there was no way I was going to do that. I had been to a couple of meetings years before and there was something about the concept of "powerlessness" that felt terribly wrong to me.

One day I happened to glance at myself in the bathroom mirror. There was a stranger looking back at me. She was

ates can be tolerable. The harder part is to keep yourself from putting the chains back on. You've worn them for so long they feel normal. You feel naked without them.

But once you've responded to the wake-up call, you're not the same person anymore. Once your lion rises from slumber, it'll never rest quietly again. Your S has had a taste of freedom and power. Even if you relapse, chances are you will try and try again, until you get it.

lifting a bottle of codeine-laced cough syrup to her mouth, ready to top off the 100-proof vodka she had guzzled straight from the bottle just moments before. I paused with the bottle half to my lips and thought, "This isn't me." My mind was made up in that instant. I was not drinking again, ever. But how?

I remembered LifeRing and went quickly to my computer. I spent days reading posts, searching the archives, absorbing all the ways other people had achieved and maintained sobriety. One of the most amazing things I discovered through LifeRing was that I wasn't alone. That other people understood the unbelievably huge physical and mental effort involved in giving up drinking. People who wanted to share this struggle for sobriety and who didn't judge me. Their support came from one side of the country to the other and from overseas, at any hour of the night or day.

LifeRing and the power of my own made-up mind have enabled me to put my life back together again. Today there is not a day that goes by that some small thing doesn't happen that reminds me of the horror of the 20+ years I spent addicted to alcohol – and of the absolute joy of sobriety.

-Alceon, Fresno, California

Motivating Yourself to Start

Getting free of substances is a positive act. To motivate yourself to get free and stay free, it helps to have a positive attitude. Here are some tips, tricks, and exercises that people have tested and used in a wide variety of contexts. Any one of them may help you get in the proper positive frame of mind to wake up and empower your sober self. Pick one that appeals to you and put it into practice.

- *Visualize your new life.* When you are free of substances, you will have more time, money, energy, and other resources. What will you do with them? Visualize yourself as a person free from the desire to use substances – a person doing something pleasant, clean, and sober. What is the weather? Where exactly are you? What are you wearing? What do you have in your hands? What do you hear, see, smell, taste, feel? Who are you with? Fill the vision with as many concrete details as you can think of. Hold on to the vision and to the feeling. Let your mind's eye linger on the details. Write it down. Professional athletes use visualization to prepare themselves mentally to reach a higher level of performance. You can use the same technique to help yourself get sober.

- *Find something to laugh about.* It's hard to be miserable and stressed-out when you're laughing. There are cases of people with serious degenerative diseases laughing themselves healthy. Even if you don't see anything funny in your own life at the moment, work at finding something that takes you out of your dumps and tickles your funny bone. The Internet has dozens of humor sites. Bookstores have humor books. Video stores have comedy sections. You can't drink and laugh at the same time, it'll blow out your nose. Laugh!

- *Forgive yourself for your substance use.* In the movie *Good Will Hunting*, Matt Damon's character is carrying a raw psychic scar that makes him defensive and hostile and gets him into repeated trouble. Robin Williams, playing an unconventional psychologist, finally leads him to see that "it's not your fault." Damon is responsible for the trouble he's caused and has to pay the price. But the inner pain that drove him to do it is not his fault. See if that isn't true for you also. Maybe your substance use had costly consequences for others; you have to answer for that. But your motives for beginning substance use were probably innocent. None of us can predict at what point we'll become addicted. Forgive yourself, let it go, move forward. You'll find that getting and staying free of substances is easier if you let go of guilt and shame for having started.

- *Do what you can do.* Planning a successful outcome won't get far if it depends on other people changing what they do first. Think about how you can achieve your goal by doing what you can do. When you think about it, you may have an amazing ability to tune out other people and get what you want. Put that ability to work in making positive changes in your life.

- *Turn off your television.* Commercial TV and radio are designed to stress you and make you feel incomplete so that you will go out and shop. These media are also a big pipeline for alcohol ads, and for programs that show people smoking, drinking, and using drugs – toxic visual stimuli that are fuel for your inner A. If you have noncommercial, listener-sponsored channels, limit your TV watching to those. Even there, be choosy about what movies you watch and try taking a break from the daily news. Yes, you want to be an informed citizen, but right now your priority is to be a sober citizen, so reduce the sources of stress in your life and turn off the boob tube.

- *Reframe negatives into positives.* In political campaigns, everything depends on the framing or spin. The art of moving people to vote your way lies in framing the issue in such a way that only one outcome, yours, appears reasonable. You can apply this principle to your project. Instead of thinking about quitting, think about getting free. Instead of dwelling on the weight of the monkey on your back, focus on how strong you are to still be alive and kicking after carrying the hairy beast all these years. Instead of worrying about whether you'll ever have fun again, anticipate how much fun you'll have when you can rock and roll without falling down drunk and can remember it the next day. Some people get great results by monitoring their internal dialogues to spear negatives. They write down any negative thoughts and then rework them into positives. For example, "I'll never get past my personal 'happy hour' without drinking" becomes "My urge to drink is only really strong for about an hour, so if I get past that danger zone, I'll be OK for today."

- *Get exercise, eat better.* Our body has natural chemicals – endorphins – that improve our mood and help us tackle our problems. You can stimulate your inner endorphin flow with exercise. It doesn't much matter what it is, just do some. Start out slow, build up gradually. If you're feeling bloated or hungry all the time or are filling up with junk food, do the obvious thing: eat better. You'll feel better, you'll look better, you'll think better of yourself, and you'll find it easier to get moving forward and leave substances behind you. There is no junkier junk food than addictive substances.

- *Get a good night's sleep.* When you're trying to get moving on something new and important, it's really helpful to have had a good night's sleep. Sleep experts advise that you do nothing in bed besides having sex and sleeping. Prepare for the next day before lying down. Try a hot bath, a warm glass of milk, or natural herbal supplements. Don't use the bed to watch TV, listen to radio or music, or read. Turn off all the lights. When you've slept well, you'll be in a better frame of mind, more likely to take action that improves your life.

- *Connect and communicate.* It's stressful to bottle up things you want to say. It's stressful to be cut off from other people. Substance use tends to make us say things we don't mean, whereas the things we do mean get stuffed. Substance use tends to connect us with people in ways that make us feel more alone than ever or to isolate us altogether. It may take quite a bit of time and effort to set all of that straight, but you can make a start. Pick one thing that frustrates you that you mean to say to another person and say it. Find a way to be helpful to another person – even in a very small way – and do it. You'll be amazed by the improvement in your outlook.

- *Believe in yourself.* If you didn't have a powerful survival instinct, you probably wouldn't be alive now, with all the substances you've put in your body. Is the person you've become, with all this substance use, the real you? Isn't there a better you inside? Focus on that better you, believe in that better you, become that better you. Use your belief in your better you to get free of the substance-using you that you've become lately.

- *Rehearse freedom.* Different people have different ways of stopping. Do a mental preview of putting away your last bit of addictive substances. Plan it out in detail. What will you do with the leftover liquor or other drugs? What will you do with your paraphernalia? Who, if anyone, will be with you? What will you do for support? Will you use medical treatment? Will you use a treatment program? Think it out and rehearse it mentally. When it actually happens, it may be quite different from your plan, but rehearsing it ahead of time will make it easier and will make you more confident.

- *Make a talisman of your strengths.* A talisman, or an amulet, is a small object that represents some person or principle that brings the wearer strength and good luck. You have lots of strengths. You wouldn't be alive carrying that monkey on your back all this time if you didn't have strong legs. Remember some strength or achievement from your pre-using days. Try to bring this memory into sharp focus, with color and sound. Now choose a talisman (a pebble, a seashell, a piece of jewelry, a photo, a tattoo, anything) that represents that positive memory in your mind. Touch the talisman and recall the memory often until it becomes strongly linked in your mind. Carry the talisman with you to remind you that you are a strong, competent person.

- *Consider sobriety as an adventure.* Getting sober is an adventure. Listen to Helen Keller: "Life is either a daring adventure or it is nothing. To keep our faces toward change and behave like free spirits in the presence of fate is strength undefeatable."[8] When you use substances, you face endless repetition of the same boring ritual. When you leave substance use behind, you become open to change. When you use, you are chained to your drug. When you break that chain, your spirit is released from its cage. When you use substances, you are defeated every day. Your life is nothing. When you get free, you have strength undefeatable. Getting free of drugs is a daring journey into a new land filled with adventure. It can take your breath away, exhilarate you, and make you happy to be alive.

There are many other pointers, tips, exercises, and tools that people use in a great variety of contexts to get themselves mentally and emotionally ready to change their lives. They all have in common the positive reinforcement of your better self. There is no reason why you should not borrow any or all of these tools to energize your S.

As you move toward action to get free of substances, you may encounter some popular myths about addiction that will tend to paralyze you if you accept them. They are the notion that addiction is rooted in defects of character and that addiction is the result of an addictive personality. Both are mistaken.

Addiction is Not
A Defect of Character

One of the most paralyzing notions that stands in the way of recovery is the belief that you became addicted because of defects in your character. If you believe this, you will have a hard time ever getting free of addictive substances because character, by definition, is unchangeable; it is who you are.

For many decades now, laboratory animals have been teaching experimenters that this belief is mistaken.

Theories of character, and similar higher-level psychological, sociological, and theological theories, may well explain why a person starts to use addictive substances – for example, to medicate an emotional pain, to fit in with peers, to raise or lower self-esteem, and many other motives.

But they can't explain why a person continues to use the substances even when it's clear that the medication only makes things worse, that the peers have grown up and moved away, and that your other motives for starting no longer apply. These theories, in short, may explain the beginning of substance use but they don't explain addiction.

In a laboratory some fifty years ago, chimpanzees who had been made addicted to opium tugged the experimenter to the cabinet where the drug was kept and assumed the position for receiving the injection. Since that time, uncounted numbers of laboratory monkeys, dogs, cats, guinea pigs, and especially rodents, among others, have been teaching scientists that substance addiction has a physiological dimension.

Eliot Gardner, a leading neuroscientist, summarizes this lesson by pointing out that theories of addiction based on human society don't apply to laboratory animals, yet these creatures readily become addicted to the same drugs as humans do. He says, "This argues compellingly for a profoundly important biological basis for substance abuse."[9]

Experimenters routinely transform healthy, normal, wild-type animals into addicted animals. All that is required is to introduce a sustained high dose of the addictive substance into their bloodstream. In a matter of days or weeks, the animals become chemically dependent.

The addicted animal may press a lever thousands of times to get more of the substance. It will ignore food, water, sex, cold, and electric shock to get more. When its supply is cut off, it will show physiological and behavioral withdrawal symptoms. It will demonstrate craving, place cue preference, relapse behavior, and many other phenomena also seen in humans.[10] Not only mammals but even fruit flies can be made dependent and can yield lessons about dependence in humans.[11] The same is true in nematodes (tiny transparent worms).[12]

Many details about how addiction happens at the molecular level remain unknown. Scientists in several countries are busy working on these problems. But the Big Picture of the etiology of addiction has been known for decades. Chronic ingestion of alcohol or other addictive substances generates the pattern of changes in the brain that drive the behavior we call addiction.[13] Addiction is caused by the chemical action of addictive substances on the brain.

We can't change our character. But we can stop putting addictive substances into the brain. Brain recovery begins rapidly.[14] Once we get free of the substances, we can figure out more effective ways – methods that don't involve addictive substances – to medicate the pain, win acceptance from our peers, and do whatever else we thought we were accomplishing by putting substances into the body.

Every Personality Type Is Liable to Become Addicted

Another myth that discourages people from getting free of addictive substances is the belief that there is an addictive personality. If you think you have or are such a personality, you will probably never get free of addiction; all you ever do is to substitute one addiction for another.

Fifty years of psychometric studies in humans, looking for a psychological profile that supposedly predisposed people to become addicted, have failed to turn up an addict personality.[15] These decades of experiments teach that the problem of addiction does not lie in some supposed preexisting personality state but in the chemical action of the substances themselves.[16]

Individuals with all character types are equally liable to become addicted if they put addictive substances into their body. If you have ever spent time in a treatment program or a support group, you can verify the diversity of characters by your own observation.

Although many humans who start using addictive substances have a preexisting mental health issue that they are trying to "medicate," this is only one of many pathways toward addiction.[17] Perfectly normal healthy human beings, if they ingest addictive substances in sufficient quantity, will arrive at the same place.[18]

Most people today understand this point when discussing nicotine. They appreciate that you can smoke only a limited number of cigarettes before you will get hooked on nicotine. (Some of the newest research suggests that a single cigarette is enough to get the addictive process started.)[19] Your religious and spiritual beliefs, your childhood, your personality, probably have little to do with it. Similarly, the same is true with cocaine or heroin. People understand that these are highly addictive substances and that if you put them into your body, you take the risk of becoming hooked.

Where people tend to go off track is with ethanol. There is so much myth and noise surrounding alcoholism that the nature of ethyl alcohol as an addictive substance is often forgotten. There is no scientific reason for a distinction. Alcohol is an inherently addictive substance, as are nicotine, heroin, methamphetamine, and the other well-recognized chemical hookers.[20] If you put it in your body at all, you take the risk of becoming addicted. If you put enough into your body, you will become addicted.

The word alcoholic simply means a person who has become addicted to the drug ethyl alcohol. As Dr. James Milam wrote in his classic work on alcoholism, the alcoholic's prior personality or character had nothing to do with it.[21]

Understanding the neurobiological roots of addiction is very far from fatalism as has sometimes been argued. On the contrary, the character theories are fatalistic. Character is immutable. Addiction is not. The neurobiological understanding points directly to a lever for change that we ourselves can activate immediately. The key to defeating addiction is to stop putting the substances into our body.

The Power of Habit

Pavlov's famous dog was shown meat whenever a bell rang. The sight of the meat made the dog salivate. After enough repetitions, the bell was rung without showing the dog meat. The dog salivated anyway.

Salivation is an unconscious process. Conditioning – habit formation – can and does control unconscious bodily processes. If the dog had formed the will not to salivate when the bell rang without meat, his salivary glands would have disobeyed him.

In another experiment, a rat was hooked up to an IV. At the sound of a tone, the rat's bloodstream got a dose of liquid containing common bacteria. The rat's immune system immediately detected the intruders and launched a defensive attack. After a number of repetitions, experimenters again sounded the tone but this time dosed the rat with sterile liquid. Even though no bacteria were present, the rat's immune system again launched an attack.[22] If the rat had been able to will its immune system not to attack, its system would have disobeyed.

The Power of Self-Conditioning

Developing an addiction has much in common with these conditioning experiments, except that we are both the experimenter and the rat. For months or years, we put the same high-octane substances into our bodies the same way at the same time in the same place. No wonder that when we are in that place at that time, our brains experience a powerful craving. We can no more will the craving to stop than the dog could curb its glands or the rat its antibodies.

Clever experiments with laboratory animals have shown that it is sheer habit, not so much wanting a reward that triggers the start of conditioned using.[23] This is important because it helps explain why people feel overwhelmed by the urge to use even when they hate the substance and don't anticipate pleasure from using it.

Such is the power of habit. But this is also the weakness of habit, by which habit can be broken. We are not only the laboratory animal, we are also the experimenter.

At certain times and places, our power of choice is severely impaired. Our A rules us with a chemical whip. We are not having the craving; the craving is having us. But at other times, we have windows of freedom and opportunity when we can make choices that empower our S. This is the meaning of Dr. Shavelson's excellent observation that our drive to be free of the substance can overcome our drive to use the substance "when the timing is right."

For me personally, the Pavlovian bell rang around 6 PM at home. That was "happy hour" – a misnomer, if ever there was one. In that setting, at that time, I was for all practical purposes powerless to resist drink. But at 10 AM one day in a downtown clinic, I entered into a contract with the Kaiser treatment program that called for me to be in a group room every day directly after work. And I went. By the time the evening session was over, two hours later, the peak of my craving cycle was well past. I was filled with S-reinforcement and I could safely go home.

After thirty-three years of drinking, I expected greater agonies. I had thought of my drinking as a steady-state entity, a condition that was essentially the same at all times and in all places. I had not realized, until my life experience in the program proved it to me, that this condition had its hot spots and its cool areas. It towered over me in some times and places. In other situations, it could not rule me. To gain the upper hand, I needed to capitalize on my freedom when I had it, so as to avoid returning to the situations where I would lose it.

Addiction is neurochemical, but the power of addiction over us is situational. The most dramatic demonstration of this point came with the heroin use of Vietnam veterans. Thousands of U.S. soldiers began heroin use in Vietnam and became addicted while there. Relatively few of them continued to use once they returned to the States.[24] The very different home environment empowered them to resist the chemical pull of the drug.

Much of the power of treatment programs and support groups derives from the situational effect.[25] These are settings where consumption of harmful addictive substances (with the deplorable exception, in many settings, of nicotine) is not acceptable and does not occur, thereby habit and its conditioned urges are undermined, and the seeds of new and sober habits are sowed. It almost does not matter what other content fills these settings, so long as the situation is substance-free.

To be sure, the power of addiction is not confined to the triggers of time and place. Stress, which can occur anywhere and at any time, is a real danger. Negative emotional experiences, interpersonal conflict, boredom, and other emotional challenges can do people in. But breaking the power of habit, by learning to avoid or to reinterpret the time and place where we conditioned ourselves to commence our substance use routine, is a necessary foundational skill for all else.

That skill is well within the power of those who want to attain it. The British psychologist Allen Carr says that much of the foreboding that people have about the difficulty of quitting addictive substances is unfounded and that when we free ourselves from these self-fulfilling prophecies, leaving the substances behind is really not so difficult.[26] My experience – and the experience of many other LifeRing members – tends to support that theory.

Different Styles of Breaking the Habit

Some people stop substance use suddenly, without lengthy deliberation. They've had enough, and they hang it up and go on with life. Other people agonize about it for years. They quit and restart, quit and restart, until it finally takes. Whichever style works for you is good.

Here are some points to think about:

- If you have been using alcohol or opiates heavily, you may need medical assistance during the initial withdrawal period. There is a risk of seizures, delirium, and other medical harm. Check with a doctor or with a public health clinic. Many health insurance policies will cover a few days of medical detoxification, even if nothing more. An alcoholic friend of mine, unsure what symptoms he would have when going cold turkey off alcohol, sat in the waiting room of the emergency department of a local hospital with a novel.

- If you have access to a chemical dependency treatment program, you will want to investigate that option. A program, inpatient or outpatient, gives you a time and a place free of substances. It puts you in a room with other people who are also getting free of their substances, which is very helpful and may give you useful information about how to stay substance-free long term.

- If you don't have access to a treatment program, or you're not comfortable with your options, you can still get free of the substances. Most people who do get substance-free do it without treatment. Use treatment if you can get it, but don't ever let the unavailability of affordable and acceptable treatment stand in your way.

- If you retain a supply of the substance or of other addictive substances, you may find it much more difficult to stay free of them. It may be much safer to dump them, all of them, down the toilet. Paraphernalia needs to be hammered before disposal, so that it doesn't climb out of the garbage by itself and jump back into your hand late at night. Put out empty bottles for recycling.

- Some people find it very helpful to have a sober companion when dumping their substances, to be sure that they go down the sewer directly instead of taking a detour through your body.

- Organized support groups can be very helpful, but be aware that the 12-step groups only appeal to about 5 percent of the people who try them. If you find that this approach is not your cup of tea, you're not alone. LifeRing support groups, described in the next chapter, have a different atmosphere, which you may find a better fit. Support is also available via the Internet.

- If organized support groups don't appeal to you, you may be able to find support in other social networks. Does your family support your freedom from substances? Maybe you can find support for sober living in a sports team, a classroom, a gardening club, a motorcycle club, a choir, a senior center, a church, a temple, a mosque, a synagogue, an ashram, a gym, a hiking club – you get the idea. Any activity that you enjoy and that puts you in contact with sober people strengthens your S and weakens your A.

There's more about these issues in the *Recovery by Choice* workbook, discussed in Chapter Five. You can also get advice – lots of it – over the Internet. The important thing to remember is that just as there are many ways into substance addiction, there are also many ways out. If one door doesn't work for you, open another. If you fall on your face, pick yourself up and try something else. There's no wrong way to stop putting addictive substances into your body. Whatever works to help you live free is good.

Develop Your Choice Muscles

Addiction, as has been said many times, severely impairs our powers of choice. But the paralysis of volition in a living person is never total. As long as people are alive, some parts of their volitional anatomy can still function, and this functionality varies with time and place.

If choice is a muscle – and I believe this is a fitting metaphor – then it gains strength by doing work. A course of recovery therapy that makes every decision for you provides no material for your choice muscle to work on, except perhaps the isometric exercise of opposing the prescribed decisions. If that is foreclosed, the paralysis remains unabated, and the choice muscles atrophy.

Here is a tool that you can use to exercise your choice muscle. This is from the first chapter of the *Recovery by Choice* workbook.[27] The members of my workbook study groups have used this tool many times to sharpen their decision-making skills in a wide variety of situations. It's called the Sobriety Priority T-Chart, also known as an A-S chart.

You draw a big T on the paper. You begin by writing your issue across the top of the T. Keep it tight and practical. Do I move in with Alex? Should I take Monday off? Do I enroll in summer school? What if I enter the poetry slam? You get the idea.

Then underneath, on the left side, you write all the ways that saying yes to the question would tend to increase the

Like a Big Family

LifeRing is people helping people to get and stay clean and sober. There is no guilt or blame involved. We each formulate our own plan for recovery. No one else can keep me from going to the corner market and drowning in a gin bottle. I must perform my own daily sobriety maintenance but do so with the help of my sober friends. We help each other maintain our sober lives through example and discussion. It's a tough job, but it beats the alternative. Without LifeRing, I am convinced that my quality of life would be significantly lower. I'd very possibly be a despondent drunk rather than a sober, relatively happy and productive member of society.

– Mark H., San Francisco, California

odds of your using substances. In other words, how it would reinforce your A. On the right side, write all the ways it would help you stay free of substances and strengthen your S.

So for example, the poetry slam. This contest is being held in a bar, so that's a factor for the A (left side of the T). On the other hand, three of your sober friends will be with you, so that's a plus for the S (right side). You'll have to pass through a cluster of smokers outside the door – a point for the A. But the air inside will be smoke-free, a point for the S. The prize is a bottle of wine – count one for the A. But participating will make you feel good about yourself as a poet – count one for the S. Being seen inside the bar may make people think you're a drinker: A. But being seen and heard as a poet may get people to show you more respect: S. If you win, you can ask for a bottle of Pellegrino instead of the wine and make a point: S. Here's the question: If you don't win, will you feel like drinking?

Working the A-S chart helps you analyze the consequences of every decision for the tug-of-war between the A and the S inside you. It also helps you make detailed action plans. Take this example: I will sit at a table with my sober friends and not at the bar. If I win, I'll trade the prize for something without alcohol. We'll get out of there as soon as the slam is over.

If you decide to go to the event, you can take the chart with you to remind you of the details. When you're done, you can review the chart and see if you missed anything. If you decide not to go, you can make a plan to enter a different poetry slam in a safer location, such as a coffeehouse.

You can do this kind of chart on the back of an envelope with a stubby pencil. With a little practice, you can do it in your head. You'll be looking at every issue from the angle of whether it leans toward your A or your S. You'll work your way out of volitional paralysis.

Neuroimaging studies show that substance use impairs the executive (decision-making) areas of the brain, so it's extra-important to become active in this area. Exercising your power of choice, like limbs that have got stiff and muscles that have atrophied from disuse, is the only way to restore proper functioning. You can make mental A-S charts many times a day. In time, evaluating every issue in terms of its A-S value and making decisions based on the Sobriety Priority will become second nature.

Getting ready to leave addictive substances behind is very largely a matter of building up one's sober confidence.

So far, we've seen that the foundation for confidence is already present in every addicted person. The drive to get free of the substance, the S drive, is one defining element of the addiction experience.

In this chapter, we have looked at ways to encourage the S to gather itself up and take charge. Now let's have a closer look at the LifeRing process and how it works.

Notes

1. Shavelson, Hooked, p. 204.
2. Ibid., p. 281.
3. http://www.artofeurope.com/shelley/she5.htm.
4. Granfield and Cloud, Coming Clean, p. 179.
5. In my recovery, I have heard variations of my story from quite a few other parents. Benjamin Rush, the Surgeon General of George Washington's armies, recounts the case of a farmer who came home in a hurry to save his crops from rain and overheard his young son saying, "Mother, Father's home and he's not drunk." The man never again touched a drop. Recounted in Ibid., p. 7.
6. William R. Miller and William White, "Confrontation in Addiction Treatment," Counselor (October 4, 2007), http://www.counselormagazine.com/content/view/608/63.
7. Anne Geller, "Comprehensive Treatment Programs," in Substance Abuse: A Comprehensive Textbook, 3rd ed., 1997, pp. 425-429; Diana M. Doumas, Christine M Blasey, and Cory L. Thacker, "Attrition from Alcohol and Drug Outpatient Treatment Psychological Distress and Interpersonal Problems as Indicators," Alcoholism Treatment Quarterly 23, no. 4 (June 9, 2005): 55-67.
8. http://womenshistory.about.com/od/disabilities/a/qu_helen_keller.htm.
9. Gardner, "Brain-Reward Mechanisms" p. 48.
10. See, for example, G. F. Koob and F. E Bloom, "Cellular and Molecular Mechanisms of Drug Dependence," Science 242, no. 4879 (November 4, 1988): 715-723, doi:10.1126/Science. 2903550; Veronique Deroche-Gamonet, David Belin, and Pier Vincenzo Piazza, "Evidence for Addiction-Like Behavior in the Rat," Science 305, no. 5686 (August 13, 2004): 1014-1017, doi:10.1126/Science.1099020; Peter W. Kalivas, Jamie Peters, and Lori Knackstedt, "Animal Models and Brain Circuits in Drug Addiction," Molecular Interventions, 6, no. 6 (December 1, 2006): 339-344, doi:10.1124/Mi.6.6.7.
11. Ulrike Heberlein, "Research," Ernest and Julio Gallo Research Center, http://www.galloresearch.org/site/HeberleinLab/. Dr. Heberlein was kind enough to show me around her laboratory. Of particular interest was the "Inebriometer," a device for measuring fruit flies' degree of intoxication.
12. Steve McIntire, "Welcome to the McIntire Lab," Ernest and Julio Gallo Research Center, http://www.galloresearch. org/site/McIntireLab/.
13. Lovinger and Crabbe, "Laboratory Models of Alcoholism: Treatment Target Identification and Insight into Mechanisms."
14. Sachio Matsushita and Susumu Higuchi, "[A Review of the Neuroimaging Studies of Alcoholism]," Nihon Arukoru Yakubutsu Igakkai Zassh Japa-

nese Journal of Alcohol Studies & Drug Dependence 42, no. 6 (December 2007): 615-621, Doi:18240649.

15. "The alcoholic should be assured throughout treatment that his personality did not cause his disease and that he is in no way responsible for it." James R. Milam and Katherine Ketcham, Under the Influence: A Guide to the Myths and Realities of Alcoholism (New York: Bantam, 1983), p. 156. "The idea of a preexisting 'alcoholic personality' has been debunked . . . by numerous prospective studies . . . The 'alcoholic personality' is the consequence, not the cause, of alcoholism." Katherine Ketcham and William Asbury, Beyond the Influence: Understanding and Defeating Alcoholism (Bantam, 2000), p. 56, "Over the years, our studies have shown no clinically significant differences between the sons of alcoholics ... and sons of nonalcoholics . . . on measurable personality variables," Marc Schuckit, "Reactions to Alcohol in Sons of Alcoholics and Controls," Alcoholism: Clinical and Experimental Research 12, no. 4 (1988): 465, doi:10.1111/j.1530-0277.1988.tb00228.x. "Fifty years of both psychological ... and longitudinal studies ... have failed to reveal a consistent 'alcoholic personality.' Attempts to derive a set of alcoholic psychometric personality subtypes have yielded profiles similar to those found when subtyping a general population ... That is, alcoholics appear to be as variable in personality as are nonalcoholics." Hester and Miller, Handbook of Alcoholism Treatment Approaches: Effective Alternatives, p. 90.

16. Gardner, "Brain-Reward Mechanisms," p. 49.

17. Kessler et al., "Lifetime and 12-month prevalence of DSM-III-R Psychiatric Disorders in the United States. Results from the National Comorbidity Survey."

18. Stephen T. Higgins, "Principles of Learning in the Study and Treatment of Substance Abuse," in Marc Galanter and Herbert D. Kleber (eds.), The American Psychiatric Publishing Textbook of Substance Abuse Treatment, 3rd. ed. (Arlington, Va.: American Psychiatric Publishing, 2004), p. 65.

19. Joseph R. DiFranza, "Hooked from the First Cigarette: New Findings Reveal That Cigarette Addiction Can Arise Astonishingly Fast. But the Research Could Lead to Therapies That Make Quitting Easier," Scientific American (May 2008): 82-87.

20. Gardner, "Brain-Reward Mechanisms," p. 48.

21. Milam and Ketcham, Under the Influence.

22. R. Ader and N. Cohen, "Conditioning of the Immune Response," Netherlands Journal of Medicine 39, no. 3/4 (October 1991): 263-273, doi:1791889; N. Cohen, J. A. Moynihan, and R. Ader, "Pavlovian Conditioning of the Immune System," International Archives of Allergy and Immunology 105, no. 2 (October 1994): 101-106, doi:7920010.

23. Rita A. Fuchs, R. Kyle Branham, and Ronald E. See, "Different Neural Substrates Mediate Cocaine Seeking After Abstinence Versus Extinction Training: A Critical Role for the Dorsolateral Caudate-Putamen," Journal of Neuroscience, 26, no. 13 (March 29, 2006): 3584-3588, doi:10.1523/ JNEUROSCI.5146-05.2006.

24. L. N. Robins, J. E. Helzer, and D. H. Davis, "Narcotic Use in Southeast Asia and Afterward. An Interview Study of 898 Vietnam Return-

ees," Archives of General Psychiatry 32, no. 8 (August 1975): 955-961, doi:1156114; Lee N Robins and Sergey Slobodyan, "Post-Vietnam Heroin Use and Injection by Returning U.S. Veterans: Clues to Preventing Injection Today," Addiction (Abingdon, England) 98, no. 8 (August 2003): 1053-1060, doi:12873239; L. N. Robins, "The Sixth Thomas James Okey Memorial Lecture. Vietnam Veterans' Rapid Recovery from Heroin Addiction: A fluke or Normal Expectation?" Addiction (Abingdon, England) 88, no. 8 (August 1993): 1041-1054, doi:8401158.

25. A fine collection of illustrations on the power of situations to govern behavior is in Malcolm Gladwell, The Tipping Point: How Little Things Can Make a Big Difference (Back Bay, 2002), Chs. 5 and 6.

26. Allen Carr, The Easy Way to Stop Smoking [Rev. and updated]. (New York: Sterling, 2004).

27. Martin Nicolaus, Recovery by Choice: Living and Enjoying Life Free of Alcohol and Drugs, a Workbook, 3rd ed. (Oakland, Calif.: LifeRing Press, 2006).

▼

Chapter Three

HOW LIFERING WORKS

I was an only child, and we moved a lot. As a result, I became a rugged individualist, a lone wolf, a lonesome rambler, a tumbling tumbleweed – you know the type. Groups were not for me. When my doctor at the Kaiser program said I had to go to recovery support groups twice a week, I groaned inside. But I went.

The LifeRing groups turned out not to be so bad. I found them easy to take. You sit in a circle. You talk about what's been going on in your life. The atmosphere is conversational, like a living room with friends. Nobody attacks you, tries to convert you to anything, or hammers you with advice.

LifeRing meetings are so easy to take that I came to wonder how they worked. Something about them was definitely working for me and for other people I met who became regulars there. All kinds of people are finding them beneficial. After I got clearer about the conflicted nature of addiction and the inner battle between the A and the S, explained in the first chapter, I began to understand. The answer is positive reinforcement from the S to the S.

LifeRing meetings can happen face-to-face (warm bodies together in a room) or online (people alone with a computer

Why LifeRing Works Better for Me

I resonate with LifeRing's positive, empowering philosophy. Positive thinking, its discussion of enjoyable sober activities, pleasures, one's productive pre-alcoholic life, etc. Positive, too, is in the basic LifeRing philosophy that says there is a good sober person in each of us needing reinforcement, not just a reprobate addict needing reformation. But most importantly, LifeRing translates those positive expectations into a statement of personal responsibility. I was empowered to construct a recovery plan crafted for my situation and my personality. I am responsible to make it work.

I also found AA's religious imagery a barrier. I believe my grounding in a love of nature – one that includes joy, wonder, and even a bit of mysticism – provides me internal support. But why deify that self-transcendence into "God, as we understood Him," invoked at every meeting via ritual, prayer, and testimonial? There is nothing supernatural there.
If no alternative existed, I could have worked my way around those barriers. But an alternative did exist, LifeRing worked well, and it didn't preclude my looking over the fence – any fence – for thoughts.

– Jim R., Oakland, California

connecting via chat rooms, e-mail lists, social network, bulletin board, forum). Some people connect face-to-face, some connect online, some do both. Some people don't connect at all but follow LifeRing ideas from LifeRing books, particularly the *Recovery by Choice* workbook. Here's how the connection process works.

The LifeRing Meeting

LifeRing groups are peer-to-peer sessions. The group facilitators (in LifeRing we call them convenors (*con-VEE-nurs*) are persons in recovery who have volunteered to take a turn leading the meeting. No degree, certificate, or license is required, and there is no pay. This means, among other things, that no one will give you a diagnosis or tell you what to do. They will bring a wealth of personal experience and a nonjudgmental, empathetic, supportive attitude.

Reinforcing Our Sober Selves

The main purpose of our meetings is to reinforce the desire to get clean and sober that lives within each of us – the S. You will observe the S in the others, and they will recognize it in you. In the meeting, people talk from their S, and they talk to the S in the others present. The meeting basically consists of S-to-S communications – ideally, a thick web of them, at some point connecting everyone with everyone else.

Here are some key points about the meetings.

- *No preaching, lecturing, or speechifying.* You will find in the average Life¬Ring meeting little in the way of abstract discussion. Most of the time is spent by people narrating and analyzing specific events that they were involved in during the week. Although it's important to get a grip on big principles, the key to success at living free of substances is the thoughtful handling of the flow of small decisions.

- Most begin with *"How was your week?"* The "How was your week?" topic that most LifeRing meetings use also asks people to look ahead and make plans for their coming week. This format is a good workbench for making better small decisions.

- *They focus on the present.* We're concerned with last week and next week because these are the immediate framework of the here and now. Our lives are works in progress. We weave our destiny moment by moment. The more light we shed on the present moment, and the more eyes we bring to it, the greater our freedom and our power to do the right thing.

- *You build your personal program.* If you listen to people's newsreels of their past week, you may find useful information that helps you face similar challenges. Gradually, as you collect more of these little nuggets, you can assemble them in a meaningful mosaic that constitutes your personal recovery program. (There is more about this topic in the next chapter.)

- *Meetings encourage feedback and cross talk.* Possibly, you may hear something in the meeting that stimulates you to contribute an experience of your own. Please share it, even if this is your very first meeting. People often learn more from what they say than from what they hear. We also encourage comments that anyone else has on everyone's weekly experiences. It's not about one recitation and then another, but rather a general atmosphere of talking together across the table.

- *There's no shame or shaming.* Your sober presence at the meeting entitles you to respect. Your desire to be clean and sober – your S – brought you there. Your best thinking made you decide to get free of substances. You have no reason to be ashamed for being here. Your efforts to get substance-free validate you as a person. They also are a valuable resource for the group. From your Day One, you are not only a pupil but also a teacher.

- *Addiction is not a sin.* People in LifeRing groups tend to have a matter-of-fact attitude about substance addiction.

Chemical dependency is not a sin that you have to confess and atone for. It happens to people with all kinds of personalities, including people who are warm and caring, brilliant and generous. LifeRing meetings exist not to judge you or shame you or guilt you for your substance-influenced past but to support you in building your substance-free present and future. The point is to make a fresh start.

- *It stays positive.* The LifeRing approach is thoroughly positive. LifeRing works by giving encouragement and support to your sober qualities and efforts. You are reinventing yourself as a person who has a life without drinking or using, and in that process you are supporting others in doing the same. What you are doing is worthwhile and important, not only for you but for the group and for the whole community.

- *You're a grown-up.* Although you may count your sober time as a rebirth and celebrate sober baby birthdays, you are an adult and need to understand some adult truths. The tooth fairy will not come in the night and take your problems away. Only you can get you sober. The group cannot get you sober. Its purpose is to support you in getting yourself sober. Your purpose as a group member is to give others the same support you would want for yourself.

- *It's your responsibility.* The bottom line is that your recovery is always your responsibility. It's your work and yours alone. The session is successful if at the end your resolve to stay clean and sober feels a little stronger and better armed than it was when you came in.

- *It's confidential.* People in the group will respect your privacy and confidentiality. Please respect theirs. It is up to you what you share in meetings and to whom you disclose the fact of your own participation. Whatever you heard and whom you saw in a meeting stays in the meeting.

- *The credit is yours.* At the end of the typical LifeRing meeting, members will give each other a round of applause for staying clean and sober. Just as the responsibility and the work are yours, the credit is yours also. The LifeRing group process helps you feel good about yourself as a clean and sober person, to rebuild your sober self-esteem, and to discover and bring out your sober potentialities.

Labels Are Optional

Labels at LifeRing meetings are optional. Some people introduce themselves in the way they learned in the 12-step environment: "Hi, I'm Alex, alcoholic." Others just say their first names: "I'm Alex." Some use other terms and descriptions. That's completely up to you, and neither the convenor nor anyone else will pressure you about it. However, it's always good manners to say your first name.

Some people feel that labels like alcoholic help them remain abstinent by reminding them that they have a special condition that does not allow them to drink. Others feel the label stigmatizes them and robs them of the confidence they need to remain abstinent. Some people relapse despite or because of the label. Some people relapse despite or because of not using the label. Research indicates that statistically, labeling oneself doesn't seem to make any difference.[1] But statistical averages are meaningless in an individual case.

The label is optional in LifeRing not so much because we have a libertarian attitude generally but because recovering individuals need the latitude to choose the approach that is going to be most effective for them in staying free of the substances.

If you find that labeling yourself *alcoholic* or *addict* makes you feel strong, clear, and determined in your S, then by all means use it. If you find the label starting to fade and turn against you, by all means drop it. The label is not and should not be a fetish. What counts is what works today to empower your sober self.

How Was Your Week?

Formats may vary, but most LifeRing meetings most of the time use the "How Was Your Week" format:

- Participants sit in a circle. We try to keep meetings small enough so that this is possible. Everyone can see everyone else.

- The convenor reads or asks someone else to read a short opening statement that lays out the ground rules. This takes a minute or less.

- The convenor then turns to someone in the room or asks for a volunteer, with the question, "How was your week?"

- The person briefly tells the highlights and heartaches of his or her life since the last meeting, insofar as these events have to do with staying clean and sober. The person also looks ahead at possible recovery challenges coming up for the coming next week.

- Other group members may ask questions, share similar stories, or make positive comments about the first person's narrative. A conversation involving any number of group members may develop.

- When the conversation about the first person's report of the week is finished, we go on to the next person: "How was your week?" More conversation may follow.

- When we have gone all around the room in this way and the hour is over, we give each other a round of applause, and the meeting is done.

That's it. This very simple format is what goes on at most LifeRing meetings wherever they may be in the world.

Here's a small sample summary of how-was-my-week narratives that I heard in one recent LifeRing meeting in Oakland:

- How was my week? My boss made me go to the office party, even though there was alcoholic punch and I was just a week sober, and I did it and I didn't drink. I feel great.

- I got together with my sober buddy and we watched the Raiders game and didn't drink, for the first time I can remember.

- I drove home and there were my parents in the living room smoking crack. I ran out of the house and got back in my truck and peeled out of there.

- My sister and I talked and hugged each other for the first time since my daughter killed her daughter in a car accident when she was drunk, following in my footsteps. Now that I'm sober, we're talking again.

- I have no money now, nothing at all, and I went to my mom and asked her if I could move back home, and we cried.

- The week has been a roller coaster of feelings. Sometimes I felt ecstatic, other times I thought I was going insane. But I'm sober.

- Today is my birthday, and if I make it to bed sober it'll be my first sober birthday since middle school. It's scary and exciting.

Focusing on current events makes for a low entry barrier. If you can remember back a day or two, you can participate. You needn't have done any book reading or be eloquent about general recovery topics. It's normal for people to speak at their first LifeRing meeting.

Focusing on current events also means that the content of the meeting varies from week to week with the flow of life. Meetings become an ever-changing unscripted reality show, but better, because you not only observe, you participate. We have had people ask to participate even though they had no addiction issue, simply because LifeRing meetings provide a form of interesting, stimulating companionship.

An X-Ray of the Meeting Dynamic

How, you may ask, can this simple conversational format possibly generate the kind of internal dynamics necessary to help a person who is addicted to substances get free of them? The answer, in a nutshell, is positive S-to-S reinforcement.

If you could see inside the assembled heads in the meeting, you would notice that they each contain the A and the S: the basic conflicting elements that make up the personality of someone in the state of addiction. As the meeting proceeds, you would notice that the S is actively engaged in the process, while the A is sidelined. People are speaking from their S to the S in other people, and the content of their messages is of interest to their sober selves. The messages are rich in practical advice, inspiration, healing laughter, and hope; they expand the horizon of possibilities. As a result of this S-to-S connectedness, the S in each participant experiences growth, reinforcement, and expansion. Meanwhile the A, finding no engagement, connection, or nutrition, suffers atrophy and loses ground.

At the conclusion of each meeting, the sober self in each participant is more powerful than it was at the start. Over time, the S achieves a resilient dominance within the person. The person becomes transformed. Sobriety ceases to be an uphill struggle and becomes second nature.

In another work, I sketched this process graphically with diagrams.[2] The gist of it is that the process of sober-to-sober connectedness, which is the core and essence of the LifeRing

---

I Like the Format

The interactive meeting format in LifeRing allows me to get immediate feedback and support from my peers when I have an issue that threatens my sobriety, challenges my emotional health, or is an obstacle to living a happy life. I have a high degree of trust in the regular LifeRing attendees and know from experience that their suggestions are well-meaning and wise.

I also like the idea of getting support from a group, rather than a single person. I have experienced instances where a single "sponsor" gave bad advice. I find this risky, especially to someone early in recovery who is more apt to follow this advice blindly. I find the wisdom of my peers to be more helpful than that of a single person.

I also appreciate the absence of long speeches that you get at other types of meetings. There are usually plenty of short tales and pained looks from new members early in recovery. That is sufficient to remind me of the perils of relapse. I don't need tawdry details of people's drinking history; this sometimes romanticizes the old behavior as much as it serves as a deterrent.

– John B., San Francisco, California

meeting, reinforces and empowers the sober selves in each of the participants.

The Neurobiological Dimension

The sober self-empowerment process also has a neurobiological dimension. It isn't just our mind that's being changed; it's our brain.

The pioneer Canadian neurobiologist D. O. Hebb found that circuits in the brain become physically more robust, faster, and more efficient in proportion as they are activated. From this discovery came the famous Hebb's Law, expressed in a nutshell as "neurons that fire together, wire together."[3]

The opposite is also true: neurons in brain circuits that aren't activated will disconnect. The brain literally rewires itself to fit the use that we make of it. These are real anatomical changes, visible (in autopsy) with a microscope.

The LifeRing meeting process represents a kind of Hebb's Law on the interpersonal scale. By communicating with one another (firing together), the S circuits in each person become stronger, more robust, and more energetic. Meanwhile the A circuits atrophy. As the meeting participants discuss their current events, one activated brain area after another gets disconnected from the A network and switched over to the domain of the S. The activation of the interpersonal circuits brings with it – and drives – the actual Hebbian rewiring process in the brain of each participant.

This is the underlying process in the LifeRing meeting. It is the neurological dimension of the LifeRing slogan, "Empower Your Sober Self."

Our brain imaging devices are still too crude to follow the directional flow of complex brain circuits from one area of the brain to another.[4] But one day, we will be able to watch this process on a screen as the meeting proceeds.

Horizontal Synergy

Real people live their lives in complicated networks of relationships, some of which are peer based (horizontal), and some of which are authoritarian (vertical). They have bosses, or they are bosses; they have parents, or they are parents; they serve a god, or they think they're god. That's fine. All that's required for the LifeRing horizontal synergy engine to work is for people to leave their vertical entanglements – and the corresponding attitudes – at the door.

Clients in treatment programs have told me many times that the most helpful part of the program was their informal sessions with the other clients. Yes, the sessions with counselors might have been good too, but the most consistently powerful sessions in helping them get straightened out were with the other clients. In those get-togethers, they were spontaneously establishing the horizontal S-to-S synergy that powers LifeRing meetings.

Feedback and Cross-Talk

An important feature of the LifeRing format is our attitude toward cross-talk. Cross-talk is the somewhat stilted name given in recovery circles to the give-and-take of conversation. Really, cross-talk is feedback.

LifeRing meetings allow and encourage cross-talk. After a person has shared the highlights and heartaches of the week, anyone else in the room may ask a question or make a direct comment. These responses provide the first speaker with direct peer feedback. Ten words of peer feedback are often worth a thousand words of lecture. Feedback is a powerful force for change. The LifeRing meeting process has this force for change built in.

Meetings without feedback – a series of stand-alone monologues – are like having jumper cables running between cars but only connecting one wire. It takes two wires for power to flow. Horizontal synergy requires a two-way connection.

We do place one limitation on feedback (cross-talk) in LifeRing meetings: it must be neutral or positive. We do not allow attacks or confrontation; those methods are not only ineffective, they're also harmful.[5] You can read more about the hows and whys of positive cross-talk in the LifeRing convenor's handbook, *How Was Your Week?*[6] The rules are not strange or difficult; they are the unwritten rules that most people naturally adopt in ordinary friendly conversation.

Mirror Neurons

There is also a deeper reason why LifeRing meetings focus on the present. In 1996, Italian neuroscientists accidentally discovered in monkeys a previously unknown kind of brain cell that fired when the monkey observed a human pick up a peanut. It was not the sight of the peanut that stimulated the cell but the sight of the person performing the action of picking it up.[7]

Since that time, an enormous research effort has been invested in these mirror neurons, and similar cells have been located in the human brain. They may fire not only at the sight but also at the sound and narration of events that have a behavioral (action) component.

Mirror neurons have been called empathy neurons. They provide a channel by which I experience your action as if I were performing it myself. They are the neurophysiological basis of social togetherness. When others tell vivid, detail-filled narratives of their week, the feeling of resonance that occurs arises, very probably, from mirror neuron activation.

Mirror neurons can also work against recovery. Many people have told me that they drank or used other drugs immediately after attending 12-step meetings that contained vivid, detail-filled narratives of the speaker's history of taking addictive substances. These recitals, called "drunkalogues" or "drugalogues," are a standard element of the story formula in that setting. Detailing your substance use history is called "qualifying."[8] Apparently, some of the speakers qualify so effectively that they fire up the addiction-related mirror neurons of audience members and send them flying to the nearest bar or dealer.

Needless to say, activating and empowering the inner A is not an appropriate function for a sobriety support group meeting. This is another reason why the main focus of LifeRing meetings is on the sober here and now. Our purpose is to fire up the mirror neurons that secure our freedom from substances – the mirror neurons of the S.

The Spiritual Dimension

Participating in the LifeRing meeting process develops the most rewarding kind of spirituality – the positive feelings that connect us with other people.

Some people use the word *spiritual* to designate supernatural beliefs that are more properly called religious. We don't do religion in LifeRing meetings. Our membership is about as churchgoing as the average, but religious or anti-religious discussion is off topic during our meetings, the same as political discussion.

What I mean by *spiritual* here is just the human relationships that rise above the economic, political, clinical, or otherwise utilitarian. At the core of this kind of higher relationship is caring and connecting.

A LifeRing meeting is like an extended family that meets around a table to touch base. Then we each scatter into the world, meet with various adventures, and come back to the table to connect again. "How was your week?" is a way of saying, "I care." For a person newly emerging from the dark, lonely night of addiction, having a place in the circle connected with a group of faces who care provides a critical boost to the survival spirit.

Some meeting participants are prodigious in their capacity for empathy. There is no misfortune or misdeed that they do not meet with words of acceptance and encouragement. While they were in their addiction, they may have displayed all sorts of narcissism and meanness. Now that they are sober, these traits have yielded to their opposites. They become like den mothers or den fathers, taking in every sort of wounded stray, and enveloping them in the balm of human kindness.

Others achieve a helping spiritual connection without softness. They listen to a newcomer's troubles with a clear, comprehending gaze. They don't need to say, "Been there, done that." Their eyes, their calm expression, say it for them. The newcomer only has to glance into those steady eyes for an instant to feel understood, accepted, supported.

LifeRing meetings often produce a free flow of humor. The spirit of laughter – spontaneous, uncontrollable, sometimes riotous laughter – brings people together and heals wounds like no other force. People who can laugh at themselves become strong. People who can expose their foibles for others to laugh at become almost invulnerable. Among the most valued meeting participants are those who have the magic touch of starting a chain reaction of laughter in the group.

The usual LifeRing closing ritual promotes the spirit of mutual support and empowerment. We know that freedom from addictive substances is more than a matter of "just say no." We appreciate how much effort, how much psychic work, sometimes real agony, goes into maintaining our freedom and rebuilding our lives, particularly early on. The outside world little understands or appreciates what we do. But we understand. Each of us who is clean and sober today is a hero. We have triumphed today over one of the most pernicious, deadly disorders that afflicts people. And so, in closing the meeting, we give each other and ourselves a heartfelt and well-deserved round of applause.

In this chapter, we have looked at a method of positive reinforcement that involves a group setting. The power of social reinforcement, so deadly when directed toward the use of addictive substances, is liberating when applied to the sober potential, the S, inside the addicted person. Although the LifeRing group setting is casual and conversational, serious motivational business is taking place. The sum of these dynamics is to move the S from a subordinate, suppressed, imprisoned position to a predominant, hegemonic, liberated role: in short, the empowerment of the sober self.

Support group meetings, however, occupy only an hour or so out of twenty-four. They provide a jolt of S-energy that will dissipate over time unless the S meets with support and validation during the intervals between meetings. The meeting time may be too short to give the individual's own issues the deeper consideration that they require. In the next chapter, we look at sober survival outside the meeting context, using as a primary tool the *Recovery by Choice* workbook.

Notes

1. Hester and Miller, Handbook of Alcoholism Treatment Approaches: Effective Alternatives, p. 95.
2. Martin Nicolaus, How Was Your Week? Bringing People Together in Recovery the LifeRing Way (Oakland, Calif.: LifeRing Press, 2003), Ch. 2. A short animated PowerPoint slide show illustrating the process is online at http://lifering.org/the-a-and-the-s/
3. See, for example, Daniel J. Siegel, The Developing Mind: Toward a Neurobiology of Interpersonal Experience (New York: Guilford Press, 1999), p. 26.
4. Koob and Le Moal, Neurobiology of Addiction, p. 362.
5. Miller and White, "Confrontation in Addiction Treatment."
6. Nicolaus, How Was Your Week?
7. Martin Nicolaus, "The Role of Mirror Neurons in Addiction and Recovery," presented at the 2007 LifeRing Congress, Denver Colo., and at the 2007 NAADAC Conference, Nashville, Tenn., 2007), http://www.unhooked. com/discussion/index.htm#mirror .
8. Ernest Kurtz, Not-God: A History of Alcoholics Anonymous (Center City, Minn.: Hazelden, 1991) p. 215.

Chapter Four

BUILDING A PERSONAL RECOVERY PROGRAM

Addictive substances insert themselves into mainstream processes of the brain. As a result, substance use can warp many different areas of our lives: our bodies, our feelings, how we spend our time, our relationships with others, and so on. When we finally shake the substances off and purge them from our systems, we probably still have some work to do. We're also in a stronger position to look at any issues we may have that arose before substances entered our bodies and our lives.

Because the impact of substance use varies with the individual, each participant in LifeRing puts together a personal recovery program (PRP). This chapter discusses why we do it and how we do it. Much of this work takes place between meetings, and we can also do it on our own.

Why Build a Personal Recovery Program

Fitting the treatment to the patient is the standard procedure in medicine. It has, however, not been the usual approach in treating chemical dependency.[1] It is therefore useful to hear the voices of some important students of the chemical dependency field who have come to the conclusion that a personalized treatment approach is as essential here as it is in standard medical practice.

Quality treatment programs in the substance field use an individualized approach. A comprehensive study of treatment programs by the National Institute on Drug Abuse (NIDA), a federal agency, found as its leading principle:

> No single treatment is appropriate for all individuals. Matching treatment settings, interventions, and services to each individual's particular problems and needs is critical to his or her ultimate success in returning to productive functioning in the family, workplace, and society.[2]

In other words, an individualized approach is essential for treatment effectiveness. This same rule applies where the client presents with co-occurring disorders (addiction plus a mental health issue). A statement of overarching principles issued by the Center for Mental Health Services and the Center for Substance Abuse Treatment of the federal Substance Abuse and Mental Health Service Administration (SAMHSA) states the following:

> Treatment should be individualized to accommodate the specific needs, personal goals, and cultural perspectives of unique individuals in different stages of change.[3]

The same finding emerged from a meta-analysis of hundreds of treatment outcome studies by Professors Reid Hester and William R. Miller of the University of New Mexico. The best design for a recovery treatment program is based on *informed eclecticism*, offering the patient a choice of different evidence-supported methods, looking for a good fit for the individual. The authors write:

> There does not seem to be any one treatment approach adequate to the task of treating all individuals with alcohol problems. We believe that the best hope lies in assembling a menu of effective alternatives, and then seeking a

system for finding the right combination of elements for each individual.[4]

In other words, the treatment professional ought to have a toolkit comprising a number of different approaches and assemble them in a combination that works for the individual patient.

William White, the historian and a senior trainer of substance abuse counselors, reaches the same conclusion from a historical perspective:

> With our two centuries of accumulated knowledge and the best available treatments, there still exists no cure for addiction, and only a minority of addicted clients achieve sustained recovery following our intervention in their lives. There is no universally successful cure for addiction – no treatment specific.[5]

Because there is no silver bullet that magically cures everyone, a deeply individualized approach is a clinical necessity. The editors of *Substance Abuse: A Comprehensive Textbook*, a monumental compendium that attempts to define the state of the science, reach the same conclusion:

> Each patient or client develops problems in unique ways and forms a unique relation to the substance of choice. Common sense dictates that treatment must respond to the needs of each individual.[6]

Indeed, responding to the needs of each individual is only common sense. One hallmark of a substance abuse treatment program that operates in a professional manner is its focus on building and carrying out a personalized treatment program for each patient.

It would be absurd if the individuals whose recovery it is were to set for themselves a lower standard than that which professionals have recognized as necessary. If a professional needs to respond to the needs of each individual, then the individual can do no less in his or her self-help work. If "one size fits all" does not work in professional treatment, it certainly has no place in self-treatment.

LifeRing embraces the modern, evidence-based principle of individualized treatment and applies it to self-treatment. Apart from the prime directive – not to put addictive substances into the body – which we all share, LifeRing dismisses the notion that any single program is appropriate for all our participants. Matching our program to our individual problems and needs is what each of us does and should do. Building a LifeRing Personal Recovery Program is what both science and common sense indicate.

The *Recovery by Choice* Workbook

LifeRing contains several pathways for reclaiming our lives from addictive substance use. The first pathway we have already discussed in the previous chapter, namely participation in LifeRing meetings, face-to-face or online. In this chapter, we focus on the pathway of workbook study, using the *Recovery by Choice* workbook, and other ideas for a Personal Recovery Program.[7]

The main focus of LifeRing meetings is to process the everyday decisions that we are making in our sober lives. Here are the issues I confronted last week; here is what I did and am doing to solve them in a clean and sober manner; here is what I will be facing next week; here is what I intend to do in order to prevail as a person who is free of substances. The sequence of such everyday decisions constitutes the person's recovery plan. We may not always call it that, but what people are doing is writing their own recovery plan, week by week, in their heads. They are answering the essay question, "How Do I Live Sober?" without using pencil or paper.

My Leap of Faith

On the evening of Friday, October 26, 2007, I looked into the eyes of my two beautiful toddlers and poured out the remainder of my last drink. After I put them to bed, I sat down at the computer and googled "quit drinking."
The first result was lifering.org. I opened it to find LifeRing. What was this –"Recovery by Choice"? I was intrigued, explored the site further, and soon discovered that a face-to-face meeting was held every Saturday in Burlingame. In other words, I had the opportunity to go to my very first support meeting in about twelve hours, just minutes away from my home. My heart raced. My palms sweated. Could I actually go through with it? Alone?
I decided to take a chance at entering the website chat room. There was another first-timer online and he (or she, I didn't know) was actually considering showing up at the Burlingame meeting, too. Again, my heart raced and my palms sweated. What was I doing? What was I thinking? I wanted to get sober . . . not get abducted!
After I calmed down and continued to "chat" with my new online acquaintance, I agreed that if he (or she) promised to try to make it that I'd do the same. I took one of the biggest leaps of faith walking into that meeting the next day . . . and so did my new sober friend, Amy. What met us was a roomful of support, understanding, love and acceptance. I have continued to attend LifeRing meetings ever since, and they have helped to redirect the course of my life.
I started drinking when I was thirteen. I would like to help teenagers realize that alcohol, drugs and tobacco are not a true "rite of passage," no matter what our society or their peers may try to tell them. My aim is to assemble resources and support for teenagers to find their true calling, and do it clean and sober.

— Trish M., Pacifica, California

The *Recovery By Choice* workbook is a tool that allows people to do the same program-building work and answer the same question using pencil and paper.

When we speak at a meeting or hear someone else speak, the words aren't recorded anywhere and we may soon forget them. When we write them in a book, they're preserved for future reference.

When we only work on our program orally, from meeting to meeting, our work tends to proceed more or less in random fashion. What we think about depends to a great extent on who happened to be at the meeting and what people happened to talk about. When we work in a book, we can proceed in a more organized way. Using the book, we can decide the whole sequence and content of our recovery planning in a comprehensive manner.

When you're done with the book, you have a written product that you can carry with you, consult and revise as required, and share with others. Working with the book gives you the advantages of permanence, organization, and control – in a word, structure.

Some people only attend LifeRing meetings (face-to-face or online) and never crack open the workbook. That works fine for them. The workbook is not the LifeRing "Bible" and it isn't even "suggested." It's just one available tool. Other people only work the workbook and have never attended a LifeRing meeting. (The workbook is filled with content that originated in LifeRing meetings.) Book work alone – the technical name is bibliotherapy – works fine for them.

The Nine Work Areas
for a Personal Recovery Program

The general strategy of building a PRP is to expand the area that the sober self (S) occupies, at the expense of the addict self (A). This is, of course, the same concept that underlies the process inside the LifeRing meeting. For the sake of practical convenience, I'm going to divide the global territory into a series of nine specific work areas or domains. Each domain has its own chapter in the *Recovery by Choice workbook.*

1. *The body.* Give yourself a medical checkup. Have a look at any visible and hidden body damage from substance use, as well as a broad range of related concerns, such as nutrition, nicotine use, coffee, sugar, teeth, physical diseases, mental health issues, pregnancy, old age, death. Conclude by making a checklist of concerns and making a plan to go see a doctor or another health care provider or to get more information as you feel appropriate.

2. *The immediate environment.* This concerns environmental cues and triggers for substance use at home, at work, in transit, and in your social life. You create a map of your hot spots, rank them in order of their danger for you, and make a plan for avoiding them or dealing with them. Consider creating a safe, substance-free space for yourself. A daily exercise that enhances freedom from substances concludes the chapter. There is space for comparing your concerns today, three months from now, and a year from now.

3. *Time and activities.* What activities fill your daily schedule? Which of these activities are linked in your life to substance use? Which of these activities should you avoid for now? Which activities can you learn to do now without

substances? There are worksheets to help you find patterns in your substance use and to find alternate activities to fill your time. There is a detailed worksheet for learning to do any particular activity clean and sober.

4. *People.* Some people in your life support your freedom from substances, some don't know that it's an issue for you, and some try to drag you back. Learn to identify these three kinds of people and develop strategies for dealing with them. What defines supporters of your sobriety? What can you ask them to do? Should you reveal yourself as a person in recovery to people who don't already know? How can you deal with people who try to get you to go back to substance use? What if you are in an intimate relationship with someone who feels threatened by your new freedom from substances? Make a plan for developing substance-free relationships.

5. *Feelings.* Learn to recapture old sober sources of pleasure and develop new ones that don't involve substance use. Learn to recognize your feelings, cultivate a more vibrant emotional life, handle roller-coaster experiences, manage the sudden return of repressed emotions, deal with cravings and other seemingly overwhelming emotions, learn to work with the powers you already have, and make a plan for resolving issues that predate your substance use.

6. *Lifestyle.* To one extent or another, your substance use may have affected your work, housing, living situation, social life, housekeeping, personal appearance, sex life, finances, legal situation, and other lifestyle aspects. Make a plan for changing any area where you feel that substance use has had an unwelcome impact.

7. *History.* You had a life before you started using substances. Can you reconnect with who you were then and resume where you left off before you started using substances?

This domain involves tools for understanding and getting past your commencement of substance use, understanding the neurobiological dimension of addiction, assessing the costs and benefits of substance use in your life, assessing credit and blame, repairing harms, and letting go emotionally of this period.

8. *Culture.* Culture is the larger environment in which you maintain your freedom from substances. You become aware of cultural messages via television and other media, and you have a look at the economics and politics of substance use. You look at the subcultures to which you belong, or which you could become part of, and assess them from the standpoint of whether they help or hinder your sober life's course. You make a plan for becoming an active participant in your cultural setting.

9. *Treatment and support groups.* If your path to freedom from substances leads you through treatment and support groups, it will be helpful to have realistic expectations and to insist on getting what you need to support your recovery.

There's also a big chapter on relapse, but that isn't a separate domain; it's a synopsis of all the others. It should go without saying that the nine domains are interrelated in many ways and that any issue in your life may pop up in two or more domains. The fact that some issues are prominent in multiple domains is a clue that highlights their importance when it comes to setting priorities. You may also find that you have no work to do, or very little, in one or more of the domains, or in sections of domains, because your situation in that area was not seriously affected by your substance use and no remedial work is required. It's your call.

This Beautiful Clarity

The setting was idyllic: a beautiful beach, a glorious setting sun, a gentle breeze, a charming man beside me, and a glass in my hand. Just like all the ads one sees on TV and in magazines for living the perfect life. The big difference was that the glass in my hand held not wine or some umbrella-clad cocktail, but pure, fresh, sparkling water.

As I became aware of this iconic situation I asked myself a question: "If I could have a drink – an alcoholic drink, that is – right now, would I want it?" The answer came back to me loud and clear: "No way. This is just perfect the way it is. Drinking alcohol now would interfere with this beautiful clarity I feel, and just get in the way. Why on earth would I want to spoil this?"

At that moment I understood that I had really integrated sobriety into my life, and that I need never be afraid to get out into the world and live my life fully. I no longer needed the crutch of booze. This was something that I had learned using the LifeRing approach to sobriety – figuring out in my own way my own program of recovery, the one that best fitted my needs and lifestyle.

The LifeRing approach to getting and staying clean and sober resonated powerfully with me. The positive support from my fellow attendees, the conversations, and the laughter in the meetings, have always been a great source of inspiration.

I am approaching my tenth anniversary of abstinence. The thought of drinking is barely a flash of consciousness now. Way to go!

– Gillian E., San Francisco, California

Abstinence, the Common Element in All LifeRing Personal Recovery Programs

The common element in all LifeRing PRPs is abstinence from the addictive substances. The legend at the top of every page of the workbook reads the following: "Sobriety is my priority. I don't drink or use no matter what." Abstinence is one point where the LifeRing approach is in complete agreement with the 12-step groups and most treatment programs.

Abstinence is also the number-one choice among people who have no use for 12-step programs or 12-step treatment. Here are some examples:

- Author Anne M. Fletcher interviewed 223 study subjects who had successful recoveries. Practically all were unaffiliated with 12-step groups, and all but one elected abstinence.[8]

- Out of a sample of forty-six alcoholics and other addicts who recovered without treatment or support groups in a study by Professors Granfield and Cloud of the University of New Mexico, all but two practiced abstinence.[9]

Although it's common for people who are unhappy with their substance use to go through a period of trying to reduce or to moderate their intake, the most popular strategy is to stop completely. Abstinence is popular with so many people with such a wide diversity of philosophies and life experiences for a number of reasons. The main reasons are that abstinence is safe, sustainable, less work, and more satisfying.

- *Abstinence is safe.* If a person who cannot moderate mistakenly drinks or uses, the consequences are liable to be painful. Even if that individual does not quickly land in an emergency room, it's likely that there will be a gradual slide into excessive use with major problems. People have died from this mistake. But if a person who could moderate mistakenly abstains, there is no harm done. Nobody needs the addictive substances. People who have had a history of substance use are simply safer to stay away from them, period.

- *Abstinence is sustainable.* When we abstain from the substances, the urges to use them gradually atrophy, like a fire burning out, and they lose all their fascination. But when we put them into the body occasionally, we throw gasoline on the fire, and we keep their appeal alive. They tend to destabilize our thinking, depress our self-confidence, and derail our recovery motivation.

- *Abstinence is less work.* We fight the battle of the urges once, when we stop, and maybe at occasional flare-ups during times of stress, but the basic trend is for the cravings to fade over time. If we put substances into the body from time to time, we wake up the whole craving syndrome and have to start from Day One all over again. It's exhausting and for what? Do we want to spend the rest of our lives fighting this war over and over? Abstinence lets us fight the big battle once and thereafter enforce and enjoy a permanent peace.

- *Abstinence is satisfying.* To have a body and a mind that aren't polluted by addictive substances, to have senses that are chemically unimpaired, to lead a life that has meaning and gives satisfaction without artificial enhancements, to enjoy real bodily and mental wellness – these are deep and enduring pleasures. No drug high even comes close.

The distinction between abstinence and moderation is fundamental to the LifeRing self-empowerment approach. Self-empowerment means that we have or we can achieve the

Staying Sober My Way

LifeRing doesn't require me to label myself in any way. I did not have to say "my name is" and I did not have to say "I am" anything.

As it states on the web site, LifeRing "welcomes people regardless of their faith or lack of it." I am a Christian. I feel very comfortable with LifeRing. LifeRing did not expect me to believe or not believe in anything. My personal beliefs are my own business, and I like the way that LifeRing allows me to keep my privacy.

I can be as anonymous as I choose to be. And that helps me to feel safe. I like that.

I got practical support. I learned ways of increasing my coping skills. I received caring feedback. Without anyone expecting that I "had to" take their advice. I could make up my own mind about what parts to use or disregard. To choose what would work for me. So I could figure out the best way for me to stay sober.

And I emphasize – for me. Not for everybody else. There was no "one way." The assumption seemed to be that each person was unique, and what worked for one person may or may not work for someone else.

I have used the LifeRing online resources – the discussion forum, the email lists and the chats – as my primary means of support to stay sober. I like the fact that I don't have to travel to a meeting. I can sit at home (even in my pajamas!) and get online sobriety support anytime, day or night, by simply typing on my computer. It's great!

I have been free from alcohol dependency for over 7 years now. That feels good. LifeRing works for me.

– Gal, Seattle, Washington

power to abstain from Drink No. 1. No divine assistance is necessary. Self-efficacy is the power to affirm zero. That affirmation may seem difficult at first, but with time and practice it becomes easier, and eventually it becomes natural and effortless. If we never take Drink No. 1, we never have to worry about Drink No. 2 and the rest.

Empowerment to abstain from Drink No. 2 is an addict's delusion. The first thing that Drink No. 1 will do is to dissolve the inhibitions against taking Drink No. 2. Many LifeRing participants can testify that their encounters with the "just-one genie" ended in disaster for them. It may happen instantly or it may happen gradually over months, but sooner or later control will go, struggle as you will. Taking Drink No. 1 is equivalent to throwing one's self-efficacy out the window. It's a decision to abandon control, to surrender one's power, and to stop caring what happens.

As if human example were not clear enough, experimenters have demonstrated the whole dynamic in laboratory rodents. First, the animals are rendered dependent on the substance. They press a lever to get more, hundreds or thousands of times. Then experimenters cut off their supply; hitting the lever now does nothing. Long after the animals get over their withdrawal symptoms and lose interest in the lever, the experimenters give them a single priming dose. Surprise! The animals quickly start hammering on that lever again, just as if they had never stopped.[10]

All of this holds not only for alcohol but also for all the other drugs of addiction.

Building a Personal Recovery Program on Your Own

If you are a person who wants to stop consuming addictive substances, you will probably find yourself building your personal recovery program without being consciously aware of it. For example, your dealer phones. You tell your dealer not to call anymore. What have you done? You've removed an environmental trigger, and you've distanced yourself from a person who is an opponent of your recovery. You've placed an important stone or two into the mosaic of your new identity.

Most people proceed in this random fashion, facing challenges as they come up; and the capacity to respond purposefully to such unexpected occasions is an important element in any good recovery program. Still, the idea of a PRP suggests something more systematic and structured. How can you go about it, if you don't like workbooks and you don't like meetings, even online? Here are some suggestions:

- *Begin where it hurts.* Let's say you decided to get sober because your doctor showed you bad liver numbers. Start with your body. Go for a healthy diet. Eliminate trashy foods. Investigate vitamins and supplements. Start healthy exercise. At each point, write down your thoughts, your research, and your decisions. That's a beginning.

- *Follow where your starting point leads.* To continue with the example, your new healthy diet may require renegotiating your living arrangement with people close to you. Do your significant others support your new life? As you begin to exercise, you will need to arrange your schedule differently. Which of your current activities needs to be dumped to make time for healthy activity? Besides exercise, what other upgrades could be made in your daily schedule? Do you really need to spend so much couch time watching TV? Isn't there some activity you used to like to do (maybe swimming) that you can start up again, or some new activity you've always wanted to do (play the guitar?) but put off because the substances were more important? You'll see that your starting point was like a pebble dropped into a pool, with ripples spreading out in all directions. Again, keep track of your changes, write them down.

- *Work on your internal changes as you make external changes.* Each new issue you encounter brings up feelings inside you – often feelings you didn't know you had. For example, you try to negotiate your living arrangement with a significant other, and you find the S.O. is supportive and understanding. You are filled with appreciation and love, and you are motivated to deepen the relationship. Or your S.O. is acting stupid and hostile. You experience feelings of conflict, doubt, and alienation. Or there is no one else in your life and you feel intensely lonely. Can you handle this powerful emotion without using addictive substances? Do you have the nerve and the resources to get professional help if your better sense tells you the situation calls for it? As you go through these passages, write it all down.

- *Let your emotional changes lead you toward further developments in your behavior.* The point of making changes in life is to feel better in your skin. Now you're eating well, exercising, feeling healthier, but feeling depressed by your job or by the people in your life. Don't get stuck here; stay proactive. Research a job change, a career change, a return to school, whatever it may take to make you happier about your work life. Don't like the people now in your life? Figure out what kind of people make you happier, and figure out how to spend more time with them. Write it all down.

- *Review and revise as you proceed.* The beauty of having written it all down is that you can look back over any point later and either underline it or scratch it out and revise it. The exercise will help you see your life in a three-dimensional way and make you a deeper philosopher. You will see that because you have examined it and changed it, your life has become worth living.

- *At some point, open up your PRP to others.* Some people are very shy and private, and that's OK, but if you're active in your pursuits, you are very likely to run into a person, or several, whom you can trust. Open up about the changes you are making and the issues you've encountered. You may be amazed at the degree of understanding and empathy that you encounter. In effect, you'll be building your own personal recovery support group. Even just one other person who knows and understands can make a world of difference.

If you've done all that, you've essentially followed the main outlines of the *Recovery by Choice* workbook. No matter what your actual starting point is – a bad lab result from your doctor, or a penetrating remark from your child, or any other wake-up call – you will find that each change in your behavior calls for other changes, that behavior and feelings mutually affect one another, that you will make new connections, and that moving through this passage with your eyes wide open will make you a happier and wiser person.

The Challenges and Rewards
of a Personal Recovery Program

Building a PRP is challenging. It requires greater effort than following a factory-issue linear program. The *Recovery by Choice* workbook supplies questions to ask yourself, but there's no answer sheet. The point of the book is not to test your knowledge about addiction in general, or about the addiction recovery programs that other people used, but to help you discover what is going to work for you. The same is true, obviously, if you work on your own without a text to guide you.

To build a PRP, you have to think hard about yourself and your world. Of course, you can discuss your issues at a LifeRing meeting and get the benefit of other eyes, but no one is going to tell you what to do. What worked for someone else in a different situation may not be the solution for you in your situation. Because there's no answer book, there's no way to cheat. Because no one else is going to grade your work, there's no point in giving answers that you think will please the teacher.

The only test of your work comes from life itself. Are you feeling the grip of the addictive substances loosening from your body and your mind? Are you living life more fully and with more engagement? If so, your program is successful. If not, there is a bug in your program, and you need to track it down and revise your plan accordingly.

Building a PRP
Is Not Everyone's Cup of Tea

Some people say, "I don't want to do what I want to do; I want you to tell me what to do!" Of course, as soon as someone tells them what to do, they rebel. Catch-22. Such people find the LifeRing approach terminally frustrating. It contains no authority figure to which they can shift blame, other than themselves. One of my favorite reader responses to the *Recovery by Choice* workbook was from a reader who said she really hated it – and that it was the most useful book she had ever worked through.

Others say, "I don't want to figure out what will work for me, that's too much thinking." They don't want to do recovery, they want to have it done to them, like a patient etherized on a table. Recovery will probably elude them as long as they maintain this passive attitude.

Some people are so down on themselves that they cannot get their minds around the self-help concept, on which building a personal recovery program is founded. Poor me, I'm too sick (dumb, crazy, and so on) to figure out what's good for me. I've tried "my way" and I've always failed. Such people have not recognized the S inside themselves, or they have been convinced that they have no such thing, even though they would not be alive in its absence.

Fortunately, there are other groups where they can be served. LifeRing does not aspire to be all things to all people. We are for that special population that tends to be anti-authoritarian and insists on figuring things out for themselves – in short, the typical alcoholic or addict and the average American.

Although the challenge is great, the rewards are high. Generally speaking, constructing a personal recovery program has these benefits:

- *Self-Knowledge.* You've thought hard about who you really are and what you want out of life. You have a better picture of yourself, without the confusion and self-deception that come with substance use and stereotyped recovery formulas.

- *Comfort.* This program is tailor-made for you. It fits you well. You're comfortable in it, and you move with ease. You're happy to be seen in it and to tell other people about it. You're likely to stay with it for a long time.

- *Portability.* This program resides in you, not in the environment where you happen to reside at the moment. It is anchored in your core personality structures. Wherever you go, it goes with you.

- *Investment.* This is not a program you've got off the shelf. It's something in which you invested a lot of effort. You feel a sense of ownership in it and identification with it. You are it and it is you.

- *Resilience.* You've put your personal program together yourself, bit by bit, and you know how and why it works for you. If your circumstances change, you are able to adapt it as required. If something goes wrong, you're back on your feet quickly.

- *Self-Efficacy.* You've demonstrated the ability to free yourself from substance use, one of the more difficult challenges in life. You have good reason to be confident that you can continue to remain free of the substances and that you can go ahead and tackle other problems that life puts in your path.

- *Good feeling.* You've examined your life and you've found a solution that works for you. Other people have helped and deserve your thanks, but their help would have amounted to nothing without your own strong motivation and hard work. You deserve the credit, lots of it.

In short, the challenging process of building your PRP will bring out the best in you. You may end up paradoxically thinking of the substance-using period in your life as not such a bad thing, because in the process of closing that chapter, you examined your life more deeply than before and gained a clarity and sense of wellness that otherwise might have eluded you.

Self-Help and Professional Help

Dr. Judith Herman at Harvard spent twenty years study-ing victims of trauma – women who had been raped, soldiers in combat, victims of political terrorism, and others. One might think that these shattered persons would benefit from an authoritarian, structured healing approach where a trusted, experienced person basically held them by the hand like chil-dren and told them what to do. Not so, Dr. Herman found. Just the contrary:

> The first principle of recovery is the empowerment of the survivor. She must be the author and arbiter of her own recovery. Others may offer advice, support, assistance, affection, and care, but not cure. Many benevolent and well-intentioned attempts to assist the survivor founder because this fundamental principle of empowerment is not observed. No intervention that takes power away from the survivor can possibly foster her recovery, no matter how much it appears to be in her immediate best interests.[11]

Just so must we, who are emerging from the trauma of sub-stance addiction, become the authors and arbiters of our own recoveries.

In the words of Dr. Linda Dimeff and Dr. Alan Marlatt at the University of Washington, experts on relapse in chemical dependency, the most successful client in resisting relapse is the one who "confidently acts as his or her own therapist."[12] If you follow the LifeRing approach, you will in fact become the author and arbiter of your own recovery and act confidently as your own therapist.[13]

Lori Ashcraft, Ph.D., a senior clinician in a private treat-ment program, found that the same patient-centered ap-proach is effective in a mental health setting:

When given a chance, people who were asked and involved in creating their treatment would regularly pre-
scribe for themselves treatment that would work. Sometimes my only contribution to their success was believing
in them until they believed in themselves."[14]

Dr. Vaillant, whom I've quoted earlier, for several years led
an addiction recovery clinic, in addition to the research study
he headed. His experience was that the dominant factor in
determining the success or failure of treatment was not the
kind of treatment used but rather the role of the patient. His
experience and data, he wrote, "bear powerful witness that
alcoholics recover not because we treat them but because they
heal themselves."[15]

Self-efficacy – an evidence-based expectancy that a person
can handle life's challenges – is a powerful predictor of successful long-term abstinence from addictive substances.[16] This
is true even in people with severe mental disorders.[17] People
with a low sense of self-efficacy succumbed to temptations
and tended to relapse quickly and frequently.[18] LifeRing participation, in which you empower your S, builds your sense of
self-efficacy and makes you more successful in building a life
free of addictive substances.

You will heal when and because you heal yourself. But this
does not mean that you work on your recovery in voluntary
isolation or that you reject professional help. On the contrary.
Recovery means, in very large part, reestablishing safe and sober relationships with other people. Being in charge of your
own recovery also gives you the freedom and the power to
draw on the broadest possible range of professional assistance
that may be available to you.

There are more tools, methods, approaches, and resources
on the psychological marketplace than any one person can
possibly know about. There are many thousands of professionals with good insights, attitudes, and approaches who

may be able to offer you something useful to add to your personal program. Sharing of experiences about different care providers, pharmaceuticals, and schools of psychology is a recurrent topic at LifeRing meetings and in online groups, and the *Recovery by Choice* workbook contains repeated references and reminders to consult professional help when appropriate. Effective people demonstrate competence by acquiring the help they need when they need it.

Like a passenger coming off an airplane after a long hijacking ordeal, you may find that the end of substance use is the beginning of self-repair. To one extent or another, you may have suffered physical or emotional damage or damage to your relationships. You may have done damage to others, and your life may be in disarray in various ways.

Fortunately, now that you are no longer impaired by mindaltering substances, you are much more capable than before of facing these other issues. You have available to you the supportive framework and the collective experience of LifeRing support groups, face-to-face and online, should you choose to go there. You have available to you the content-rich, nonlinear, networked structure of the *Recovery by Choice* workbook and other sources, helping you to organize your work into manageable domains and to build your personal recovery program in a coherent format that you can revise and share with others. You have the power and the freedom to build new relationships and to utilize available professional help whenever you feel it appropriate.

In the next chapters, we'll have a look at some of the major ideas that dominate the current recovery marketplace.

Notes

1. Arnold Washton and Richard Rawson, "Substance Abuse Treatment Under Managed Care: A Provider Perspective," in The American Psychiatric Publishing Textbook of Substance Abuse Treatment, 3rd ed., 2004, p. 547.
2. National Institute on Drug Abuse, Principles of Drug Abuse Treatment: A Research-Based Guide (National Institute on Drug Abuse, 1999).
3. Substance Abuse and Mental Health Administration, "Overarching Principles to Address the Needs of Persons With Co-occurring Disorders" (Substance Abuse and Mental Health Administration, 2006), http://www. coce.samhsa.gov/cod_ resources/PDF/OverarchingPrinciples(OP3).pdf.
4. Hester and Miller, Handbook of Alcoholism Treatment Approaches: Effective Alternatives, p. 33.
5. White, Slaying the Dragon, p. 342.
6. Joyce H. Lowinson, Substance Abuse: A Comprehensive Textbook, 3rd ed. (Philadelphia: Lippincott, 1997), p. xi.
7. Nicolaus, Recovery by Choice: Living and Enjoying Life Free of Alcohol and Drugs, a Workbook.
8. Anne M. Fletcher, Sober for Good: New Solutions for Drinking Problems – Advice from Those Who Have Succeeded (Boston: Houghton Mifflin Cookbooks, 2002), p. 21.
9. Granfield and Cloud, Coming Clean, p. 21.
10. Roy A. Wise, "Addiction," in Steven's Handbook of Experimental Psychology, 2002, pp. 801-839; World Health Organization, Neuroscience of Psychoactive Substance Use and Dependence, p. 54 (citing studies); Koob and Le Moal, Neurobiology of Addiction.
11. Judith Lewis Herman, Trauma and Recovery: The Aftermath of Violence – From Domestic Abuse to Political Terror (New York: Basic Books, 1997), p. 133.
12. Linda Dimeff and Alan Marlatt, "Relapse Prevention," in Handbook of Alcoholism Treatment Approaches, 2nd ed., 1995, pp. 176-177.
13. Beeder makes this point forcefully for patients with co-occurring disorders: "As in the treatment of other populations, the importance of empowering the patient to take responsibility for his or her own behavior and treatment cannot be overemphasized." Ann B. Beeder and Robert Millman, "Patients with Psychopathology," in Substance Abuse: A Comprehensive Textbook, 3rd ed., 1997, p. 554.
14. Lori H. Ashcraft and William A. Anthony, "Breaking Down Barriers," Behavioral Healthcare (April 2008), p. 8.
15. Vaillant, The Natural History of Alcoholism Revisited, p. 384.
16. Alan Marlatt, Kimberly Barrett, and Dennis Daley, "Relapse Prevention," in The American Psychiatric Publishing Textbook of Substance Abuse Treatment, 2nd ed., 1995, p. 357.
17. Jazmin I. Warren, Judith A. Stein, and Christine E. Grella, "Role of Social Support and Self-Efficacy in Treatment Outcomes Among Clients with Co-

occurring disorders," Drug and Alcohol Dependence 89, no. 2/3 (July 10, 2007): 267-274, doi:S0376-8716(07)00045-2.

18. Albert Bandura, Self-efficacy: The Exercise of Control (New York: Freeman, 1997), p. 364; Goldstein, Addiction: From Biology to Drug Policy, p. 241.

Chapter Five

▼

ABOUT POWERLESSNESS

In the fourth century A.D., at the dawn of the Dark Ages, not long after Christianity became the official religion of the remnants of the Roman Empire, there lived two wandering teachers.

One was a Christian monk named Pelagius. Born in the remote provinces of the British Isles, he found his way to the imperial capital and also visited and taught in Carthage and in Palestine. He led an exemplary life of poverty, modesty, and virtue. Even those who opposed his teachings respected his lifestyle. He preached that God had endowed human beings with the power and the freedom to make moral choices, both for evil and for good.

The other teacher was by his own public admission a fornicator, a thief, and a drinker, among other vices, in addition to being the father of an illegitimate child. He was a Manichean – a religion that holds that everything composed of matter, including all living beings, is dark, corrupt, and evil but that the forces of light, which exist outside material things, will eventually prevail. His sudden midlife conversion to Christianity and his quick promotion to bishop of the North African city of Hippo aroused so much popular skepticism that he felt it politic to write a 160,000-word "Confessions" in his own defense. He preached, in opposition to Pelagius, that man was powerless to choose virtue and could only choose sin; whatever human beings achieve that is good, they achieve exclusively through the power and grace of God, and God alone deserves the credit.

When my chemical dependency counselor on my Day One in 1992 held up for me the two schedules of the two kinds of recovery support group meetings – the groups that became LifeRing and the 12-step groups – I had no inkling that I stood before a modern edition of the dispute between the virtuous monk Pelagius and the converted sinner Augustine of Hippo.

Choice or Powerlessness

In the first chapter, we saw that inner conflict – Dr. Jekyll versus Mr. Hyde – is a core experience of the addicted person.

Inner conflict is a Pelagian concept. If you have the power of choice between good or evil, you will experience inner conflict. Both antagonists will exert some force on you, pushing you this way and that. To make a choice means to resolve a conflict.

In the film *A Beautiful Mind*, based on the life of the brilliant mathematician John Nash, the Nash character (played by Russell Crowe) suffers psychotic hallucinations: people who seem real and who control his life but exist only in his mind. His psychiatrist tries to persuade him to submit to a round of heavy shock treatments that risk turning him into a vegetable.

Says the doctor, "You can't reason your way out of this . . . because your mind is where the problem is in the first place."[1] That is an Augustinian viewpoint: the mind is 100 percent diseased.

But Nash finds a small place in his mind that is not damaged – an inner island of sanity – and he proceeds to build from there. The strategy works for Nash. He expands his sane base, reconnects with real people, renders his imaginary people small and powerless, and goes on to regain his functioning, his family, and his professional standing. He ultimately wins a Nobel Prize.

The idea that a mind can be divided into parts, one bad, the other good, is a Pelagian idea. Even if the good part is only 1 percent, all hope lies there.

The Augustinian Doctrine of Alcoholics Anonymous

The first step of Alcoholics Anonymous (AA), which forms the primary text of more than 70 percent of American addiction treatment programs, is absolutely Augustinian. It says flatly that "we are powerless over alcohol."

Not that we have within us both the power to go down with alcohol and the power to get free of it. *Not* that we are in inner conflict about our use of alcohol. *Not* that our power to get free of alcohol is at times as fierce and vigorous as our obsession to drink. *Not* that our urge to drink and our power not to drink are in a frequently changing balance. *Not* that there is dissonance within us about the substance. *Not* that we are powerless *if* or powerless *when*.

No balancing, no qualifications, no conditions, no exceptions. Just powerless over alcohol. Only an A. No S.

The identity between the AA doctrine of powerlessness and the teaching of Augustine is not coincidental. Augustine himself – no stranger to the fermented grape – formulated the doctrine of powerlessness over alcohol in a nutshell: "For no one can be continent unless Thou give it."[2] No one can abstain from alcohol or moderate intake, except by the power and grace of God. That's the AA approach.

The Augustinian doctrine came down to Bill Wilson, the cofounder of AA and author of the 12 steps, through a Christian fundamentalist evangelical sect known as the Oxford Group, in which Wilson was active when he began to work with alcoholics. A number of religious scholars have previously traced the Augustinian roots of the AA Step 1 powerlessness clause.[3]

The Problems of the Zero-Power Doctrine

What I'm concerned with here is not the fact that the zero-power clause is a religious doctrine. There are lots of useful religious ideas (for example, "Thou shalt not kill"). What troubles me is the mismatch between this doctrine and the inner reality of the person suffering from addiction and approaching recovery.

In the real mind of the addicted person, there are two forces at war, a bad one and a good one. The good one is the basis of hope. The 12 steps recognize only the bad one. In the Augustinian paradigm of Alcoholics Anonymous, there is no force for good inside you.

Many consequences flow from this fundamental belief that addicted people have no possibility of doing the right thing on their own.

In a typical scenario, the initial therapeutic encounter between client and counselor quickly becomes confrontational. The 12-step counselor starts by trying to get the client to identify as powerless. The client resists this oversimplification, which ignores or insults the client's own best efforts at self-help. The therapist responds that the client is in denial. Client and therapist start out with a power struggle where the therapist seeks the client's unconditional surrender. The client tends to lock up or go away.[4]   Bad start.

The counselor could have begun by eliciting the client's inner conflict, bringing out the aspect of the client's inner dynamic that constitutes a pole of healthy striving, and building a therapeutic alliance with that energy. This is the basic strategy of strength-based treatment approaches such as Motivational Interviewing, Cognitive Behavioral Therapy, Solution-Focused Therapy, and others. It is also the basic philosophy of LifeRing.

The zero-power doctrine also infects the internal atmosphere in 12-step self-help groups. Here is the gist of what a great many people have reported to me from their experiences in such groups:

- If you take credit for your efforts to stay clean and sober, you are admonished – the credit belongs to God alone.

- If you express confidence in your own ability to stay sober, you are attacked for lack of humility.

- If you managed to stay clean and sober for any length of time on your own, you were only a dry drunk – a term of contempt.

- If you try to use your mind to understand your situation and figure out what to do next, you are told that your mind is a dangerous place.

- "Your best thinking got you here," which is literally true, is thrown at you in a sarcastic tone, implying that there is no power of sound thinking in your mind.

- Your "self" is considered inherently selfish. Alcoholics have no power to help themselves. There is no hope inside. All help comes from outside, from God.

The zero-power doctrine also narrows the long-term recovery pathway. If you start from zero power, zero sanity, and below-zero moral judgment, you're not going to be allowed much of a voice in shaping your recovery pathway. Your program is laid out for you in steps 1–12. The steps are only "suggested," but in the way that a parachute is suggested before jumping out of a plane. These will be your recovery clothes, whether they fit you or not. You will be told that this is the only way. Yours is not to reason why. The program is not only to get you sober but to govern the rest of your life. If it works, the program gets all the credit. If it fails, you get the blame.

This whole chain of consequences – and more – follows from the Augustinian premise that there is no power for good inside you.

If you begin from the starting point that there is also power for good inside you, as well as a power for bad, then the whole approach is different. If you have stayed sober on your own, you deserve applause for that. If you are confident about your ability to stay sober, you deserve support. If you use your powers of reason to analyze what you need to do to stay sober, you deserve affirmation for that. You will be encouraged to use your rational, social, and emotional intelligence to make choices about your recovery pathway, to exercise and strengthen your decision-making powers, to build a personal recovery program, to achieve self-efficacy, and to gain a deep understanding of your life. You will gain the freedom to follow any life philosophy of your choice. If it fails, you need to revise your plan and try again. When it works, the credit is yours.

All this and more follows from the Pelagian premise that there is not only bad but also good inside you, just as there is in everyone else. The latter is the LifeRing approach.

Augustine Won the Battle But Pelagius Won the War

After a struggle of several decades in the fourth and fifth centuries A.D., the partisans of Augustine decisively won the battle to define Christianity. They argued that the sin of Eve, which caused God to expel the primal pair from the Garden of Eden, tainted all of their descendants and rendered mankind powerless to rise out of sin, except by the grace of God.

Augustine's critics pointed out that the original sin doctrine, although attributed to an Old Testament origin, led to the same position as the Manichean teaching that all things made of matter were dark, corrupt, and powerless.

But the official state church of the Roman Empire – which, perhaps not coincidentally, had inherited the lucrative monopoly of the Roman vineyards and was the liquor industry of its day – locked onto the Augustinian doctrine. It made Augustine a saint. It damned Pelagius as a heretic, drove him into exile, and suppressed his writings. The powerlessness doctrine became known as the doctrine of original sin.

Not for nothing is this period called the Dark Ages.

None but theologians today remember Pelagius's name. But the fate of Pelagius's ideas is another story altogether. A survey of world religions in the twenty-first century shows that even though Augustine won the battle, Pelagius won the war. Islam, Judaism, Buddhism, Hinduism – every major religion except Western Christianity – rejects the doctrine of original sin and accepts that humankind has the power to do good as well as evil. (The Eastern Orthodox church also rejects it.)

Even within Christianity, in its Catholic as well as Protestant branches, there is a huge divide between the official doctrine up high and the practical theology of the faithful on the ground.

One contemporary theologian observes, "No doctrine inside the precincts of the Christian Church is received with greater reserve and hesitation, even to the point of outright denial, than the doctrine of original sin."[5]

It's not just the secularists but also the believers who make up the resistance. The idea that all of mankind is indelibly tainted and morally bankrupt forever because of one innocent misstep by one woman with a piece of fruit and a snake in a garden a very long time ago is hard even for fundamentalist Christians to swallow.

The original sin doctrine means among other things that newborn infants are already filled with sin, and if they die before they are baptized, they go to hell. John Calvin, the Protestant reformer, said it with characteristic clarity: "Infants bring their own damnation with them from their mothers' wombs; the moment they are born their natures are odious and abominable to God."[6] It is a spiritual geneticist theory; it posits that damnation comes in the genes, like eye color and hair color, but absolutely so, with never a tick of random variation.

Preaching original sin without embellishment in most churches today would be a disaster; it would empty the pews.[7] Even modern-day evangelicals, doctrinal purists though they may claim to be and generous dispensers of brimstone and hellfire that they are, tend to exempt the babies and make allowance for "islands of righteousness" within a human nature that is 99 percent depraved. These are fundamental concessions to Pelagius.

The Christian theologian R. C. Sproul, after surveying what believers actually believe, writes, "The seminal thought of Pelagius survives today not as a trace or tangential influence but is pervasive in the modern church."[8]

Linda Mercadante, professor of theology at the Methodist Theological School in Ohio says it more strongly: "The idea of original sin . . . has been decidedly disowned by American culture."[9]

In short, even though original sin is the official church party line, the real working theology of most adherents of Christendom, even among the clergy, quietly affirms people's power of moral choice, not only for evil but also for good, much as

I Was Scared

I came to Life Ring as a very scared person, thinking I knew everything and not knowing I was an addict and if I wanted to keep my job I had to do something. I tried several 12-step programs but because I am a Christian I could not accept a lot of their ways of doing things and that is when I came across LifeRing. I loved it because my faith was not challenged but was accepted. I stayed and later became a convenor, and now I have ten years clean. I have met some very nice and lifelong friends in this program and believe me it works. All you have to do is want it.

– Bettye D., Nashville Tennessee

most secular humanists do. The Popes remain Augustinian, but the people are Pelagian.

How the Powerlessness Doctrine Drives Out Newcomers

The doctrine of powerlessness is more exposed to view in the recovery world than it is in the churches. In theology, it gets buried in the fine print for seminary students. In recovery rooms, it's the first clause of the first step on the giant posters that hang in countless meeting rooms and treatment programs. It's very likely the first thing that strikes the newcomer's eye. And it's probably one of the main reasons why those newcomers leave in hordes.

As I pointed out in the Introduction, AA's own internal membership surveys show that 80 percent of first-time participants at AA meetings walk away within thirty days. Ninety percent leave within ninety days. At the end of one year, out of one hundred who started in AA, only five are still attending.[10]

The AA doctrine of powerlessness is by far the biggest reason for rejecting AA. This was the clear finding in Professors Granfield and Cloud's study of people who recovered without treatment or support groups.[11] The reaction of this group ranged from the restrained ("You're not as powerless as these groups preach") to the earthy ("Having read their credo, I thought it was bullshit.")[12]

In the stories and short testimonials of LifeRing members distributed throughout this book, you will find that rejection of the zero-power clause ranked high in their decision to seek an alternative to the 12-step approach.

Katherine Ketcham, a 12-step advocate and clinician, admits, "It is the rare alcoholic who accepts 'the higher power malarkey' without any quibbling." She estimates that it drives "many thousands" away.[13] Of course, the "higher power malarkey" is only necessary because of the zero-power starting point.

Preaching powerlessness to people who want to get sober may not be quite as repellent as preaching the odious and abominable nature of newborn infants (John Calvin), but it's in the same category. Nobody who earnestly wants to change for the better needs or wants to be told they're powerless to do so.

The whole thrust of the counseling profession – outside the 12-step orbit – runs in exactly the opposite direction: toward decreasing the client's feelings of powerlessness and encouraging the client in the direction of self-efficacy and self-responsibility.[14]

Life Is Good Now

I had been attending AA meetings for well over two years with little or no results – sobering up for a month here or a month there, each time falling farther into oblivion. The AA process seemed to heighten my desire to imbibe rather than subdue it. I wanted to be empowered and felt that the teachings of AA stripped me of any self-control over my addiction yet offered no substitute for inner strength.

I had all but given up but, after three hospital stays for intensive detox, including a close brush with death, I conducted a Web search and discovered the LifeRing chat room.

At first I was skeptical, having been through an endless stream of therapists, group therapy, and outpatient programs. But, as I became involved, I found myself drinking less and, after several false starts at sobriety, stopped drinking completely. Yes, I faltered at times and experienced several relapses but each time I slipped, instead of retreating into my insular world full of self-loathing and hopelessness, as had been my history, I found myself rushing back to LifeRing. I listened to members' advice, gleaning insights from those that had sustained the same sort of damage as I, yet had remained sober for years, even decades.

Now I try to contribute to this unique environment as best I can; helping others while helping myself, being there for the newcomers, and trying to lend support whenever needed. The candor and non-judgmental camaraderie among this brave and insightful group of people has given me the inner strength that I thought was lost forever. Life is good now – and I have LifeRing to thank for it.

– Shawn B., New York City, New York

The First Drink and the Second

A few years ago, I composed an April Fool's Day article, in which a fictitious Roman Catholic bishop started up a 12-step group for alcoholics who wanted to moderate their drinking. Said the imaginary bishop:

> To claim that God only has power to help alcoholics abstain, but not to moderate, is blasphemy. In this new group, each individual will find a Higher Power who helps him or her stop after the first drink. God can certainly help you recover from alcoholism and become a social drinker again.

Of course, there is no such bishop and no such group. But it's worth asking why. If God is all-powerful, it should be an easy matter for Him to help the alcoholic become a moderate drinker again. Why must surrendering to God mean abstinence?

There is nothing in the 12 steps that requires abstinence. There is nothing in the Christian Bible that requires abstinence, either. The Oxford Group, where the AA founders got their theology, had no such requirement.[15] Why aren't there groups that use the 12-step program to learn to stop after that first drink?

The reason, apparently, there are no 12-step groups of alcoholics achieving moderation is that even God seems to be powerless to produce this outcome with any reliability. Once an alcoholic has taken the first drink, God mostly strikes out. The whole edifice of the 12 steps, with its seven mentions of God, its moral inventories, its amends, and all the rest of it, isn't strong enough to reliably stop the average alcoholic from taking the second drink. After the first drink, the Higher Power isn't.

But before the first drink, the higher power isn't necessary. The majority of alcoholics stop drinking without subscribing to this AA doctrine. Even people who begin AA routinely stop drinking before their first meeting. Some treatment programs put all applicants on a waiting list and require them to have a certain amount of sober time before admission.

I've seen it time and again: people demonstrate by months or years of abstinence on their own that they have the power to stop drinking and then enter a program that tells them they don't. One patient told me that a 12-step counselor tried to get him to say that he was lying about having had a long period of abstinence on his own.

The spectacle of a group of sober people in a recovery room contritely labeling themselves powerless over alcohol is a case of extreme dissonance between words and actions. If they were really powerless over alcohol, they would be off drinking instead of participating in a sobriety meeting.

The fact that they are in the room sober proves that they had the power to say no to the bottle at least on this occasion. They deserve recognition and credit for that, not humiliation. If alcoholics were truly powerless over alcohol, AA meetings would be impossible.

An alcoholic who is truly powerless over the first drink will soon be a dead alcoholic. Such an alcoholic cannot work or sustain any activity other than drinking. They cannot say "not now" or "not here" to a bottle. Powerlessness is a reality only for late end-stage alcoholics, who have nothing left to live for.

Despite the best of intentions, when 12-step practitioners push the powerless-over-alcohol clause on their clients, they are guilty of attempted "S-icide" – killing the client's S, instead of empowering it. The treatment professional who overlooks the client's S – or tries to step on it – is working to facilitate relapse instead of recovery.[16]

I Finally Feel Like I Can Be Myself

I was four years into my recovery and was sporadically going to twelve-step meetings when I said enough is enough. I did not relapse but I stopped going to twelve-step meetings because I could never fully buy in to much of what they preached.

When I found LifeRing, I immediately become captivated by its "three S" philosophy of Sobriety, Secularity, and Self-help. I also loved the fact that I could process in group, meaning that during the meeting I could interact with my fellow members and deal with stuff on the spot. Sitting in a circle appealed to me also so that I could see everyone's eyes instead of their backs.

LifeRing has provided me with a totally new outlook and confidence in my sobriety and life. I finally feel like I can be myself and I look forward to sharing the wisdom of my recovery with others. Do I sound like a powerless person to you?

– Michael W., Victoria, B.C., Canada

Feelings of Powerlessness Lead People to Drink

The psychiatrist Lance Dodes at Harvard has made a practice of listening carefully to his patients, most of whom suffer from one or another addiction. He noticed that there was a common thread in their narratives about initiating drinking or other substance use. They resorted to substances when a situation arose in their lives where they felt powerless.

The frustration and stress of feeling helpless were unbearable, and they had learned that the mere decision to drink (even before the actual intake) made them feel as if they had achieved a measure of control, if not over the situation, at least over their mood.[17]

Dodes' observation spotlights an important psychological fact: feelings of powerlessness are powerful in producing relapse. Powerlessness and helplessness are among the most stressful of emotions. Stress, both in laboratory animal experiments and in human experience, is an engine that can produce reinstatement of long-extinguished addictive consumption patterns.[18] Consequently, the effort to persuade addicted individuals that they are "powerless over alcohol," particularly if this effort is conducted in a confrontational manner, is most likely to provoke in this person an urgent and immediate desire to drink.[19]

The 12-Step Gauntlet of Negative Emotions

Research shows that stress and other negative emotions are important risk factors in producing relapse in the newly sober. Negative emotional states are by far the leading cause of relapse.[20] In this regard, the clinical wisdom of exposing people who are newly sober to the experience of the 12-step program is open to question.

The 12-step program, as others have pointed out, is a gauntlet of negative emotional encounters.[21]

- In step 1, as we have seen, there is the stress of feeling powerless.

- In step 2, there is the stress of being labeled insane ("Came to believe that a Power greater than ourselves could restore us to sanity").

- In step 3, people are asked to surrender themselves, again raising the feeling of powerlessness.

- In step 4, people are told to take a "moral inventory," implying that they are morally deficient and setting the stage for feelings of shame and guilt.

- In step 5, people are supposed to focus on all their "wrongs."

- Step 6 centers on the person's "defects of character."

- Step 7 has to do with "shortcomings."

- In step 8, people are asked to look at all the harm they have caused to other people, underlining what Bad Persons they are.

- In steps 9 and 10, this is repeated and deepened.

- Step 11 implies that people are too clueless to figure out what to do with their life.

- Step 12 calls on people to recruit other alcoholics to undergo this same series of exposures.

Based on the 95 percent dropout rate documented in the AA membership surveys, the percentage of newcomers who actually complete all 12 steps must be quite small.

A study needs to be undertaken to follow people as they work the 12 steps and keep track of the step at which relapse or walkaway from the program occurs. Based on many anecdotal reports I have heard, my hypothesis is that step 4, the "moral inventory," is the biggest relapse generator for those who get past the "powerless" clause of the first step and the "insanity" clause of the second.

The small percentage who survive this obstacle course of negative affect deserve the utmost respect. Their drive to be clean and sober – their inner S – was so strong that it overcame every challenge on this parcourse. Like the survivors of a Marine Corps boot camp, or of a fraternity hazing ritual, they have reason to be proud.

But if the research on the impact of negative emotional states on relapse rates means anything, they achieved their sobriety not because of but in spite of the 12-step encounter. Fortunately, the social support that the 12-step organizations provide serves to buffer to some extent the emotionally hazardous aspects of the 12-step program, or there would be nothing to redeem the experience.

Powerlessness for Women and Minorities

The term powerlessness has a political dimension, and this aspect has not been lost on those for whom lack of power is a primary reality. As is apparent from the observations of Dr. Dodes, discussed previously, the feeling of powerlessness or helplessness is very widespread, and no sector of the population has a monopoly on it.

But among women and minorities in the United States, powerlessness has a special currency, to the point where many see powerlessness as a core dimension of growing up and surviving as an average member of these populations.

The founders of AA were white males of upper socioeconomic status. Bill Wilson, the author of the 12 steps, was a blue-blood Republican who quit a job rather than join a union and hated Roosevelt and the New Deal. There was no question that he had a gigantic ego, as he himself admitted, and that "deflation" of this ego was necessary for him to get a realistic grip on himself and stay sober.

I Am Responsible

As the years of caring for my ailing father stretched toward a decade, I turned increasingly to alcohol to escape the stress and sadness and pain. After my father's death, my downward spiral continued as I sought to numb my grief.

Growing up in the 1960s and 70s, my identity was rooted in the empowerment politics of the leftist and feminist movements. I knew that to break out of my self-destructive habits, I needed to become empowered within myself and through the support of others. I needed to nurture my self-esteem, not to be told that I was powerless.

One lucky day, my therapist handed me a copy of the LifeRing workbook, *Recovery by Choice*. I was intrigued and eager to learn more. Shortly thereafter, I attended my first LifeRing meeting. I have been attending ever since.

In LifeRing I have found a community of friends who exchange ideas and mutual support to help each other along our paths to sobriety. Crosstalk in meetings is an integral part of that. I have learned so much from others' shared experiences, struggles, and feedback. At each LifeRing meeting, I am inspired by comments and insights that shed light on my own journey. LifeRing has helped me discover and sharpen the tools that work for me in my own recovery.

I have also found support in my failures as well as for my successes acknowledgment that recovery is a process, often with slips and missteps along the way. When I relapsed, this support helped me to keep sight of the big picture, to pick myself up and get back on track, to learn from my mistakes and move on, instead of getting stuck in shame and self-criticism.

While the support of others has been essential, I also have learned that I am ultimately responsible for my own recovery. Only I can get and keep myself sober, and I am the only one who can make the decision not to drink.

I didn't really relate to the name at first, but now I do: LifeRing has truly been my life ring!

— S.W., San Francisco, California

The doctrine of powerlessness and its twin, surrender, along with the "medical business" (of which more later), were probably appropriate components of his personal recovery program and that of many of his early AA friends, at least at first.

The subtitle of the first edition of the AA Big Book was *The Story of How More Than One Hundred Men Have Recovered from Alcoholism.* Wilson even insisted on writing the patronizing Big Book chapter "To the Wives" himself – refusing to let his wife have a hand in it.[22]

Ask any woman: ego-deflation would be beneficial to quite a few men that she knows. But for everyone?

In 1976, Jean Kirkpatrick founded Women for Sobriety. She was the first person to declare publicly that the ego-deflation model of AA was not a good fit for most women. Women's egos were not too big, she said, they were too little. They didn't need deflation; they needed building up. They didn't need to surrender; they needed to become empowered. Kirkpatrick found that with every AA meeting she attended, she felt a greater desire to go out and get drunk.[23]

Kirkpatrick's courageous initiative in articulating a philosophy of sobriety through empowerment met with a resounding echo among women. Although her organization has had its struggles, nearly a decade after Kirkpatrick's death, the recognition that powerlessness is not an appropriate prescription for everyone is gaining wider recognition. Charlotte Kasl, among other writers, in her monumental *Many Roads One Journey*, picked up and extended Kirkpatrick's core insights, developed them further, and popularized them.

Kirkpatrick is the spiritual mother not only of her own Women for Sobriety organization but also of each of the abstinence-based AA alternatives that followed, including Life-Ring.

People of color, women, and homeless folks have always known they are powerless. When some white person stands up and reads the first step in a 12-step program, a black person hears the call to powerlessness as one more command to lie down and take it.[24]

That's the voice of the African-American spiritual leader Rev. Cecil Williams, then pastor of Glide Memorial Church in San Francisco, a religious community that opens its doors, especially, to all powerless, marginalized, and outcast people and offers them comfort, support, and hope.

Rev. Williams's observation underlines the point that powerlessness as a healing perspective is narrowly limited. It may be a suitable component of the personal recovery programs of some individuals, but as a general formula it not only fails to fit, it can also provoke counterproductive negative emotions that lead people further into addiction, rather than out of it.

The Addict Needs to Fight, Not to Surrender

One of the standard openers of 12-step treatment is to demand that the client "surrender" – to God, to the program, to the counselor. The question is, to which of the two powers inside the recovering person is the demand for surrender addressed? If the demand is addressed to the A, it is futile.

If confronted with overwhelming force, such as in a professionally orchestrated intervention, addiction may pretend to surrender and go through the motions of compliance – but only as a survival tactic, in order to prevail again at a later time.

Addiction never, ever surrenders so long as its host organism is alive. The only way to subdue it is to starve it, and even then it remains in a minimal-power state, like a long-dormant thistle seed, waiting for a change in climate that will allow it

Connected with LifeRing

Twenty-five years ago, I lost a business in which I was the president of a small corporation. I was a raging alcoholic, living in a car with no job, no prospects. My son took me to detox and I was in a recovery home six months. I was absolutely unable to stand 12-step groups and their religiosity and powerless theme. So I "went out" for five years. Again, my sons did an intervention. I went to the Kaiser Chemical Dependency Recovery Program, and through a counselor there I got connected with LifeRing. LifeRing has become my support system. I've met incredible loving, funny, brave, inspiring friends in LifeRing. Now I have two and a half years clean and sober. I know I need LifeRing and the support I get – I am so deeply appreciative that it is there for me.

– Ginger S., Mountain View, California

to emerge and rule again. To ask the addict self to surrender is to reveal the utmost naïveté about the nature of addiction.

But if the demand for surrender is addressed to the sober self, it is perfidious. The addicted person's sober self has spent too long in the posture of surrender, already. Its vital need is to get off its knees, stand up, and assert itself.

The doctrine of powerlessness over alcohol, which is the starting point and the cornerstone of the 12-step program, is a religious doctrine out of the Dark Ages of Christianity. Its theological foundation, the doctrine of original sin, has been repudiated not only by modern Christianity in its actual practice but also by American culture and by the American counseling profession.

As a therapeutic approach, powerlessness mates with the reality of the addicted person like a square peg with a round hole. It overlooks and denies the freedom-seeking side of the addict's inner experience, the force that has kept the person alive despite addiction, the foundation on which the person's chance of recovery rests. The powerlessness doctrine leads to unnecessary confrontations and to missed opportunities in treatment. It evokes an emotional state that engenders urges to use addictive substances, and it initiates a series of further emotional stresses that constitute well-known relapse risks. Powerlessness may be an appropriate therapeutic element in the personal recovery program of some privileged individuals, but as a general prescription it is a poor fit and has a high potential of creating harm.

Yet there is something to be learned from this peril. The wrong of the powerlessness doctrine lies in its absolute application, which derives from its origin as religious dogma. If we take from this encounter an appropriate measure of respect for the power of addiction, we can come out stronger and wiser. There are situations where the addiction exceeds our power to resist it; survival means avoiding those situations. Even after many years of sobriety, the addiction can come back to life, even quite suddenly, if we put addictive substances into our body.

Therefore, in rejecting the doctrine that addiction is all-powerful and we are nothing, we must not fall into the opposite error of contempt for the power of addiction, as if addiction were nothing. Everything depends on knowing the situation and knowing ourselves.

The doctrine of powerlessness over alcohol is one of the major themes a newcomer is liable to encounter on the chemical dependency recovery marketplace. In the next chapter, we'll have a look at another dominant theme: the theory that alcoholism is a disease.

Notes

1. http://www.amazon.com/Beautiful-Mind-Jennifer-Connelly/dp/ B000FVQLQQ/ref=sr_1_1?ie=UTF8& s=dvd& qid=1219 639963& sr=8-1.
2. Augustine of Hippo, Confessions, vol. 10, Pusey Translation., http://ccat.sas. upenn.edu/jod/augustine/Pusey/book10.
3. Kurtz, Not-God, pp. 178, 182; Linda A. Mercadante, Victims and Sinners: Spiritual Roots of Addiction and Recovery (Louisville, Ky.: Westminster John Knox Press, 1996), pp. 109-110, 116.
4. See Hester and Miller, Handbook of Alcoholism Treatment Approaches: Effective Alternatives, Ch. 6.
5. Edward T. Oakes, "Original Sin: A Disputation," First Things: The Journal of Religion, Culture, and Public Life (November 1998): 16-24.
6. Cited in Ibid.
7. Ibid.
8. R. C. Sproul, Augustine and Pelagius, http://www.leaderu. com/theology/ augpelagius.html. See also, R. C. Sproul, The Pelagian Captivity of the Church, Modern Reformation, vol. 10, no. 3 (May/June 2001): 22-29, http://www.bible-researcher. com/sproul1.html.
9. Mercadante, Victims and Sinners, p. 116.
10. McIntire, "How Well Does A.A. Work? An Analysis of Published A.A. surveys (1968-1996) and Related Analyses/Comments."
11. Granfield and Cloud, Coming Clean, p. 109.
12. Ibid.
13. Ketcham and Asbury, Beyond the Influence, pp. 202-203.
14. Christine Le, Erik P. Ingvarson, and Richard C. Page, "Alcoholics Anonymous and the Counseling Profession: Philosophies in Conflict," Journal of Counseling and Development (July 1, 1995), http://unhooked.com/sep/ aacouns.htm, p. 603.
15. Mercadante, Victims and Sinners, p. 62.
16. Somewhere between 7 and 15 percent of patients in substance abuse treatment are harmed rather than helped by it. Rudolf H. Moos, "Iatrogenic Effects of Psychosocial Interventions for Substance Use Disorders: Prevalence, Predictors, Prevention," Addiction 100, no. 5 (May 12, 2005): 595-604, doi:doi:10.1111/j.1360-0443.2005.01073.x.
17. Lance M. Dodes, The Heart of Addiction (New York: Harper-Collins, 2002).
18. Koob and Le Moal, Neurobiology of Addiction, Ch. 1.

19. Marlatt, Barrett, and Daley, "Relapse Prevention," p. 357.

20. Ibid., p. 353.

21. Le, Ingvarson, and Page, "Alcoholics Anonymous and the Counseling Profession: Philosophies in Conflict."

22. Charlotte Davis Kasl and Charlotte S. Kasl, Many Roads, One Journey: Moving Beyond the Twelve Steps (New York: Harper-Collins, 1992), p. 142.

23. Quoted in Ibid., p. 166.

24. Cecil Williams and Rebecca Laird, No Hiding Place: Empowerment and Recovery for Our Troubled Communities (Harper San Francisco, 1992), p. 9.

▼

Chapter Six

ABOUT THE DISEASE THEORY OF ALCOHOLISM

We have never called alcoholism a disease.
– AA cofounder Bill Wilson, 1961

When my friend Wendy came back from her first AA meeting, she took away with her two key concepts. One, that alcoholism is a disease. Two, that if she relied on a Higher Power, the disease could be arrested.

If that had made sense to Wendy and she had kept coming back, she would have heard the definition of alcoholism as a disease repeated hundreds of times, as an accepted and unquestionable truth, even more fundamental than the 12 steps.

The steps are said to be just suggestions, even if compelling ones.[1] But the disease concept is beyond suggestion. To many people both inside and outside AA, the definition of alcoholism as a disease is carved in stone. The theologian Mercadante observed:

> Today, the assertion that alcoholism is a disease is "sacred." It has achieved a level equivalent, in theological terms, to dogma: a fundamental, non-negotiable, undergirding belief. Alcoholism as disease is so foundational that one cannot deny it without distancing oneself from the believing community.[2]

None of this impressed my friend Wendy, an independent thinker. To her ears, the word *disease* meant a medical diagnosis, like diabetes, hypertension, heart disease, and the like. She felt that her drinking was more like a bad habit, similar to smoking cigarettes, than like a disease. She also felt that the disease label would unfairly stigmatize her.

Although Wendy was a Christian believer, she was raised in a denomination that went to doctors. The idea of curing diseases through faith didn't resonate with her.

As a result, Wendy became one of the 95 percent who tried AA and left. She also stopped drinking and remains sober.

In this chapter, I'll tell the fascinating story of how the disease concept of alcoholism came to be part of AA's teaching. You'll see the psychological utility as well as the economic and political interests behind the disease concept. You'll learn why the AA version of the disease model of alcoholism has failed to persuade many thoughtful people, including people within the medical and scientific communities. You'll see that leading advocates of the disease model themselves undermine its credibility because their approach to treating alcoholism has little in common with accepted modern medical practice. Finally, I'll present a brief summary of the pros and cons of the disease model and suggest a guideline for making up your mind whether to embrace it or not.

If you become part of LifeRing, you'll have complete freedom of opinion on the disease issue. LifeRing as an organization does not take a position on it. Sometimes we have debates within the organization between partisans of different lines on it. Our experience is that people who love the disease model, people who hate it, and people who are on the fence about it can all stay clean and sober. And that's what matters.

The "Medical Business"

Addressing a group of Catholic clergy in 1961, AA co-founder Bill Wilson said,

> We have never called alcoholism a disease because, technically speaking, it is not a disease entity. For example, there is no such thing as heart disease. Instead there are many separate heart ailments, or combinations of them. It is something like that with alcoholism. Therefore we did not wish to get in wrong with the medical profession by pronouncing alcoholism a disease entity. Therefore we always called it an illness, or a malady – a far safer term for us to use.[3]

In this, Wilson was not entirely accurate. The first printing of the Big Book in 1939 used the term *disease* along with *cure* and *ex-alcoholic*, but these terms were replaced with illness and other language in subsequent printings.[4] For the next thirty years, until Wilson testified before Congress in 1969, Wilson's consistent usage was *illness* or *malady*.

This careful choice of words was grounded, as Wilson's 1961 statement to the clergy makes clear, in the desire not to "get in wrong with the medical profession." Anyone could use the metaphorical terms *illness* or *malady*, but jurisdiction over the definition of *disease* lay with the medical establishment.

Disease as the Hammer to Induce Powerlessness

Wilson's main interest in medical terminology was tactical and psychological. He was making little headway converting drunks using the religious appeals of the Oxford Group. Dr.

William Silkworth, who had treated Wilson in his clinic, advised Wilson to "give them the medical business and give it to them hard."[5]

Learning that he had a fatal illness and that his condition was hopeless, the newcomer would be "shattered." His hard shell would be broken and his ego "deflated." He would see that his condition was totally "hopeless" and that he was utterly "helpless." The disease analogy reduced the alcoholic "to a state of complete dependence" on his caregiver, like a dying cancer patient who is "abjectly dependent" on his physician.[6] He would then be open to hearing the AA message.[7] That at least was the theory.

In other words, the "medical business" was a psychological tactic to convince the alcoholic of his powerlessness. In Wilson's own phrase, "We have torn some pages from the Book of Medicine" for these purposes.[8] Beyond these few torn-out pages, Wilson's writings show little interest in the book of medicine. Although he says repeatedly that alcoholism is a three-fold illness – of the body, the mind, and the spirit – the approach is not medical in any modern sense. Alcoholism, Wilson wrote, is "an illness which only a spiritual experience will conquer."[9]

The term *spiritual experience* had a vivid meaning for Wilson. Wilson was a practicing Spiritualist who interpreted many an experience as spiritual, where others had their doubts. He believed that he could hold conversations with the dead, that spirits could levitate tables, and that the dead could guide his hand in writing texts.[10] His famous "white light" experience, which marked the beginning of his sobriety, was likely induced by a cocktail of barbiturates, belladonna, and other medications administered by Dr. Silkworth. But to Wilson, it was a spiritual revelation.[11] Wilson was also an avid reader of Mary Baker Eddy's *Science and Health with Key to the Scriptures*, the bible of modern faith healing.[12] He had visited a Christian Science practitioner in an effort to get sober before joining the Oxford Group.[13]

Healing of medical disorders through religious faith – the core teaching of Eddy's church – was also a central teaching of the Oxford Group. The Oxford Group gave the religious-medical model a further twist. It redefined all sin – including, of course, drunkenness – as a "spiritual disease."[14] Its leader, Frank Buchman, described God as the Great Soul Surgeon and made liberal use of medical metaphors in his religious teaching. A typical Oxford Group formulation was "Sin is a disease with consequences we cannot foretell or judge; it is as contagious as any contagious disease our bodies may suffer from."[15]

The appeal in AA's step 6 to "have God remove all these defects of character" is an application of the Oxford Group's soul surgeon metaphor, as is the plea in step 7 to ask "Him to remove our shortcomings." This envisions God with a scalpel cutting out the moral failings that – in Wilson's view – made the alcoholic want to drink. In short, there was little or nothing in Wilson's worldview that resembles modern medicine. Not surprisingly, the Journal of the American Medical Association dismissed the Big Book on its publication in 1939 as having "no scientific merit or interest."[16]

Enter the Alcohol Industry and Marty Mann

That same year, the scientifically prestigious but financially starved Research Council on Problems of Alcohol (RCPA) in New York caused a scandal when it announced that it had accepted a research grant from the alcohol industry. A condition of the grant was that RCPA research in the next period would

A Heartwarming Experience

I am a sixty-three year old man who has been in recovery for a little more than ten years. Being from a very dysfunctional family, my childhood was almost unbearable. I began drinking at a very early age to cope with deep depression. I also began using other drugs. I used alcohol and drugs for forty-one years before my addiction forced the issue of recovery or death. My marriage was also hanging by a thread. I entered the Kaiser C.D.R.P. (Chemical Dependency Recovery Program) for my initial treatment. There, I was encouraged to attend 12-step programs. This was difficult, because the 12-step programs make little sense to me. I didn't feel like I belonged; even though I knew I was one of these people. I am not a religious person, which added to my discomfort. In 2004, I attended the LifeRing Congress in Berkeley to hear William White speak. It was there that I was introduced to LifeRing for the first time. I attended a meeting in Vallejo Ca. and was so impressed with this approach to recovery; it was like a breath of fresh air. I became a regular attendee. LifeRing has become a large part of my life. I have started two new meetings in the area. I intend to start meetings and encourage other addicts to do the same.

– John D., Benicia, California

switch from alcohol to "the disease of alcoholism (inebriety) and the alcoholic psychoses (alcoholic insanity)."[17]

This was a 180-degree turnabout. The council had been focused on studying the risks and dangers of the substance alcohol. However, funding for that focus had run dry. The alcoholic beverage industry had emerged from the shadow of illegality only six years earlier, with the repeal of Prohibition. In the ensuing climate of triumph for the advocates of drinking, the industry undertook a complete makeover of its public image.

On the scientific front, the industry wanted researchers to stop targeting the harmful effects of alcohol and the social, economic, and political issues surrounding it. It wanted to locate the problem not in the bottle, but in the man. The theme the industry wanted the researchers to develop was that normal people drank alcohol without harmful consequences, but a small minority had the disease of alcoholism and therefore could not drink safely.

The industry had money, and it got its way.[18] At the 1943 conference of the RCPA, where the organization defined its program, representatives of the liquor industry outnumbered temperance advocates 11 to 3.[19] The new RCPA reframed the debate from *alcohol* to *alcoholism*. Instead of exposing the dangers of the substance to society, the focus became the vulnerability of a few special individuals. The alcoholism paradigm, as the historian White puts it, "blessed the drinking of the majority while it provided a rationale for radical abstinence by an alcoholic minority."[20] It thereby took the heat off the industry.

Burnham, the medical historian, puts it this way:

> The great victory of the alcoholic-beverage business was to turn the idea that there is an illness, alcoholism, into the negative of social action that might diminish the profits on the sale of the beverages. As Thomas F. McCarthy, president of Licensed Beverage Industries, Inc., noted in 1947, specialized scientists generally agreed that "the root of the 'problem drinker's disease' lies in the man and not in the bottle. The 'problem drinker' is a medical problem – and he won't be cured until the scientists and doctors

figure out a way." The money spent on individualizing the problem paid off handsomely over the years – not in solving drinking problems but in diverting public attention away from the industry.[21]

In other words, by establishing that there was a disease called alcoholism, the industry pointed the finger of social blame away from the alcohol industry and toward the drinker.[22]

Alcohol industry money funded not only the RCPA but also a cluster of alcohol projects based at Yale University, beginning in the early 1940s. These included a clinic, a scholarly journal, and the Yale Summer Schools, a combination summer camp and cadre school for evangelists of the industry's disease paradigm.[23]

Of the summer school students, none was brighter and more energetic than one Marty Mann. Mann came from a socially prominent and affluent family. But as a young woman, she drank away her assets and her marriage, faced ruin, and attempted suicide. After sobering up in AA, Mann built a career in public relations for a department store.

The new focus on alcoholism-as-a-disease at the Yale projects met with considerable scientific ambivalence. But Mann was not a scientist. As a public relations professional, she was not deterred by scarcity of scientific proof.[24] In 1944, she launched a new career: an initiative to popularize the disease concept.

With alcohol industry seed money, she founded the National Council for Education on Alcoholism (NCEA, today NCADD). The council's first and most prominent principle under Mann's leadership was, "Alcoholism is a disease."[25]

Mann's declared mission was to break down the moral paradigm, under which the alcoholic was defined as a bad person who must be punished and replace it with a medical paradigm, which sees the alcoholic as a sick person who can be helped.

From the beginning, the attractive, articulate, and PR-savvy Mann got her message across in the mass media. She was by all accounts a dynamic, brilliant, charming, and powerful speaker, and the media covered her every public move. She was also a tireless campaigner.

Mann gave an average of two hundred speeches per year for twenty-four years. She crisscrossed the country dozens of times. She carried the message that alcoholism was a disease directly and indirectly to hundreds of thousands, perhaps millions, of people.

Moreover, she always connected herself publicly with AA. Wherever she went, membership in local AA groups snowballed.[26]

Wilson, who had given Mann the green light to break her anonymity and identify herself publicly as an AA member, always regretted it. He expressed his foreboding in 1955 in the AA *Grapevine*:

> In nothing flat, her own full name and picture, plus excellent accounts of her educational project, and of AA, landed in nearly every large paper in North America. The public understanding of alcoholism increased, the stigma on drunks lessened, and AA got new members. Surely there could be nothing wrong with that. But there was. For the sake of this short-term benefit, we were taking on a future liability of huge and menacing proportions.[27]

Dr. Tiebout, the major theoretician in the AA camp at the time, shared this foreboding. In a letter, he confided privately in the same year:

> I cannot help but feel that the whole field of alcoholism is way out on a limb which any minute will crack and drop us all in a frightful mess. To change the metaphor, we have stuck our necks out and not one of us knows if

he will be stepped on individually or collectively. I sometimes tremble to think how little we have to back up our
claims. We are all skating on pretty thin ice.[28]

In fact, the science lagged far behind the publicity. Dr. Silkworth's argument that alcoholism was a type of allergy, hence
a proper medical disease, persuaded nobody in the medical
profession.[29] Wilson later distanced himself from it.[30]

Jellinek's 1960 book, *The Disease Concept of Alcoholism*,
helped with the public perception that there was a scientific
foundation – at least for those who did not read it. Jellinek,
who was skating on thin ice himself (his claim to have a Ph.D.
was bogus), suggested that there was not one alcoholism but
several, only two of which deserved the "disease" label; and he
hedged his findings with numerous qualifications.[31]

But when Wilson in 1961 tried to distance AA from the
disease term ("We have never called alcoholism a disease"), he
was probably already in a minority among AA participants.
Thanks to Marty Mann, AA groups were filling with new
members who never thought of alcoholism as anything else.

Disease Is the Money Word

Mann's public relations campaign soon picked up new
backers: investors in the alcoholism treatment industry. Fig-
ures of speech like *illness* and *malady* didn't cut it for them.
In order to make alcoholism treatment eligible for insurance
company reimbursement and public funding, alcoholism had
to be classified as a genuine disease.

As the historian of AA, Ernest Kurtz, observed, health insurance policies at that time did not cover the costs of alcoholism treatment:

> Changing that became the top agenda item of the treat-
> ers, and bringing about that change involved convincing

medical and insurance and especially public authorities as well as the public at large that alcoholism was a genuine disease. The effort was huge, and members of Alcoholics Anonymous, as well as members of Al-Anon and anyone who had any however tenuous contact with treatment or alcoholism, alcoholic or not, were mobilized into partici-pating.[32]

They were mobilized in a protracted political campaign to convince the American Medical Association (AMA) and Congress to declare alcoholism a disease. In the phrase of the historian William White, they formed an "invisible army."

> The contributions of recovered alcoholics to the success of the modern alcoholism movement were often hidden behind masks of personal discretion or AA anonymity. Acts that pushed the movement forward were often per-formed by people not recognized as bringing personal passion to their contribution."[33]

The AA doctrine of anonymity, presented as a self-effacing, humble, modest spiritual principle, became a cover under which thousands of undisclosed AA members in the existing institutions of government, press, medicine, and related fields agitated in favor of the disease paradigm. The anonymity rule gave this orchestrated economic and political campaign the outward appearance of a spontaneous grassroots movement.

AA and the Alcohol Industry

The alcohol industry was not in the least bothered by AA's involvement. On the contrary. AA members working in the new alcoholism movement were reinforcements for the in-dustry's image makeover campaign. The historian Burnham writes that the alcoholics themselves worked to support the industry's interest in pointing to the problem in the man rather than in the industry's product.[34] In parallel with Burnham's observations, the historian White writes:

> The industry saw Alcoholics Anonymous as a potential ally because the organization focused on a small percentage of late-stage drinkers and had little to say about the drinking habits of most Americans. In modern parlance, the organization was concerned about alcoholism, but not about alcohol use – or even alcohol abuse. Perhaps even more, AA located the problem of alcohol in the person, not in the bottle."[35]

Illustrating this point, Nell Wing, Wilson's long-time secretary and AA archivist, recounts that alcohol was always served at the Christmas parties in AA's world office in New York.

> AA was not against drinking, and the staff always made sure that the nonalcoholics were served drinks if they wanted them – as I remember, everybody did.[36]

At one such party, the young women AA employees were flirting with the men at the office of a national distiller across the street.[37] There has never been any apparent friction between AA and the alcoholic beverage industry – a remarkable peace.

A Political but Not a Scientific Triumph

The alcoholism movement was highly successful. In 1966, President Lyndon Johnson made history when he said, "The alcoholic suffers from a disease which will yield eventually to scientific research and treatment."[38] The following year, the AMA finally applied the coveted "*D*" word to alcoholism. The insurance industry extended health insurance coverage for alcoholism treatment.

In 1970, Congress passed the Hughes Act, which created the National Institute on Alcohol Abuse and Alcoholism and opened the floodgates of federal funding for alcoholism research and treatment. In White's words again:

> The passage of the Hughes Act marked the political coming-of-age of the invisible army of recovering and non-recovering people who had toiled as the foot soldiers of the "modern alcoholism movement." When fully mobilized, the numbers and political power of this group were impressive. The Hughes Act transformed this social movement into a new industry, which Hughes himself later referred to as an "alcoholism and drug abuse industrial complex."[39]

Although the invisible army was composed very largely of AA members, it always marched under the aegis of the NCEA and its successors. There was no official involvement by AA.

The victory was above all an economic and political watershed. No new scientific breakthroughs and no developed body of scientific evidence drove the adoption of the disease concept.[40]

The physician Enoch Gordis, head of the National Institute on Alcohol Abuse and Alcoholism, wrote:

> In the case of alcoholism, our whole treatment system, with its innumerable therapies, armies of therapists, large and expensive programs, endless conferences, innovation and public relations activities, is founded on hunch, not evidence, and not on science.[41]

But this is not surprising, Gordis points out, because the treatment approaches developed "outside the mainstream of medical science" and were influenced rather by religion, moral attitudes, psychoanalytic theories, and pop psychology.[42]

The "Medical Business" Conquers AA

When Wilson testified at a congressional hearing in support of the Hughes Bill in 1969 – after Mann's testimony – he spoke at length about his own recovery story, avoiding more general topics. He mentioned the word disease exactly once, in passing, near the end of his narrative.[43] Between the lines of this testimony, one could read a growing discomfort with the medicalization that was sweeping into AA on the rising tide of the disease movement.[44] Wilson's 1955 foreboding about "a future liability of huge and menacing proportions" was fast becoming a reality.

The medicalization that was coming into AA went beyond the few pages that Wilson had "torn from the Book of Medicine" years earlier. Dr. Tiebout had put his finger on the conceptual evolution already in a 1949 address to the American Psychiatric Association. He said: "Alcoholism is a symptom that has become a disease."[45]

Virtually all of psychiatry and psychology defined (and still defines) alcoholism as a symptom of another "underlying" disorder, such as infantile narcissism, repressed sexuality, depression, bad parenting, and personality conflicts. Alcoholism is seen as secondary to something else.

 For the Thinking Person

I really like LifeRing because it allows for individuation and that's crucial for me. I guess I'm not much of a blind follower. I know what's best for me. I'm the one that lives in my skin. The group process of LifeRing is what works for the thinking person.

– Sam, Seattle, Washington

This was also Wilson's view. As a follower of the psychiatrist C. G. Jung, Wilson held that "abnormal drinking is but a symptom of personal maladjustment to life."[46] Later, Wilson amplified *personal* to mean emotional and spiritual maladjustment, but the drinking always remained a symptom.[47]

The whole therapeutic strategy of the 12 steps rests on the belief that alcoholic drinking is a symptom of a deficient moral inventory or defects of character – in Wilson's words, the "serious character flaws that made problem drinkers of us in the first place."[48]

But the modern alcoholism movement defined (and still defines) alcoholism as a primary disease, a disease in its own right. Various other disorders, such as narcissism, sexual problems, depression, bad parenting, personality conflicts, and character defects, are either etiologically separate and unrelated or arise from alcoholism and are secondary to it.

This difference is not only jurisdictional; it affects clinical diagnosis and treatment as well as the alcoholic's own self-definition and recovery strategy. Whether Wilson liked it or not, the alcoholism movement, marching under the medical-disease banner, exerted a powerful influence back on the AA environment. The success of the disease movement provided tens of thousands of AA members with jobs in the rapidly exploding treatment industry.[49] The burgeoning industry in turn bought millions of copies of AA literature and referred its clients by the hundreds of thousands into AA meetings.[50]

The new recruits often came into AA meetings from the treatment centers. According to Kurtz, they were not there to learn. They were there to teach.

> And one of the big things about which they wanted to teach was the disease-concept of alcoholism, which old-time members realized had very little if anything to do with living AA's Twelve Steps, the heart of its program.[51]

Kurtz, White, and others have completed a prodigious research effort, demonstrating conclusively that the disease concept of alcoholism long predated AA, that AA did not invent it, and that it was carried into AA from the outside.[52] They urge AA to put some distance between itself and the disease concept and to stay neutral on the issue (exactly as LifeRing has done).

Kurtz and other old-timers familiar with AA complain that AA's close association with the treatment industry and its disease concept has changed the nature of the fellowship – and not for the better.[53]

But not completely. Newcomers are still taught the old-time religion of "get a sponsor, work the steps" at the same time as they are taught the newfangled medical-disease concept.

The fact that these two trains of thought run in opposite directions is disregarded, suppressed, or worded over. Only a relatively few observers have reflected on it. One of them is Dr. James Milam, author of the 1981 classic *Under the Influence*.[54] Commenting on the conjunction of the medical-disease theory with the moralistic-psychologistic paradigm of the 12 steps, he says that "AA stands as a colossal paradox." On the one hand, it promotes acceptance of alcoholism as a treatable disease. On the other hand, it is "a powerful obstacle to accepting the otherwise overwhelming evidence that biological factors, not psychological or emotional factors, usher in the disease."[55]

Dr. Milam, a giant among his contemporaries, fearlessly stated what has long been obvious, but few have dared to say:

> Students of the disease have tried to have it both ways, proclaiming loudly that alcoholism is a treatable disease and at the same time continuing to affix the blame and stigma for contracting the disease on the character of the unwitting victim.[56]

The resulting mishmash of religion and treatment industry boosterism engulfs practically every topic. If you ask, for example, why recoveries happen, the answer sounds like a musical chord in which one note rings, "By the grace of God" and the other, "Treatment works." Those who remark that these notes don't harmonize are hushed into silence, like a person who asks questions during a church service.

We have already seen one big reason why the disease concept is beyond discussion: it forms the basis for insurance reimbursement, a principal revenue source for the treatment industry. We now see a second reason. The stunted and mongrelized disease concept that emerged from the marriage of the medical paradigm and the religious-psychological 12-step program is beyond discussion, because any serious effort to deconstruct it would release its inner contradictions and lead to divisive arguments.

The Comparison to Tobacco

A useful historical contrast is the tobacco industry. When evidence of the harmful properties of nicotine first began to enter public discourse fifty years ago, the industry made a

I Am Not a Label

I have attended several 12-step programs and could never accept the view of labeling myself. Yes, I have an addiction, but it does not define who I am. LifeRing has let me deal with my addiction and learn to move on with life as I fight it. The support from the group and their coping skills have helped me get back into life.

– Cathy K., Nanaimo, B.C., Canada

strategic decision to try to develop a safe cigarette.[57] That was a huge blunder. The effort not only failed technically, it also highlighted by implication the unsafe nature of the product as currently sold.

The tobacco industry would have spent its money much more wisely to invest in research to establish the existence of a disease called "nicotinism" and to construct a profile of those who suffer from it, the "nicotinics" (or "nicoholics"). Had the industry succeeded in framing scientific and public opinion along these lines, the prevailing attitude today would be that cigarettes taken in moderation are harmless end even beneficial to a normal person, but there is a small minority of biologically vulnerable persons who cannot control their smoking and as a result suffer harmful consequences.

The industry might have been spared the mega-billion dollar class action lawsuits, public humiliation, and the substantial decline in consumption rates that it has suffered in the United States in the past twenty years.

Another useful contrast is heroin. Pharmacologically, alcohol and opiates have much in common in their action on the brain, and there are lines of research that could be construed as making out a disease of "heroinism," affecting a relatively small percentage of users. Social recognition of this disease would legitimize moderate use of the drug as normal in the same way as moderate use of alcohol.

But there is no above-ground industry to sponsor such studies or to popularize the results, as there is with alcohol. Consequently, alcohol use is considered normal and only a minority of users – those thought to have the disease – are steered toward treatment, but all heroin use is stigmatized and criminalized. The disease theory of alcoholism in effect widened the gap between alcoholics and users of other substances.[58]

Only in very recent years, with the revival of comprehensive concepts such as addiction, chemical dependency, or substance abuse, has this gap been partially bridged over.

The disease concept of alcoholism remains one of the most controversial issues in the addiction literature. Most alcoholism treatment providers firmly believe in the disease model. But alcoholism treatment is only a small outlying enclave in a larger world of health care and medical research, and these are only a part of the larger society on which substance addiction has an impact. In this larger world, as we will see, the disease concept of alcoholism is far from capturing a consensus.

In the remainder of this chapter, I will present a balance sheet of the disease concept – pros and cons – from the standpoint of the person seeking long-term freedom from addictive substances, so that you can make up your own mind. I repeat that LifeRing actually does what Kurtz and White wish AA would do: namely, keep hands off and not take a position on the disease concept, because it is an extraneous issue. Any opinions expressed or implied here are of course my own.

Drinking and Public Health

My friend Mike T., who had a decades-long "career" in alcoholism before getting sober, prided himself on having been a professional drunk driver. When he drove drunk, he put a matchbook cover over one lens of his glasses to eliminate the confusion caused by double vision. He never ventured out on the streets on New Year's Eve or other drinking holidays. "Too many amateurs," he said.

A recent study in the state of New Mexico found that only 1.6 percent of the population met the criteria for alcohol dependence. My friend Mike T. undoubtedly fit that category. If alcoholism is a disease, he had it. But ten times as many people (16.5 percent) engaged in excessive drinking or alcohol abuse.[59] Those are the "amateurs." They don't fit a diagnosis for the disease of alcoholism. But they account for the major proportion of alcohol-related problems, including violence, traffic deaths and injuries, family problems, and much more.[60]

This kind of finding is by no means unique to New Mexico. It's a pattern wherever alcohol is consumed. Dr. Tim Naimi, a physician with the Centers for Disease Control and Prevention in Atlanta, puts the issue this way:

> In order to prevent most alcohol-related problems, including alcoholism itself, we need to focus on excessive drinking, not just alcoholism. Focusing exclusively on alcoholism will identify only a small percentage of those at risk of causing or incurring alcohol-related harms, precludes the possibility of prevention, and is very costly, at least on a per-person basis.[61]

The disease approach focuses on alcoholism, which is primarily an individual health issue affecting a relatively small number of people. The disease approach neglects problems arising from drinking generally, which cover a much broader population.

This insight is fundamental to the public health approach to alcoholism, which sees drinking as a bio-psycho-social issue, and points to a wide range of medical, psychological, cultural, social, political, and economic measures, both preventive and remedial, that have shown effectiveness in relieving the social and individual costs of alcohol consumption.[62]

Not surprisingly, the alcohol industry, which promoted the disease model and is at profound peace with it, has reacted with undisguised hostility to the public health perspective.[63]

Professor Lorraine Midanik, Dean of the School of Social Work at the University of California at Berkeley, points out that the disease focus leads people to concentrate on fixing the individual, instead of fixing the social, economic, and political conditions that generate addicted individuals.[64] The treatment industry and the alcoholic beverage industry are allies, she points out, in the ongoing political maneuvers to reinforce and to tighten the disease focus and to marginalize public health perspectives.[65]

In sum, then, the disease concept has a very powerful plus: it opens up some sources of treatment funding for individuals who seek professional help concerning their substance use, or who are assigned by authorities to seek such help, and who are covered by insurance, or have the money to pay out-of-pocket, or are eligible for government benefits where available. A moral or penal model would not offer professional help, and in cases where substance use was linked with lawbreaking, the offender would be dealing only with other prisoners and prison staff.

In contrast, the disease model only focuses on one small segment of the problem – mainly individuals who are fairly late in their substance-using career. It does not address what it calls "normal" substance abusers, particularly those who make excessive use of alcohol, thereby causing major automobile

Didn't Fit with 12-Step Programs

I was a drug addict, alcoholic, sex addict. I've been in recovery for nine years. I got a few 24 hours and would relapse. This went on for years. I was a dope dealer and knew I couldn't drink, every time it got me in trouble. I got hooked on meth, coke. Been in jails and institutions. I tried 12-step programs but didn't fit in there. Then I found LifeRing. It's truly amazing. I fit here. I get support. I got great caring friends. Thank you all.

– James G., Nashville, Tennessee, 2 years clean and sober

accidents, domestic violence, heart disease, obesity, and other public health hazards.

The public health model also embraces individual treatment, but it frames this within a much larger context of prevention and regulation, and it arguably would have caught the person earlier and would in the aggregate reduce the incidence of the disease and the number of persons needing to be treated for it.

Does the Disease Theory
Reduce Social Stigma?

One of Marty Mann's main selling points was that reframing alcoholism as a medical rather than a moral issue served to reduce the social stigma from which alcoholics suffer. The public would look more kindly on a person who was sick, who suffered from a disease, than on one who was healthy but malicious, undisciplined, obnoxious, egotistical, and otherwise a Bad Person.

But there are diseases and diseases. The great cultural critic Susan Sontag observed that diseases vary greatly in their social acceptability. Tuberculosis, in its day, was a diagnosis that sent the patient into hiding. Today, despite extensive public education campaigns, people with HIV/AIDS are still often heavily stigmatized.[66]

Diseases that stigmatize the victim, Sontag said, are those whose etiology is poorly understood, so that the victim is open to blame, and for which no widely effective treatment is known. A disease isolates its sufferer when its nature remains a mystery and when it is believed without recourse.[67] Then patients go into denial. Families construct elaborate defenses. Lies and secrets multiply.

Alcoholism and other drug addictions fit squarely under this heading.[68] Numerous public opinion surveys show that Mann and her alcoholism movement were successful in gaining public acceptance for labeling alcoholism a disease – but mostly as lip service, and with no reduction in negative attitudes toward the alcoholic.[69]

To a certain extent alcoholics-as-persons-having-a-disease became more troublesome, expensive, egotistical, pretentious, and all-around blameworthy in the public mind than when they were looked on as healthy people who were bad actors. In some surveys, respondents who agreed that alcoholism was a disease were more likely to blame the alcoholic as a weak-willed person than those who did not agree with the disease label.[70]

None of this is surprising. Benjamin Rush, the Surgeon General of George Washington's revolutionary armies, and one of the pioneers of the disease concept, defined chronic drunkenness already in 1784 as "a disease induced by a vice."[71] Like HIV/AIDS, the mere labeling of alcoholism as a disease does nothing to remove the stigma of its presumed licentious acquisition.

A case in point is homosexuality. Beginning in 1952, while Marty Mann was in middle age, until seven years before her death in 1980, the American Psychiatric Association's Diagnostic and Statistical Manual (DSM) classified homosexuality as a disease.[72] Mann was herself a homosexual. She lived in a stable, long-term lesbian relationship.[73]

During the same period that Mann was advocating adoption of the disease label in order to free the alcoholic from stigma, representatives of the gay communities were lobbying the medical authorities to lighten the stigma of homosexuality by *removing* it from the disease classification.

This is not to say that Mann's efforts to lift stigma were unavailing. On the contrary, she accomplished a great deal in this direction. But the active ingredient was her public appearance as a healthy, energetic, witty, totally appealing sobered-up alcoholic. It's not the dead label of the disease but the live face of the cure that won over the public.

Mann's organization also sponsored a series of celebrity comings-out (as alcoholics) and set the stage for the later public self-disclosures of prominent recovered alcoholics, such as Elizabeth Taylor, Kitty Dukakis, and Betty Ford, which were hugely important in changing the alcoholic's negative public image.

In summary, the disease model has the potential for reducing the stigma from which addicted persons suffer, but this will not happen until the nature of the disease is freed from mystery, from linkage with character defects, and from spiritualist hocus-pocus: in short, from the 12-step paradigm. Until then, the most effective antidote to public fear and loathing of the sufferer was the former sufferer's own fearless and affirmative public display of the reality of a fulfilling life freed from the substances.

In a perverse way, the inherent mysticism of the 12-step disease concept – a three-fold illness caused by defects of character that render the victim powerless and that only a spiritual transformation can arrest – deepens the sufferer's stigma by making the condition and its cure incomprehensible. Mystery is the womb of stigma. AA-cofounder Wilson said it himself: "A. A. is an utter simplicity which encases a complete mystery."[74]

The Disease Concept and Abstinence

One of the primary didactic utilities of the disease concept of alcoholism in the hands of its advocates was and is to hammer home the need for complete abstinence. In Dr. Tiebout's words, "The alcoholic must be brought to accept that he is the victim of a disease and that the only way for him to remain healthy is to refrain from taking the first drink."[75]

That formula has been repeated countless times, and virtually all of the individuals in 12-step alcoholism treatment have had it drummed into their heads. A huge and bitter controversy erupted in the 1970s in academic and research circles about whether this was factually true.[76] The argument continues to this day under the heading *abstinence* versus *harm reduction*.

I'm all for abstinence, but I'm astonished that advocates of abstinence rested and still rest their case on analogies with chronic diseases such as diabetes, heart disease, and hypertension. What are they thinking?

Diabetes is linked with excessive consumption of sugar, heart disease with overindulgence in animal and dairy fats, and hypertension with too much sodium. None of these diseases requires abstinence from the noxious agent.

- An authoritative Web site for diabetics advises that in the event of a hypoglycemic incident, the sufferer should promptly consume sugar; for example, "5 or 6 pieces of hard candy, or 1 or 2 teaspoons of sugar or honey."[77]

- Wellness tips for sufferers from atherosclerosis (heart disease, hardened arteries) include the advice to "Cut down on foods rich in animal fats, particularly fatty meats (beef, pork) and high-fat dairy products."[78] Abstinence from such foods is not suggested.

- Sufferers from high blood pressure where salt is a factor are advised to "decrease sodium."[79]

The authoritative medical counsel for these diseases is to minimize, moderate, control.

There are valid and important similarities between alcoholism and these diseases, both as to etiology (pathologies arising from consumption) and as to treatment (noncompliance with medication regimes, relapse rates, and so forth).[80] But these comparisons with diseases not involving addictive substances do not sustain the case for abstinence; they undermine it.

The disease model has also been used with great evidentiary support at the highest scientific levels in the case of heroin, as a rationale why abstinence is impossible and why substitution of a chemically analogous but less harmful drug (methadone) is the only medically feasible remedy.[81]

Observers have noted for many years that the disease model has its dark side. It serves as a popular rationalization not only for abstinence but also for relapse and continued drinking. The idea that "I am powerless to control my drinking because I have a disease" provides a perfect lubricant for the alcoholic mind to slide back helplessly into the pit.

Let me be clear. I am a hard-core believer in abstinence, and the LifeRing organization has abstinence written into its indelible fundamental charter. I am quite open to medical research and to medical metaphors. However, the specific pharmacological action of the drugs of addiction is to my mind both necessary and sufficient to explain what my experience also tells me; namely, that I have the power to abstain from the first drink, but not from the second. By contrast, I have little trouble abstaining from the second Snickers bar, the second rib eye steak, or the second teaspoon of sodium chloride.

The loose analogies with diabetes, hypertension, and other chronic diseases not involving addictive substances are not helpful for maintaining abstinence and can even be counterproductive.

The Disease Concept and the Supreme Court

Leroy Powell was a married man living at home in Austin, Texas, who had been arrested numerous times for drunk-

Spending Time with Sober People

My drug of choice was crystal methamphetamine. I started using when I was 17 years old. After many twists and turns I ended up awaiting trial on a felony. My lawyer suggested I enroll in a drug program voluntarily before the state enrolled me involuntarily. At the beginning, I was not really feeling it. The program I was in required two self-help meetings per week. We were given the option of AA, NA, or LifeRing. LifeRing quickly became my only self-help group. The people at LifeRing turned out to be very similar to me. We were all mostly lost, confused and looking for answers and help. Part of the problem is that we don't always know the questions we are seeking answers to. With the open format, we can work with the group to achieve what we are seeking. These meetings are not advice sessions or "you must do this to succeed" meetings. They are an open format, dedicated to sharing with others what has and has not worked for us. This includes our weekly struggles, triggers, and cravings as well as how we handled them or didn't. If someone relapses, we still love them and hope they learned something and hopefully they will share that with us. One of the changes that the meetings help me make is spending time with sober people doing sober things. This is huge for me, as my most damaging use was brought on directly by loneliness. I am very introverted and making friends and lasting relationships is difficult at best. These meetings help with both of these issues.

As I write, I have 3 years 6 months 16 days clean. I work a total abstinence program.

– M. B., Union City, California

enness. On this occasion, he was arrested and fined $20 for violating a local ordinance against being drunk in public. He appealed, was again convicted, and appealed to the U.S. Supreme Court. His lawyers' argument was that he suffered from the disease of alcoholism, and this rendered him powerless to control how much he drank and where he drank it.

The court's opinion, written by Thurgood Marshall and seconded by Earl Warren, Hugo Black, and John Harlan, took a dim view of the disease theory.

> The inescapable fact is that there is no agreement among members of the medical profession about what it means to say that "alcoholism" is a "disease." One of the principal works in this field states that the major difficulty in articulating a "disease concept of alcoholism" is that "alcoholism has too many definitions, and disease has practically none." This same author concludes that "a disease is what the medical profession recognizes as such." In other words, there is widespread agreement today that "alcoholism" is a "disease," for the simple reason that the medical profession has concluded that it should attempt to treat those who have drinking problems. There, the agreement stops. Debate rages within the medical profession as to whether "alcoholism" is a separate "disease" in any meaningful biochemical, physiological or psychological sense, or whether it represents one peculiar manifestation in some individuals of underlying psychiatric disorders. Nor is there any substantial consensus as to the "manifestations of alcoholism."[82]

In the court's view, there was no firm basis for diagnosis of such a "formless 'disease.'"[83] The disease claim and the arguments based on it were, in the court' s words, "mystifying," "meaningless," and "unintelligible."[84]

Twenty years later, it was the same story. In 1988, the U.S. Supreme Court, reviewing the case of veterans who had been denied disability benefits because of their alcoholism, wrote:

> This litigation does not require the Court to decide whether alcoholism is a disease whose course its victims cannot control. It is not our role to resolve this medical issue, on which the authorities remain sharply divided.[85]

One can read in these judicial reactions a keen skepticism not so much toward a medical definition of alcoholism in general, but toward the particular claim that absolute powerlessness is part of the diagnosis. The powerless claim, as we saw earlier, has its root in a religious doctrine of the Dark Ages. In the hands of the early AA activists, the "medical business" was nothing more than a tactic to hammer the resistant alcoholic into a state of receptiveness to this doctrine. Modern courts, without knowing the history, nevertheless smelled the Augustinian rat in the physician's white cloak.

Why Physicians Have Trouble With the Disease Concept

An important fact about the history of the modern disease concept of alcoholism is that medical doctors were largely absent from the leadership of the movement. The sociologist Peter Conrad writes that the medicalization of alcoholism was not mainly the work of physicians but "was primarily accomplished by a social movement [Alcoholics Anonymous]."[86]

As we have seen, this is a bit unfair to say. Alcoholics Anonymous as an organization played no official role in the process. Rather, it was the alcoholic beverage industry, seconded by players in the alcoholism treatment industry, behind the public relations energy of Marty Mann and her NCEA/NCADD, that mobilized virtually the whole membership of AA and of affiliated organizations and individuals to create and drive this social movement.

But Conrad's main point, that physicians were not the principal drivers of the alcoholism-as-disease movement, is valid and important. He points out:

> Physicians were actually late adopters of the view of alcoholism as a disease... And even to this day, the medical profession or individual doctors may be only marginally involved with the management of alcoholism, and actual medical treatments are not requisite for medicalization.[87]

Conrad points out that physicians themselves were often reluctant, resistant, or irresolute on the issue of alcoholism as a disease.[88]

One has to understand here that the process by which the bureaucracies of the American Medical Association and the American Psychiatric Association add and delete things from the list of diseases is essentially political.[89] It responds to lobbying and pressure group mobilizations in both directions. Thus, the alcoholism movement mobilized to have alcoholism declared a disease. The gay movement mobilized to have homosexuality removed from the disease list.[90] There are a number of other examples, both successful and not.[91] These definitional changes may have little if anything to do with developments in scientific research or in clinical practice.

Only with this understanding can one begin to make sense of the reality that alcoholism is a disease in which large numbers of physicians do not believe. Hospital studies show, for example, that physicians frequently don't make the diagnosis of alcoholism even if the signs are staring them in the face.[92] Most trauma surgeons in emergency room settings don't screen for alcoholism at all, even though they encounter it with great regularity.[93]

Even when physicians recognize the diagnosis, they often don't like it. They say they get less professional satisfaction from dealing with alcoholics than from any other patients. Psychiatrists rank alcoholism as their least favorite illness to treat, and the general medical profession agrees.[94] A study of Canadian physicians found that only a minority believed in a biological etiology for alcoholism.[95]

As I write this, in the first half of 2008, twenty years after the U.S. Supreme Court observed that medical authorities were sharply divided over the disease issue, the ambivalence in the medical profession continues unabated.

- Charlotte Boettinger, a senior researcher at the Ernest Gallo Clinic and Research Center, a super-modern California alcoholism research laboratory founded with a grant from the winemaking firm, expresses the "hope" that a consensus on addiction-as-a-disease might be reached among her scientific peers in ten more years.[96]

- Another researcher at the same laboratory, Dr. Howard Fields, says that the refusal of many in the medical profession to "buy into the fact that addiction is really a disease of the nervous system" remains "the biggest hurdle" to progress in this area.[97]

- Markus Heilig, clinical director of the National Institute on Alcohol Abuse and Alcoholism (NIAAA), wrote in November 2007 that "the view of substance use disorders as medical conditions much similar to other chronic, relapsing disorders is still not widely accepted."[98]

The reason for this reluctance is really not that far to seek. The 12-step movement, with its "spiritual disease" concept, has done nothing to construct a medically intelligible disease model and has done much to confuse the issue. The central focus of the 12 steps on powerlessness, insanity, moral inventories, character defects, shortcomings, wrongs, amends, and the need for a spiritual awakening sends a powerful message that this is not a real medical disease. These are simply not the kind of problems with which physicians are – or should be – trained and equipped to deal.

Disease Treatment Without Doctors

The newcomer to this field who has been told that alcoholism is a disease and who enters treatment expecting to find a modern hospital or clinic where other diseases, such as cancer, heart ailments, asthma, diabetes, or hypertension, are treated may be in for a rude surprise.

Although a few islands of genuine medical treatment for addiction exist (I was fortunate to have access to one of them, thanks to my family's membership in the Kaiser Permanente HMO in Oakland, California), they are the exception, not the rule.

What I Wish For

The longer I was in AA the more I questioned the existence of God. So often I would hear people attribute their ability to get and stay sober to their higher power. In reality their success was largely their own doing with the support of others; it was the fruit of changes they made in their lives. Rather than denigrating ourselves and praising a higher power, we should praise and give credit to each other and ourselves for good choices, self-realization, and better thinking. In LifeRing, this is what we do. I know people in LifeRing who have not been to a treatment program and have not done a 12-step program. Yet, these persons have sobered up and maintained sobriety. The belief or reliance on a higher power is not necessary to be sober.

– Troy B., San Francisco, California

- The average "medical model" addiction treatment facility does not have a physician or a nurse or anyone else with an advanced graduate degree on full-time staff.[99]

- In nearly half the states, there is no standard certification or license for addiction treatment counselors, as there is for every other type of health care practitioner. You need a license to set up shop as an auto mechanic, a hairdresser, or a masseuse but not to work as an addictions counselor.[100]

- About half of the counseling staff in typical medical-model centers have not finished college. An uncounted but substantial number have not finished high school.

- Currently, there is a bill sponsored by an addiction counselors' organization that is before the California legislature. The bill declares that "addiction is a fatal disease." They propose that in order to obtain a counselor license in the future, candidates should have a high school diploma.[101] In a real medical setting, personnel with these qualifications would not be performing frontline disease treatment.

- The average salary in 2006 for substance addiction counselors was between $ 24,000 and $ 30,000, and the average staff tenure was two years. Among program administrators, over half had held their positions for one year or less.[102]

- Treatment in a typical medical-model facility will begin by instructing you to surrender yourself to the care of God.[103]

- Your treatment plan in the typical medical-model program will be prescribed for you without asking your opinion or obtaining your consent, and your plan will be identical to everyone else's. The motto is "One size fits all." If you raise questions, you will be told that you are in denial.

The patient is required to fit the program, rather than vice versa.[104]

- In an average medical-model facility, you may be permitted to smoke but not to use pain medications, even aspirin.[105]

- Available medications for the treatment of addictions, such as naltrexone, buprenorphin, and others, may not be prescribed for you, and you may be urged to discontinue medications for the treatment of related disorders, such as depression.

- In the usual medical-model facility, if you display the primary symptom of your disease by relapsing, you will probably be thrown out.[106]

- If you complete the medical-model program, you will be urged to entrust your follow-up care to a person who typically has even fewer professional qualifications and is less accountable than the staff of your treatment program, namely an AA member playing the role of "sponsor."

- If the treatment doesn't work for you, you the patient – not the treatment – will be blamed.[107]

One could understand this model in a backward country where standards were low, physicians few, education rare, resources unavailable, and superstitions widespread. But in a developed country such as the United States, no hospital or clinic for the treatment of diseases such as diabetes, hypertension, heart disease, cancer, or asthma would be permitted to operate on the model that is typical in the treatment of addiction. Patient lawsuits would drain them white. Licensing authorities would shut them down.

The bottom line is that the medical model of addiction treatment is "medical" only on the accounts-receivable side, where the claim forms and invoices are processed. At the patient interface, there is very little that deserves the name *medicine* in any modern sense. More than one surprised and outraged addiction patient has described the actual therapeutic practice in one of these medical-model addiction treatment mills as "voodoo."[108]

It's impossible to come away from either the experience or the study of addiction treatment on this so-called disease model without becoming aware that many of its leading advocates don't believe in anything resembling modern medicine. Addiction treatment is medicine with a wink and a nod. Why should anyone believe in a medical-disease model of addiction if its principal advocates don't practice it? Actions speak louder than words.

The Perfect Storm
That Made the Treatment System

In a comprehensive meta-analysis of what works and what doesn't work in alcoholism treatment, Professors Hester and Miller of the University of New Mexico came to a puzzling conclusion: the treatment approaches that had the least evidence of being effective were the ones in the most widespread use.

> The negative correlation between scientific evidence and application in standard practice could hardly be larger if one intentionally constructed treatment programs from those approaches with the least evidence of efficacy.[109]

How did we end up with a treatment system that appears as if it had been purposely designed to be as ineffective as possible?

At the time that the alcohol industry bought into the strategic center of alcohol science and began to popularize the disease-of-alcoholism paradigm (1939), there was no substantial alcoholism treatment industry as we have come to know it. There is no basis, therefore, for a claim that the alcohol industry intended to shape the treatment paradigm in any particular manner, other than to establish that there was something called *alcoholism* and that it was a disease.

The repeal of Prohibition in 1933, the formation of Alcoholics Anonymous shortly thereafter, the intervention of John D. Rockefeller that lifted AA out of obscurity a few years after that, and the political climate of the 1960s, which favored the rise of the new alcoholism movement, appear to have had separate origins that happened to coincide to make a perfect storm.

It's useful in this context to understand a basic fact about the market for alcoholic beverages. A small proportion of the heaviest drinkers drink the bulk of the beverage alcohol sold in the United States. It has been estimated that 5 percent of the drinkers drink half the total alcohol.[110] This means that the alcoholic beverage industry can't do without the small minority of people who drink to excess – alcohol abusers and alcoholics.

If you get the heavy drinkers sober and remove them from the market, the beverage industry collapses to half its size, or less. All the ads that promote responsible drinking are window dressing. What makes the alcoholic beverage industry tick is the customer who drinks to get drunk and does it practically every night. Customers like I used to be.

The strategic aim of the alcohol industry as it emerged from the repeal of Prohibition was to shift the blame for the social harms related to alcohol away from itself and its product and onto the man who used its product.

The 12-step program was and is perfectly constructed to accomplish that shift. What is the message here? You are out of control and powerless (step 1), you are insane (step 2), you are incompetent (step 3), you are morally deficient (step 4), you must confess your wrongs (step 5), your character is defective (step 6), you are substandard (step 7), you are a menace to others (steps 8 and 9), you're wrong (step 10), you're clueless (step 11), and your marching orders are to recruit other reprobates like yourself to this course of humiliation (step 12). The bottom line is this: you are to blame. A more thoroughgoing psychological blame-transferring exercise could hardly be devised.

Even without the added overlay of the medical-disease model (that tells you you're sick), the 12-step paradigm constitutes an array of fingers pointing at the drinker.

It's no wonder, as Professors Granfield and Cloud reported in their study of natural recovery, that most of their successful abstainers kept quiet about the change they had made in their lives.[111] They didn't want the baggage that comes with being labeled an alcoholic: diseased, powerless, insane, morally defective, and all the rest of it. They just wanted to get free of their drugs and get on with their lives. And they did. But it's a shame that they kept quiet, because other people could benefit from that lesson, and they themselves could benefit from sharing it.

We shouldn't be at all surprised, then, as every study has shown, that only a small minority of people who meet criteria for alcohol dependence approach the existing treatment system.[112] It's a psychologically punitive system that tends to deter people from quitting alcohol or from seeking help to do so, or both. It's an approach, coincidentally, that makes the least possible dent in the heavy-drinking core market of the alcoholic beverage business.

There's no evidence that the alcoholic beverage industry intended to create a treatment system that protects its profit center. It just worked out that way.

The Cure for the Disease Model

As I said at the outset of this chapter, the participant in LifeRing is free to decide whether to subscribe to the disease concept or to leave it alone. Had I used the term disease in the earlier chapters of this book, I would have implicitly pre-judged the issue.

Happily, every known physiological manifestation of the power of substance addiction – every aspect of its pathology – can be adequately explained without using the label disease, and I have tried to do so. There appears to be a perfectly sufficient medical and psychological vocabulary for explaining all the currently known actions and effects of addictive substances without this term.[113]

Researchers who work with laboratory animals that replicate key elements of human addictions hardly seem to find it necessary to use disease language. (This is perhaps because there is no money to be made in treating the animals.) Neutral terms such as the behaviorist concept of *habit* and the noncommittal medical term *disorder* explain as much or more than the indefinable term disease and do not carry the same political, economic, and moral baggage.

It may be objected that by avoiding the term, I have pre-judged the issue in the opposite direction. Perhaps so. Let me then sum up where these reflections have led me and lay my personal conclusions on the table.

The problem with the disease concept as we know it is its irrational 12-step envelope. The person seeking help to stop drinking usually encounters the disease concept in a setting that is saturated with religious exhortation and moral judgments. Unlike any other disease, having the disease of alcoholism means wearing the sackcloth and ashes of powerlessness, insanity, moral deficiency, and all the rest of it.

It isn't the disease per se that brings stigma, it's the disease as defined by its 12-step shell that stigmatizes the patient. Of course, stigma will attach to a condition whose owner is morally defective. Of course, someone whose own shortcomings of character have rendered him powerless is not going to get a lot of sympathy. Naturally, physicians don't believe in and don't want to touch a disease that is defined as a mysterious, cunning, and baffling spiritual misalignment. What rational physician would?

The cure for the disease theory of addiction, however, is not to throw medicine overboard, but to apply more medicine – real medicine – in place of the voodoo 12-step pseudomedical model. The religious-moralistic shell needs to be stripped from the disease concept so that its scientific core can emerge.

The 12-step concept of powerlessness is a Dark Ages religious relic, not a medically viable concept, and needs to go. Powerlessness exists, but it is relative to time, place, and situation. The addicted person can very well achieve the power not to take the first drink.

The notion of absolute reliance on an external power needs to be abandoned. Outside help is good and can be lifesaving, but the primary source of the power to recover lies within. Those who would be helpers need to direct their attention to supporting the recovering person's own natural resistance (the S).

Treatment needs to be an emotionally empowering rather than an emotionally punitive experience. Demands for surrender and assaults on the character or personality of individuals are unsupportable by evidence and need to be replaced with positive reinforcement for their sober traits.

People's capacity to experience sober pleasure urgently needs to be restored. Their capacity to think and make choices needs to be activated and exercised vigorously. Building personal recovery programs needs to become standard practice.

People's self-efficacy in coping with life's challenges needs to be built and supported. Treatment needs to be based on reinforcing inner strengths.

The disease concept need not be a tool for blaming and shaming the patient, as it is now. It need not even remain a strategy for locating the problem in the person rather than in the bottle.

A scientific disease concept is entirely conceivable based on the premise that alcohol, along with similar substances, is inherently addictive and that all of us – including those who are physically and psychologically within the "normal" range (whatever that may mean) – are at risk of contracting this disease if we put enough of the substance into our body. Alcohol is a poison, and those who consume it to excess will suffer chronic alcohol poisoning with all its consequences.

Such a disease concept not only has scientific validity, it also serves useful prophylactic functions as a public health message. Drink sparingly, if you must drink at all, because the danger of addiction lies in every bottle. Drink enough, and no matter how sweet, kind, compassionate, Aquarian, and God-loving you are, you may become alcoholic.

The shift of public opinion on nicotine within the past few decades points the way toward a new public understanding of alcohol. The concept that ethyl alcohol is a necessary and normal component of sociability, stress relief, and other positive qualities must be and can be deflated. The same claims were once made for nicotine. The notion that the good life includes a cocktail glass is as false as the notion that it includes a burning cigarette.

A disease concept based on public health foundations rather than one that shames and blames the individual could begin at last to carry away the mountain of death, sickness, crime, violence, broken families, traumatized children, and economic losses that alcohol brings us.

In the preceding chapter and here, we've looked at two of the dominant themes in the addiction recovery marketplace: powerlessness and the disease concept. In conclusion, let's have a look at another of the big topics in this area: the notion that alcoholics and other addicts are doomed to their fate by their genetic inheritance.

Notes

1. Jared Lobdell, This Strange Illness: Alcoholism and Bill W. (Piscataway, N.J.: Aldine Transaction, 2004), p. 247.
2. Mercadante, Victims and Sinners, p. 98.
3. Ernest Kurtz, "Alcoholics Anonymous and the Disease Concept of Alcoholism," Alcoholism Treatment Quarterly 20, no. 3/4 (2002): 3, 5-40.
4. Kurtz, Not-God, p. 132.
5. Lobdell, This Strange Illness p. 243; Kurtz, Not-God, p. 35.
6. To the same effect was cofounder Dr. Bob's advice, "Have to use disease – sick – only way to get across hopelessness." Quoted in Kurtz, "Alcoholics Anonymous and the Disease Concept of Alcoholism"; Lobdell, This Strange Illness, p. 87.
7. Ibid.
8. Ibid., p. 86.
9. Quoted in Kurtz, "Alcoholics Anonymous and the Disease Concept of Alcoholism," p. 2.
10. Nell Wing, Grateful to Have Been There: My 42 Years with Bill and Lois, and the Evolution of Alcoholics Anonymous (Center City, Minn.: Hazelden, 1998), pp. 55-65; Lobdell, This Strange Illness, pp. 90-91; Francis Hartigan, Bill W.: A Biography of Alcoholics Anonymous Cofounder Bill Wilson (Old Tappan, N.J., Macmillan, 2000), pp. 176-177.
11. Kurtz, Not-God, pp. 19-20; White, Slaying the Dragon, p. 129; Lobdell, This Strange Illness, p. 85.
12. Wing, Grateful to Have Been There, 25; Hartigan, Bill W., p. 63.
13. Lobdell, This Strange Illness, p. 3.
14. Ibid., p. 13.
15. A Layman with a Notebook, What Is the Oxford Group? (Oxford University Press, 1933), p. 15, http://www.stepstudy. org/downloads/what_is.pdf.
16. "Book Review," Journal of the American Medical Association 113, no. 16 (October 14, 1939), http://www.silkworth.net/bbreviews/01007.html.
17. Quoted in Roizen, The American Discovery of Alcoholism, 1933– 1939.
18. Ibid.
19. White, Slaying the Dragon, p. 195.
20. Ibid., p. 196.

21. John C. Burnham, Bad Habits: Drinking, Smoking, Taking Drugs, Gambling, Sexual Misbehavior (New York University Press, 1994), p. 83.
22. Jellinek himself noted that "the propagation of the illness conception of alcoholism may favor the interests of the alcoholic-beverage industry and, as a matter of fact, it has been intimated that the disease conception was triggered and has been fostered by those interests." He did not attempt to rebut this charge; he argued instead that it should make no difference. "No doubt, 'alcoholism as an illness' is pleasing to the beverage industry," but "their pleasure concerning the illness conception of 'alcoholism' cannot form a basis for its rejection if that conception should turn out to be valid." Elvin Morton Jellinek, The Disease Concept of Alcoholism (Ossining, N.Y.: Hill House Press, 1960), pp. 174-175.
23. White, Slaying the Dragon, pp. 183-184, 196.
24. Ibid., p. 186.
25. Ibid.
26. Sally Brown and David Brown, "Marty Mann and the Evolution of Alcoholics Anonymous [Excerpts]," 2001, http://www. barefootsworld.net/aamartymann.html.
27. Bill Wilson, "Why Alcoholics Anonymous Is Anonymous," AA Grapevine, January 1955, http://silkworth.net/grapevine/whyaaanonymous.html.
28. Quoted in White, Slaying the Dragon, p. 198.
29. Kurtz, Not-God.
30. Lobdell, This Strange Illness, p. 71.
31. Roizen, "Jellinek's Phantom Doctorate," 1997, http://www. roizen.com/ron/index.htm.
32. Kurtz, "Alcoholics Anonymous and the Disease Concept of Alcoholism," p. 40.
33. White, Slaying the Dragon, p. 194.
34. Burnham, Bad Habits, p. 83.
35. White, Slaying the Dragon, p. 195.
36. Wing, Grateful to Have Been There, p. 16.
37. Ibid.
38. White, Slaying the Dragon, p. 265
39. Ibid., p. 266.
40. Ibid., p. 198; Roizen, The American Discovery of Alcoholism, 1933–1939.
41. E Gordis, "Accessible and Affordable Health Care for Alcoholism and Related Problems: Strategy for Cost bnotes.indd 205 11/4/08 8:39:41 PM 206 Notes Containment," Journal of Studies on Alcohol 48, no. 6 (November 1987): 579-585, doi:3682832.
42. Ibid.
43. Bill Wilson, "Statement Before the U.S. Senate," July 24, 1969, http://www.hopenetworks.org/bill_w.htm; Kurtz, "Alcoholics Anonymous and the Disease Concept of Alcoholism," p. 44.
44. Kurtz, "Alcoholics Anonymous and the Disease Concept of Alcoholism," p. 44.
45. Quoted in Lobdell, This Strange Illness, p. 154.

46. Quoted in Kurtz, "Alcoholics Anonymous and the Disease Concept of Alcoholism," p. 18.
47. Ibid.
48. Quoted in Milam and Ketcham, Under the Influence, p. 140.
49. White, Slaying the Dragon, pp. 274-275.
50. Kurtz, Not-God; Chad Emrick and J. Scott Tonigan, "Alcoholics Anonymous and Other 12-Step Groups," in Marc Galanter (ed.), Recent Developments in Alcoholism: Treatment Research (New York: Springer, 2004), p. 433.
51. Kurtz, "Alcoholics Anonymous and the Disease Concept of Alcoholism," p. 44.
52. William White, "Addiction as a Disease: Birth of a Concept," Counselor 1, no. 1 (2000), http://www.bhrm.org/papers/Counselor1.pdf; William White, "The Rebirth of the Disease Concept of Alcoholism in the 20th Century," Counselor 1, no. 2 (2000): 62-66; William White, "Addiction Disease Concept: Advocates and Critics," Counselor 2, no. 2 (February 2001), http://www.bhrm.org/papers/Counselor3.pdf; William White, "A Disease Concept for the 21st Century," Counselor 2, no. 4 (April 2001), http://www.bhrm.org/papers/Counselor4.pdf; Kurtz, "Alcoholics Anonymous and the Disease Concept of Alcoholism."
53. White, Slaying the Dragon, p. 278; Lobdell, This Strange Illness, p. 239.
54. James R. Milam, "The Alcoholism Revolution," Professional Counselor, August 1992, http://www.lakesidemilam.com/TheAlcoholismRevolution.htm.
55. Milam and Ketcham, Under the Influence, p. 141.
56. Ibid., p. 142.
57. Stanton A. Glantz (ed.), The Cigarette Papers (Berkeley: University of California Press, 1998).
58. White, Slaying the Dragon, p. 197.
59. Sandra Woerle, Jim Roeber, and Michael G. Landen, "Prevalence of Alcohol Dependence Among Excessive Drinkers in New Mexico," Alcoholism, Clinical and Experimental Research 31, no. 2 (February 2007): 293-298, doi:ACER305.
60. Robin Room, "Alcohol," in Detels: Oxford Textbook of Public Health, 4th ed. (Oxford University Press, 2002), http://www. robinroom.net/alcohol.htm.
61. Jim Roeber, "Excessive Drinking, Not Alcoholism, May Lead to Most Alcohol-Related Problems" (Eureka Alerts, January 25, 2007), http://www.eurekalert.org/pub_releases/2007-01/ace-edn011807.php. A study of emergency room admissions found that most injuries occurred after consumption of one or two drinks, see Cheryl J. Cherpitel, "Injury and the Role of Alcohol: County-Wide Emergency Room Data," Alcoholism: Clinical and Experimental Research 18, no. 3 (June 1994): 679– 684, doi:10.1111/j.1530-0277.1994.tb00930.x.
62. A good summary is in Hester and Miller, Handbook of Alcoholism Treatment Approaches: Effective Alternatives, pp. 7– 8.
63. Room, "Alcohol."

64. Lorraine T. Midanik, Biomedicalization of Alcohol Studies: Ideological Shifts and Institutional Challenges (Piscataway, N.J.: Aldine Transaction, 2006), pp. 2-3, 25.

65. Lorraine T. Midanik, "What's in a Name? Proposed Name Changes of the U.S. National Institute on Drug Abuse and the U.S. National Institute on Alcohol Abuse and Alcoholism," Addiction 103, no. 1 (January 1, 2008): 1-3, doi: doi:10.1111/j.1360-0443.2007.02037.x.

66. Susan Sontag, Illness as Metaphor and AIDS and Its Metaphors (Old Tappan, N.J., Macmillan, 2001), http://www. susansontag.com/SusanSontag/books/illnessAsMetaphorExcerpt. shtml; Room, "Sociology and the Disease Concept of Alcoholism."

67. Sontag, Illness as Metaphor and AIDS and Its Metaphors.

68. "Alcoholism has not been medically respectable; it has no well-defined etiology or therapy." R. Straus, "Medical Practice and the Alcoholic," Annals of the American Academy of Political and Social Science, 315, no. 1 (1958): 117-124.

69. R. Roizen, "The Great Controlled Drinking Controversy," Alcohol Sociology Home Page, 1987, http://www.roizen.com/ron/cont-dri.htm.

70. Room, "Sociology and the Disease Concept of Alcoholism," pp. 70-71; Roizen, "The Great Controlled Drinking Controversy."

71. Quoted in White, Slaying the Dragon, p. 2 [emphasis added].

72. Midanik, Biomedicalization of Alcohol Studies, 24; Peter Conrad, The Medicalization of Society: On the Transformation of Human Conditions (Baltimore: Johns Hopkins University Press, 2007), p. 99.

73. William R. Flynn, "A Biography of Mrs. Marty Mann: The First Lady of Alcoholics Anonymous [Book Review]," American Journal of Psychiatry 159 (November 2002): 1950-1951; Sally Brown and David Brown, A Biography of Mrs. Marty Mann: The First Lady of Alcoholics Anonymous (Hazelden, 2005); R. Roizen, "Marty Mann: An Experiment That Failed," Alcohol Sociology Home Page, 1997, http://www. roizen.com/ron/mann. htm; Hartigan, Bill W., p. 8.

74. Wilson to JLK, cited in Kurtz, Not-God, p. 157.

75. Quoted in Lobdell, This Strange Illness, p. 154.

76. Roizen, "The Great Controlled Drinking Controversy."

77. "Diabetic Diet (Diabetes Diet) Information on MedicineNet.com," Diabetic Diet (cont'd), http://www.medicinenet.com/diabetic_diet/page4.htm#toce.

78. "Atherosclerosis Risk Factors, Prevention and Wellness Tips," Wellness Tips, http://www.recoverymedicine.com/atherosclerosis_ wellness_tips.htm.

79. "Diet and Hypertension," http://www.ext.colostate.edu/pubs/food-nut/09318.html.

80. A. T. McLellan et al., "Drug Dependence, A Chronic Medical Illness: Implications for Treatment, Insurance, and Outcomes Evaluation," Journal of the American Medical Association 284, no. 13 (October 4, 2000): 1689-1695, doi:11015800.

81. Drs. Nyswander and Dole, pioneers of methadone maintenance; discussed in White, Slaying the Dragon, p. 253.

82. Powell v. Texas, 392 U. S. 514 (1968), 522, http://supreme.justia.com/us/392/514/case.html.
83. Ibid.
84. Ibid., p. 524.
85. Traynor v. Turnage, 485 U. S. 535 (1988), http://supreme.justia.com/us/485/535/.
86. Conrad, The Medicalization of Society, p. 6.
87. Ibid.
88. Ibid., p. 9.
89. White, Slaying the Dragon, p. 188.
90. Conrad, The Medicalization of Society, pp. 9, 99.
91. Conrad, The Medicalization of Society; Midanik, Biomedicalization of Alcohol Studies.
92. T. D. Schneekloth et al., "Point Prevalence of Alcoholism in Hospitalized Patients: Continuing Challenges of Detection, Assessment, and Diagnosis," Mayo Clinic Proceedings. Mayo Clinic 76, no. 5 (May 2001): 460-466, doi:11357792.
93. Vaillant, "Interview: A Doctor Speaks"; G. J. Paz Filho et al., "[Use of the CAGE questionnaire for detecting alcohol use disorders in the emergency room]," Revista Da Associação Mèdica Brasileira (1992) 47, no. 1: 65-69, doi:11340453.
94. E. B. MacDonald and A. R. Patel, "Attitudes Towards Alcoholism," British Medical Journal 2, no. 5968 (May 24, 1975): 430-431, doi:1125569.
95. B. Rush et al., "Detecting, Preventing, and Managing Patients' Alcohol Problems," Canadian Family Physician MéSdecin De Famille Canadien 40 (September 1994): 1557-1566, doi:7920049.
96. Charlotte Boettinger, "UCSF News Office – Brain Imaging and Genetic Studies Link Thinking Patterns to Addiction," http://pub.ucsf.edu/newsservices/releases/200712262.
97. Howard Fields, "Alcoholism: Vice or Disease? A Conversation with Howard Fields, Part 3 of 3-UCSF Science Cafè," http://www.ucsf.edu/science-cafe/conversations/fields3/.
98. Markus Heilig, "Imagen: Implications for Addiction Science and Science Policy," Addiction (Abingdon, England) 102, no. 11 (November 2007): 1699-1700, doi:ADD2004.
99. In a representative national sample of 175 substance abuse treatment programs surveyed by McLellan et al., only one was headed by a physician. The "model" program epitomizing the 12-step "medical model" facility featured in Ketcham's treatise has neither a physician nor a nurse on staff. A. T. McLellan, Deni Carise, and H. D. Kleber, "Can the national addiction treatment infrastructure support the public's demand for quality care?" Journal of Substance Abuse Treatment 25 (2003): 117-121; Ketcham and Asbury, Beyond the Influence; David J. Powell, "It's Time for a National Approach on Staff Development," Behavioral Healthcare (March 2006), http://www.behavioral.net/.
100. Powell, "It's Time for A National Approach on Staff Development."

101. Dorothy Farnsworth, "Quality Assurance Report," CAADAC, November 6, 2007, http://www.capwiz.com/caadac/attachments/qa_final_report_12_07_fin.pdf.

102. Turnover among program directors and staff exceeds 50 percent a year. McLellan, Carise, and Kleber, "Can the National Addiction Treatment Infrastructure Support the Public's Demand for Quality Care?"

103. Joseph Volpicelli and Maia Szalavitz, Recovery Options: The Complete Guide (New York: Wiley, 2000).

104. Washton and Rawson, "Substance Abuse Treatment Under Managed Care: A Provider Perspective," p. 547.

105. A vivid illustration is in the movie *28 Days*, where the 12-step treatment staff refuses to give pain medications, even Aspirin, for a sprained ankle.

106. William White, "It's Time to Stop Kicking People Out of Addiction Treatment," Counselor (April 2005), http://www. bhrm.org/papers/AD-PDF.pdf.

107. "Harold Hughes, the political Godfather of the modern alcoholism treatment system, often noted that alcoholism was the only disorder in which the patient was blamed when treatment failed." White, Slaying the Dragon, p. 331.

108. Peter D. A. Cohen, "Is the Addiction Doctor the Voodoo Priest of Western Man?" Addiction Research & Theory 8, no. 6 (2000): 589, doi:10.3109/16066350008998990.

109. Hester and Miller, Handbook of Alcoholism Treatment Approaches: Effective Alternatives, 33; Paula Wilbourne and Ken Weingardt, "Therapeutic Outcome Research and Dissemination of Empirically Based Treatment for Alcohol Use Disorders," Translation of Addictions Science into Practice (2007): 259-276, doi:10.1016/B978-008044927-2/50062-6.

110. The top 2.5 Per Cent Drank About One Third. Charles Winick, "Epidemiology," in Substance Abuse: A Comprehensive Textbook, 3rd ed., 1997, p, 13.

111. Granfield and Cloud, Coming Clean, pp. 172-173.

112. Kessler et al., "Lifetime and 12-Month Prevalence of DSM-III-R Psychiatric Disorders in the United States. Results from the National Comorbidity Survey."

113. Roy Wise: "It remains to be proven that addiction is more than a very strong habit directed toward a harmful and socially unacceptable reinforcer," "Addiction," p. 827.

Chapter Seven

GENETIC HEADLINES
MEET LABORATORY REALITIES

My friend Kevin comes from a mixed Native American and Irish background. On his father's side, all the male ancestors as far back as anyone can remember died of alcoholism, directly or indirectly. Six of his mother's sisters died of alcoholism, and so did both maternal grandparents. It is a safe bet that if alcoholism comes in the genes, Kevin has those genes.

But Kevin doesn't drink or do other drugs. He's had a few nips now and then at ceremonial occasions, but as a general rule he doesn't touch the stuff. It just doesn't appeal to him.

Sarah was Jewish. Nobody in her family tree, going back at least four generations, has ever had an issue with drinking or other addictions. Sarah started drinking in a college sorority, started doing pills not long after, and kept this up for almost three decades. When I met her, her friends said she was drinking two liters of vodka per day. Her skin was yellowing, a sign of liver failure. She refused to consider slowing down or stopping. She died at forty-nine.

These examples touch only the surface of the problem of determining what role genetic factors play in the development of alcoholism and other addictions. Almost everyone knows heavy drinkers with a long family history of alcoholism, who very probably inherited alcoholism in their genes. But almost everyone also knows people who break that stereotype: people like Kevin who should be alcoholics by family history but who don't drink and others like Sarah who have no sign of genetic background but drink and suffer with the worst of them.

Headline Fantasies
Versus Laboratory Research

Newspaper headlines occasionally announce that the alcoholism gene has been found. Headlines appear such as "Born to the Bottle" and "Gene and Tonic: Science Proves that Alcoholics Can't Help it."[1] Popular excitement follows. But when the research is checked by other laboratories, the claims become smaller, and soon they evaporate.

A case in point is Dr. Kenneth Blum's 1996 claim in *American Scientist* to have discovered "the gene for alcoholism," along with a string of other disorders.[2] A major genetics laboratory checked his claim two years later and found "absolutely no evidence" for it.[3] This claim, along with Blum's alleged genetic test kit and a line of nutritional supplements advertised as a cure for the condition, all faded from view; even the original article has disappeared from the magazine's online archive.[4]

Studies of Twins

Tracing genetic factors for behavioral patterns in humans turns out to be an extremely difficult, complicated, and expensive business. For starters, family background is inconclusive because the drinking behavior could have been learned by example rather than acquired in the genes. The well-documented existence of nonalcoholic members of alcoholic families challenges any simple inheritance model.[5]

Studies of identical twins raised in different families are more suggestive, but far from conclusive. Twins as a class tend to be different from singletons. They suffer on the average more stress in utero. They have lower birth weight, higher rates of birth defects, lower childhood IQs, among other difficulties.[6] We need to know how different the adoptive family is from the biological family, whether the twins raised in different families were in contact, and whether they supplied each other with alcohol or drugs.[7] There are other confounding factors.[8] Some researchers consider twin studies of behavioral phenomena to be so riddled with methodological problems as to be pseudoscientific.[9]

Some researchers studying populations of twins concluded "that genes may account for about 50-60 percent of the risk of developing alcohol dependence."[10] Some studies show as low as 40 percent, whereas one study claims as high as 73 percent in men.[11] A recent critical meta-analysis of twin studies puts the maximum genetic contribution at 30-36 percent.[12] The wide range of these estimates illustrates the methodological difficulties in twin studies.

It's not only the twin studies; all research in this area suffers from the lack of scientific consensus about what constitutes alcoholism. Is there one alcoholism, as the treatment industry seems to think, or is it "a heterogeneous group of disorders," as research indicates?[13] Which elements of the 7-point DSM-IV laundry list of symptoms of substance dependence (pick any three) are most relevant to genetic research?[14]

Molecular Studies

The gold standard in genetic research today is molecular studies. This is based on technological breakthroughs in the past two decades, culminating in the successful sequencing of the human genome. Molecular linkage studies and molecular association studies are the two principal tools. Both aim to identify specific variations at points of the DNA helix that are seen when specific behavioral traits, such as alcoholism, are present.[15]

This quest has turned out to be much more difficult than anticipated. The popular notion that genes are similar to the mainspring that drives the organism like a clockwork mechanism is remote from the reality. What researchers working with the best modern technology have discovered is much more complex.

- Genes don't directly drive the organism. They work only if and when they express themselves by producing proteins. Important details about the complex chains of molecular events that intervene between genes and proteins are still unknown and under study.[16]

- Genes and the environment interact.[17] Environmental influences can and do have a say in whether genes express themselves or remain silent.[18]

- Among the environmental influences that influence gene expression is stress.[19] Specific behavior patterns can also influence gene expression.[20]

- The inheritance of alcoholism is not Mendelian, like eye color or handedness. The genetic influence exists not in the form of a single gene, like Huntington's disease, but as the constellation of a number of genes, each having only a small impact by itself.[21] The exact number of genes that may be implicated in alcoholism has not yet been established. It could be as few as eight.[22] Or it could be more than a hundred.[23] The list of candidate genes identified in one or another molecular study – but not replicated – would fill a huge table.[24]

- Promising candidate genes for alcoholism are also linked with other, more loosely defined traits, so that teasing out cause and effect becomes extremely challenging. Those traits include the following:
  - Novelty-seeking[25]
  - Antisocial behavior[26]
  - A variety of psychiatric disorders[27]
- A number of genetic abnormalities found in alcoholic brains and thought to be linked to dependence are not the cause but rather the effect of the individual's drinking.[28]
- What is inherited – if and when inheritance takes place – is not the behavior pattern of drinking to excess despite negative consequences ("the disease of alcoholism") but only a predisposition or a vulnerability to develop alcoholism if and when the person starts drinking.[29] Most people who inherit the predisposition for alcoholism will not become alcoholics.[30] (There is more about this later in the chapter.)

These problems are not unique to addiction research. They bedevil the genetic study of psychiatric disorders generally. For example, in twin studies autism is reported to be almost 100 percent genetic, leading to the expectation that the autism gene would soon be discovered. But molecular studies showed that at least twenty different genes are involved, each with a very small contribution. Almost everyone is walking around with one or more of the "autism genes."[31]

Searching for the Alcoholism Gene

The huge Collaborative Studies on Genetics of Alcoholism Project (COGA) set out in 1989 to hunt through the genome and isolate the alcoholism gene. After twelve years of research, it had little to show:

> [T]he project, funded by the National Institute on Alcohol Abuse and Alcoholism, went nowhere fast. Instead, scientists quickly discovered that the disease was even more complicated than anticipated. It is polygenic and heterogeneous, and involved numerous environmental variables.[32]

COGA has meanwhile announced some likely target areas that may indicate genetic effects, but other scientists rate the results as weak and not replicable.[33] Much more work lies ahead.[34] It seems that as the technology of genetic research grows more powerful, the picture becomes more complex and the findings become more tentative.

Guarded Generalities

Scientifically conservative statements today tend to avoid numerical estimates of the genetic risk for such a complex set of phenomena as those involved in substance dependence and speak in guarded generalities. For example:

> It is the interaction of genes, environment and developmental influences that ultimately predict vulnerability to substance use disorders.[35]

Or:

> What is clear is that many genes likely influence the vulnerability for alcoholism and that different combinations of genes are likely to be more or less salient for each endophenotype associated with the disorder.[36]

Or:

> Alcoholism is a prototypical example of a multi-factorial illness in which gene-environment interaction represents a key element.[37]

These guarded scientific summaries emphasize that alcoholism is very complex and that environmental and genetic influences interact with one another in its development.

The carrot at the end of the stick driving genetic research is the hope of finding a pharmaceutical intervention, a magic pill.[38] But with the genetic component spread over many different genes, and with the ever-present role of environmental factors, scientists are becoming skeptical that a single pill could tip the balance. More than one researcher is of the opinion that a genetic marker specific for alcoholism simply may not exist.[39]

Seeking and Giving Honest Help

What I like most about LifeRing is that the folks are genuinely talking about what is going on in their lives, and seeking and giving honest help in recovery. I don't have an issue with the "God thing" in AA. In fact, my faith is a big part of my recovery. But I find that often what is said in AA meetings seems less about heartfelt concerns and more about appearing to fit within perceived doctrine, saying what is expected. Because there is no "doctrine" in LifeRing besides abstinence and mutual help, there is none of that artificiality in the LifeRing discussions. Also, my experience is that there is a higher percentage of newly clean and sober folks at LifeRing. There are very few new people who come to my regular AA meeting. Since I believe that helping others achieve sobriety is a critical part of the recovery process, there seems to be more opportunity for that in LifeRing.

– Dan H., San Francisco

Because the initial expectations from the alcoholism-gene hunt were high and the results so far have been modest, a number of scientists not invested in this technology are now questioning whether continuing this costly research is a rational investment of scarce science dollars.[40] Although an understanding of the genetic picture is certainly useful, these scientists contend that a more balanced approach would devote greater societal resources to the public health aspects of these disorders, particularly efforts at prevention.[41] Some lay observers have even suggested that the high-tech gene hunt has degenerated into a boondoggle.[42]

In a fascinating new twist, one group of researchers now proposes that environmental chemicals such as pesticides, endocrine disrupters, and heavy metals known to affect the dopamine system, may play a role in predisposing people toward substance addiction.[43]

In short, the fine print of scientific evidence tells a more humble and complex story than the brassy sound bytes in newspaper headlines.[44]

A Genetic Trait
That Protects Against Alcoholism

The most robust and undisputed finding in genetic research of alcoholism is a negative one. It demonstrates the inheritance of a trait that protects against drinking alcohol and developing alcoholism. About half of Han Chinese, Japanese, and Koreans have a genetic trait that results in unpleasant physical reactions when they drink. They experience flushing, vomiting, upset stomach, and heart palpitations, similar to the effects of the deterrent drug Antabuse® (disulfiram).[45] A single, easily identified genetic variation (*ALDH2*) is responsible. It causes the liver to pour high levels of the alcohol breakdown product acetaldehyde into the bloodstream, and this upsets the metabolism.

Not surprisingly, the rates of alcohol consumption and of alcoholism in people with this genetic variation are very low.[46] This protective trait is much less frequent in Thais, Filipinos, Indians, and Chinese and Taiwanese aborigines.[47] A very few indigenous people in North America but somewhat larger proportions in South America also have this protective gene, and the amount they drink and their risk of alcoholism are substantially less than the average among indigenous Americans generally.[48] Some Jews also have this aversive gene, and they also tend to drink less and have a lower rate of alcoholism than other Jews on the average.[49] The protective gene is otherwise rarely if ever found in people with European or recent African ancestry.[50]

Even here, where the genetic factor is strong and clear, environmental and psychological influences also play a role. For example, a study among Han Chinese in Taiwan found that some men classified as having antisocial personality became alcoholics even though they had the protective gene. Perhaps as a demonstration of machismo, they drank their way through the physical discomfort barrier – just as some Caucasians drink through disulfiram – and ended up as alcoholics.[51]

Some Asian American college students in the United States engage in similar gene-defying behaviors.[52]

Japanese workers who experience high levels of occupational stress are also liable to drink alcohol despite the genetic discomfort.[53]

Those who override the messages from their metabolism frequently pay a high price in the form of cancers and other diseases.[54] Acetaldehyde is not only upsetting, it is also a carcinogen.[55]

In some of the literature, possession of the protective gene is characterized as a deviant, abnormal, or deficient variation by comparison with the normal genetic endowment, in which the liver processes alcohol without pouring high levels of acetaldehyde into the bloodstream.[56] Given the enormous physical, social, and economic cost of alcohol consumption, a sounder judgment might be that the alcohol-aversive gene represents the more adaptive evolutionary avenue, whereas the genetic facility for ingesting alcohol without immediate discomfort points toward an evolutionary train wreck.

The High Risk of Low Responsiveness

The most robust positive finding that demonstrates a genetic mechanism that predisposes to the development of alcoholism is much more subtle than the finding of a protective gene. It comes from the study of sons of alcoholics by Marc Schuckit and colleagues. The research shows a degree of inheritance not of alcoholism per se, but of low responsiveness to alcohol.[57]

People vary naturally in the extent to which a dose of alcohol produces signs of intoxication. Low responsiveness means that if people want to achieve the state of being drunk, they have to drink more than the average person to get there. High-responsives have to drink less. Highs are cheap dates. Lows are expensive.

Schuckit found that about 40 percent of young men aged twenty whose fathers were alcohol dependent had the trait of low responsiveness. Only about 10 percent of young men whose fathers were not alcohol dependent had the low-responsiveness trait.[58] Similar but weaker patterns were found in daughters.[59]

Schuckit was careful to eliminate from his sample men with a family history of mental illness, antisocial personality disorder, and similar confounding factors.

In interviews with his original male study subjects fifteen years later, when the men were aged thirty-five, Schuckit found that about one quarter had become alcohol dependent. But contrary to expectation, there was no significant relationship between their level of responsiveness to alcohol at age twenty and the likelihood of being alcohol dependent at age thirty-five. High-responsives were as likely to become alcoholic as low-responsives.

The only significant difference between the low-responsive and the high-responsive group of alcohol-dependent men was that the low-responsives arrived at alcohol dependence about two years earlier than the high-responsive group.[60] This earlier arrival time held for low-responsives generally, whether or not they had an alcoholic father.

Of the men in Schuckit's sample who were alcoholics at age thirty-five, more than 60 percent were not low-responsive sons of alcoholic fathers. In other words, only a minority had the genetic predisposition.

In every respect except the earlier onset, the alcoholic men with a genetic predisposition were indistinguishable from the alcoholic men without it, Schuckit found.

These concrete research findings give tangible shape to the otherwise abstract proposition that there is some degree of inherited predisposition to develop alcoholism. All other things being equal, low responsiveness to alcohol at age twenty leads to consumption of higher volumes of alcohol to get the same effect as one's peers. This may lead to social ties with other hard-drinking young people, further reinforcing the behavior.[61]

The result is that the low-responsive drinker puts a higher volume of the substance into the body. Higher volume means more molecules of alcohol doing their demolition-and-remodeling work on the brain circuits, hence an earlier onset of dependence.

That's It. No More

Five years ago, at the age of 77, I quit drinking. You might wonder what took so long. I wondered that myself. It came to me later, months later, in fact, that I truly believed I COULDN'T quit drinking. Every time I told myself to stop, I'd think: I can't! I love drinking. What'll I do at parties? The truth was there weren't that many parties; I was mostly drinking alone at home. At least I wasn't driving drunk, so I wasn't hurting anyone. One night I got really plastered during a holiday gathering while many of my family members were here, grandkids and all. It was embarrassing and humiliating, and my family was concerned, but infuriated too. When I woke the next morning, I said, "That's it. No more." It was painful to accept the shame I felt, but that helped cement my resolve. I talked to a psychologist at Kaiser. I followed his recommendation and began going to LifeRing the following week. The help of all the people at LifeRing, people with all sorts of addiction problems, was an invaluable blessing. I learned how to prepare myself for parties knowing I wouldn't drink. I figured out how to break the five o'clock habit every day. I prepared for the sudden urges. I learned to be honest in the meetings and to myself. There's good news. I wake every day with a clear head and a clear conscience and a clear reminder of what I could lose if I ever drank again. I feel wonderful. My family, friends, and increasing self-respect keep me safe and sober. Sometimes I wish I had stopped drinking sooner. I remind myself that I quit in time to mend broken fences that I created with my drinking. I am grateful for my family, friends, and the strangers who became friends through that very tough first year. Each day becomes easier, and I am living my happiest life now, even with my 82-year-old body. The joy is beyond explaining, but I am so glad it was within reach.

– Mary B., San Rafael, California

Another study by different researchers comparing alcoholic sons from alcoholic families with alcoholic sons from nonalcoholic families similarly found that the outstanding difference in the development of their drinking patterns was that those with the alcoholic pedigree progressed from first drink to alcoholism more quickly than those without.[62]

Low responsiveness to alcohol is often misunderstood as a sign that the person is invulnerable to harm from alcohol, because they can drink more than their peers without falling over. In fact, as Schuckit's research demonstrates, low responsiveness is a warning flag for the risk of alcoholism. These genetic studies provide reason to caution the offspring of alcoholic parents to refrain from drinking – or to be extremely vigilant if they do put alcohol into the body.

At the same time, the studies underline that the path of genetic predisposition is not the only road into alcoholism; it is merely the fast lane. Most of those who arrive in the land of alcoholism get there without having the genetic predisposition. It just takes them a little longer. Once arrived, the minority of alcoholics with a genetic propensity and the majority of alcoholics without a genetic propensity are indistinguishable.

The Dangers of Genetic Fatalism

A proper estimation of the genetic role is important for cautionary purposes. But despite the very modest scale of the evidence, there is a popular tendency to exaggerate the genetic role, sometimes to the point of fatalism, as if genetics were the whole of the picture. Such an overemphasis on genetic factors can have unhealthy effects.

Sarah, who died of liver failure at forty-nine, had no alcoholics in her family tree for at least four generations. She had heard that "alcoholism is genetic," and so she felt she was safe.

To the end, she continued to believe that she could not be and was not an alcoholic.

Overestimation of the genetic factor can provide drinkers with an almost foolproof denial mechanism. If alcoholism is genetic, then people who don't come from a line of alcoholic ancestors – and most people don't – needn't worry. This chain of reasoning is dearly beloved of the alcohol industry. It is wrong. It may take people who have no genetic risk a little longer to get into alcoholism, but if they persist, they will get there.

Genetic determinism can also deprive drinkers of hope. It can make them believe that alcoholism is their genetic fate, like an unchangeable character trait, and that there is nothing they can do about it. Wrong! All that was probably in their genetic fate was low responsiveness – the inability to get as high as the next person on the same amount of alcohol. The rest of the damage was optional and can be undone if caught in time.

Genetic fatalism can deprive the world of lives still unborn. My friend Tiana comes from a long line of alcoholics. She now has more than a decade of sobriety. She decided not to have children because she does not want to bring more alcoholics into the world. A more accurate understanding of the genetic factors in alcoholism might have changed her mind. Her children could very well be sober all their lives. Her genetic line includes persons with great musical, literary, and artistic abilities. The world is a poorer place for the absence of Tiana's children.

Genetic Fatalism and Eugenics

As of this writing, a credible genetic test for the predisposition to alcoholism is not on the commercial radar screen.[63] But the mere hypothetical possibility is enough to raise alarms. If a predisposition for alcoholism could be revealed in amniocentesis, the infant's life chances could be at risk. Parental bonding might be impaired. The infant could become unadoptable. Insurance companies could refuse to cover.[64] Employers could refuse to hire. Would existing privacy safeguards be strong enough to lock up this information?

A Beautiful Simplicity

The counselors at the daytime outpatient chemical dependency recovery program introduced us to support groups – both LifeRing and AA – in the first week of my sobriety. I realized that I would need some kind of support system to balance against my tendency to isolate. In those first two weeks, I attended six AA meetings and three LifeRing meetings. At my first LifeRing meeting, I realized that this was the kind of meeting where I could get the support I needed. I've not attended any more AA meetings but have been going to my local LifeRing meeting ever since. One of the beautiful things about a LifeRing meeting is its simplicity. The meetings flow so naturally that I would almost say there is no structure. But there is; it's just informal, and natural. This works well with the fact that addiction affects each person uniquely and each person finds their own path to recovery. Members share and give feedback as they need to. We take turns checking in. Time is allotted to give everyone a chance to speak if they want to. We talk about last week and next week. Sometimes a person will give some background and sometimes there are discussions about concepts of addiction and recovery. There is always crosstalk. Presently I've got two and a half years of sobriety under my belt and LifeRing is my support group.

– David F., San Rafael, California

Professor Neil McKeganey, director of the Centre for Drug Misuse Research at Glasgow University, made headlines in February 2007 when he said that authorities should take away the children of alcoholic parents.[65] It's only a small step from there to the recommendation that alcoholics should be prevented from having children in the first place.

This idea is not new; it has a history.

The definition of alcoholism as a primarily genetic disorder was a core belief of the eugenics movement that originated in the United States in the 1880s. Eugenics portrayed itself as an attempt to improve the human stock by controlling mating, much as breeders do with cattle and dogs. The movement supported laws banning interracial marriages and was a precursor of Nazi theories of racial superiority. The eugenics movement spawned legislation that banned alcoholics from marrying or compelled them to undergo castration or hysterectomy. More than sixty thousand Americans were involuntarily sterilized in this effort to eliminate alcoholism by pulling up its supposed genetic root.[66]

If one believes that genetic transmission is the primary or only cause of alcoholism and that the disease as a whole (the behavior pattern of drinking to excess despite consequences) rather than merely a predisposition is what is transmitted, then these eugenic policies make sense. One might not agree with the brutal methods and the racist ideology of the historical eugenics movement, but the logic of genetic disease transmission drives policy in that same dangerous and self-destructive direction.

Alcoholics Are Not a People Apart

One of the principal points of doctrine that people take away from AA is that alcoholics are in some fundamental biological way different from ordinary people.[67] It's as if we were a separate race from the rest of humanity.[68]

The concept of alcoholics as genetically "a people apart" stems from passages in the AA Big Book.[69] Wilson uses a biological metaphor to hammer home the need for abstinence: alcoholics cannot control their drinking because they are "bodily and mentally different."[70]

Although there are good "bodily and mental" reasons to avoid putting alcohol into one's body, there is no scientific foundation for the concept that alcoholics are born constitutionally different. The notion that alcoholics are in effect a distinct race of people only drives a wedge between alcoholics and the rest of society. It encourages alcoholics to huddle in cults and hide, as oppressed Jews had to do in the ghettos of old Poland.[71] It encourages the rest of society to hold alcoholics in contempt. These formulations only assist the alcoholic beverage industry in its campaign to convince the marketplace that "normal" people have nothing to fear from alcohol and that the potential for harm exists only in a small percentage of pitiable genetic defectives.

Alcoholics are safer – and much more accurately seen – when they are viewed as a people like everyone else rather than as a people apart, especially when we ask the public for its understanding and support. Empathy arises on a ground of perceived similarity and dies when "the other" is seen as different.[72]

The underlying assumption of genetic theories is that alcoholism causes drinking. The notion is that some persons are born with a genetic computer program that compels them to drink to excess regardless of negative consequences.

Decades of genetic and neurobiological studies not only have failed to support this theory, but they've also led to its exact opposite: alcoholism is not a predetermined disease that causes drinking. No! It's the habit of drinking that causes alcoholism.

What children may get in their genes from their alcoholic parents is a greater likelihood of having the trait of low responsiveness to alcohol. People who have lower responsiveness to alcohol, if they drink at all, need to drink more than the average to get the same effect. Having a greater exposure to the neurobiological action of alcohol in their brains, they tend to develop alcoholic drinking patterns earlier than the average.

But this predisposition is in no way required or even typical for the onset of alcoholism. The majority of persons who become alcoholics do not have the genetic predisposition. The only difference is that on the average they take a little longer to get there. Otherwise alcoholics with and without the genetic predisposition are indistinguishable.

Loving the Camaraderie

One of the important parts of LifeRing for me is the level of camaraderie. Not only do I get to share my struggles but I can also get immediate responses in the meeting on how to go about handling my struggles. I can get a choice of practical suggestions I can put to use, and I love that. I have found a place where I am comfortable and welcome and that allows me to share more freely. I have gotten to meet some wonderful people. I look forward to being in their company and talking with them. I am very thankful I have found LifeRing. It has helped me become more successful at making changes.

– J. Jones, Hayward, California

In short, the genetic research shows only a relatively minor genetic factor in alcoholism and a predominantly environmental etiology. Understanding the genetic factor is important and useful, but exaggeration of the genetic influence leads to irrational distortions in individual thinking and in social policies.

Notes

1. David Ball, "Addiction Science and Its Genetics," Addiction (Abingdon, England) 103, no. 3 (March 2008): 360-367, doi: ADD2061.
2. Kenneth G. Blum et al., "Reward Deficiency Syndrome," American Scientist 84 (March 1, 1996): 132-145.
3. Constance Holden, "Behavioral Genetics: New Clues to Alcoholism Risk," Science 280, no. 5368 (May 29, 1998): 1348b-1349, doi: 10.1126/science.280.5368.1348b.
4. Blum et al., "Reward Deficiency Syndrome"; Stephen Barrett and Harriett Hall, "Dubious Genetic Testing," Quackwatch, 2002, http://www.quackwatch.com/01QuackeryRelatedTopics/Tests/genomics.html.
5. Nora D. Volkow et al., "High Levels of Dopamine D2 Receptors in Unaffected Members of Alcoholic Families: Possible Protective Factors," Archives of General Psychiatry 63, no. 9 (September 1, 2006): 999-1008, doi: 10.1001/archpsyc.63.9.999.
6. Friedrich Vogel and Arno G. Motulsky, Human Genetics: Problems and Approaches. (New York: Springer, 1996).
7. James C. Anthony, "Epidemiology of Drug Dependency," in The American Psychiatric Publishing Textbook of Substance Abuse Treatment, 2nd ed., 1999, p. 52.
8. Stephen M. Malone, William G. Iacono, and Matt McGue, "Drinks of the Father: Father's Maximum Number of Drinks Consumed Predicts Externalizing Disorders, Substance Use, and Substance Use Disorders in Preadolescent and Adolescent Offspring," Alcoholism: Clinical and Experimental Research 26, no. 12 (December 2002): 1823-1832.
9. Matt McGue, "A Behavioral-Genetic Perspective on Children of Alcoholics," Alcohol Health and Research World 21, no. 3 (1997): 210-217; Jay Joseph, "Twin Studies in Psychiatry and Psychology: Science or Pseudoscience?," Psychiatric Quarterly 73, no. 1 (March 1, 2002): 71-82, doi: 10.1023/A:1012896802713; David Lester, "The Heritability of Alcoholism: Science and Social Policy," in Edith Gomberg, Current Issues in Alcohol/Drug Studies, (New York: Routledge, 1990).
10. Roberto Ciccocioppo and Petri Hyytia, "The Genetics of Alcoholism: Learning from 50 Years of Research," Addiction Biology 11, no. 3/4 (2006): 193-194.

11. Cited in World Health Organization, Neuroscience of Psychoactive Substance Use and Dependence, p. 154.

12. Glenn D. Walters, "The Heritability of Alcohol Abuse and Dependence: A Meta-Analysis of Behavior Genetic Research," American Journal of Drug and Alcohol Abuse 28, no. 3 (2002): 557, doi: 10.1081/ADA-120006742.

13. Show W. Lin and Robert Anthenelli, "Genetic Factors in the Risk for Substance Use Disorders," in Substance Abuse: A Comprehensive Textbook, 5th ed., 2004, p. 33.

14. Marc Schuckit, "Vulnerability Factors for Alcoholism," in Neuropsychopharmacology: The Fifth Generation of Progress, Davis, ed. (American College of Neuropsychopharmacology, 2002), pp. 1399-1411, http://www. acnp.Org/Docs/G5/Ch98_1399-1412.pdf .; Robin Room, "What If We Found the Magic Bullet? Ideological and Ethical Constraints on Biological Alcohol Research and Its Application," Robin Room, 2004, http://www. robinroom.net/magic.doc; World Health Organization, Neuroscience of Psychoactive Substance Use and Dependence, pp. 148-149; Lin and Anthenelli, "Genetic Factors in the Risk for Substance Use Disorders." pp. 35-36.

15. Ball, "Addiction Science and Its Genetics."

16. Da-Yu Wu, "Decoding Drug Abuse in Noncoding RNA?," Scientific World Journal 7, no. S2 (2007): 142-145; Donald W. Pfaff, Wade H. Berrettini, and Tong H. Joh, Genetic Influences on Neural and Behavioral Functions (Boca Raton, Fla.: CRC Press, 1999).

17. John C. Crabbe, "Genetic Contributions to Addiction," Annual Review of Psychology 53 (2002): 435-462.

18. Lovinger and Crabbe, "Laboratory Models of Alcoholism: Treatment Target Identification and Insight into Mechanisms."

19. Toni-Kim Clarke et al., "HPA-Axis Activity in Alcoholism: Examples for a Gene-Environment Interaction," Addiction Biology 13, no. 1 (March 2008): 1-14.

20. Lovinger and Crabbe, "Laboratory Models of Alcoholism: Treatment Target Identification and Insight into Mechanisms."

21. Justin S. Rhodes and John C. Crabbe, "Progress Towards Finding Genes for Alcoholism in Mice," Clinical Neuroscience Research 3, no. 4/5 (December 2003): 315-323, doi: 10.1016/j.cnr.2003.10.012; John C. Crabbe et al., The Genetic Basis of Alcohol and Drug Actions (New York: Springer, 1991); Gunter Schumann, "Okey Lecture 2006: Identifying the Neurobiological Mechanisms of Addictive Behaviour," Addiction (Abingdon, England) 102, no. 11 (November 2007): 1689-1695, doi: ADD1942.

22. Howard J. Edenberg and Tatiana Foroud, "The Genetics of Alcoholism: Identifying Specific Genes Through Family Studies," Addiction Biology 11, no. 3/4 (2006): 386-396.

23. Li Fan et al., "Genetic Study of Alcoholism and Novel Gene Expression in the Alcoholic Brain," Addiction Biology 9, no. 1 (March 2004): 11-18; John C. Crabbe et al., "Alcohol-Related Genes: Contributions from Studies with Genetically Engineered Mice," Addiction Biology 11, no. 3/4 (2006): 195–269.

24. Ball, "Addiction Science and Its Genetics."

25. Christopher Kliesthernes and John Crabbe, "Genetic Independence of Mouse Measures of Some Aspects of Novelty Seeking," Proceedings of the National Academy of Sciences 103, no. 13 (March 28, 2006): 5-18.

26. N. Hiroi and S. Agatsuma, "Genetic Susceptibility to Substance Dependence," Molecular Psychiatry 10, no. 4 (December 7, 2004): 336-344; D. E. Comings and K. Blum, "Reward Deficiency Syndrome: Genetic Aspects of Behavioral Disorders," Progress in Brain Research 126 (2000): 325-341.

27. Scott F. Stoltenberg and Margit Burmeister, "Recent Progress in Psychiatric Genetics-Some Hope but No Hype," Human Molecular Genetics, 9, no. 6 (April 1, 2000): 927-935, doi: 10.1093/hmg/9.6.927; R. E. Tarter, "What Is Inherited in the Predisposition to Alcoholism: New Model or More Muddle?" Alcoholism, Clinical and Experimental Research 24, no. 2 (February 2000): 246-250, doi: 10698381; Henri Begleiter, "What Is Inherited in the Predisposition Toward Alcoholism? A Proposed Model," Alcoholism: Clinical and Experimental Research 23, no. 7 (1999): 1125-1135; Deborah A. Finn and John C. Crabbe, "Exploring Alcohol Withdrawal Syndrome," Alcohol Health and Research World 21, no. 2 (1997): 149; Stoltenberg and Burmeister, "Recent Progress in Psychiatric Genetics – Some Hope but No Hype."

28. Fan et al., "Genetic Study of Alcoholism and Novel Gene Expression in the Alcoholic Brain"; Flatscher-Bader et al., "Alcohol-Responsive Genes in the Frontal Cortex and Nucleus Accumbens of Human Alcoholics"; Koob and Le Moal, Neurobiology of Addiction; Justin S. Rhodes and John C. Crabbe, "Gene Expression Induced by Drugs of Abuse," Current Opinion in Pharmacology 5, no. 1 (February 2005): 26-33, doi: 10.1016/j.coph.2004.12.001.

29. Begleiter, "What Is Inherited in the Predisposition Toward Alcoholism? A Proposed Model." A simple explanation is in National Institute on Alcohol Abuse and Alcoholism, "Alcohol Alert #60," July 2003, http://pubs.niaaa.nih.gov/publications/aa60.htm

30. Stoltenberg and Burmeister, "Recent Progress in Psychiatric Genetics – Some Hope but No Hype"; World Health Organization, Neuroscience of Psychoactive Substance Use and Dependence, p. 148.

31. Stoltenberg and Burmeister, "Recent Progress in Psychiatric Genetics – Some Hope but No Hype."

32. Victoria Elliott, "Addictive Cocktail: Alcoholism and Genetics," American Medical News, February 5, 2001, http://www.ama-assn.org/amednews/2001/02/05/hlsa0205.htm.

33. Ball, "Addiction Science and Its Genetics."

34. Howard J. Edenberg, "The Collaborative Study on the Genetics of Alcoholism: An Update," September 22, 2002, http://findarticles.com/p/articles/mi_m0CXH/is_/ai_106731236; Stoltenberg and Burmeister, "Recent Progress in Psychiatric Genetics – Some Hope but No Hype."

35. Lin and Anthenelli, "Genetic Factors in the Risk for Substance Use Disorders," p. 33.

36. Ibid., p. 38.

37. Ciccocioppo and Hyytia, "The Genetics of Alcoholism."

38. Room, "What If We Found the Magic Bullet? Ideological and Ethical Constraints on Biological Alcohol Research and Its Application."

39. Conor K. Farren and Keith F. Tipton, "Trait Markers for Alcoholism: Clinical Utility," Alcohol and Alcoholism 34, no. 5 (September 1, 1999): 649-665, doi: 10.1093/alcalc/34.5.649; Danielle M. Dick, "Identification of Genes Influencing a Spectrum of Externalizing Psychopathology," Current Directions in Psychological Science 16, no. 6 (December 2007): 331– 335.

40. Ball, "Addiction Science and Its Genetics"; Paula Kiberstis and Leslie Roberts, "It's Not Just the Genes," Science 296, no. 5568 (April 26, 2002): 685, doi: 10.1126/science.296.5568.685; Walter C. Willett, "Balancing Life-Style and Genomics Research for Disease Prevention," Science 296, no. 5568 (April 26, 2002): 695-698, doi: 10.1126/science.1071055; Kathleen Ries Merikangas and Neil Risch, "Genomic Priorities and Public Health," Science 302, no. 5645 (October 24, 2003): 599-601, doi: 10.1126/science.1091468. An early critic was Professor David Lester, who called the genetic theory "a triumph of fancy over fact, subversive of sound social policy." Lester also pointed out that E. M. Jellinek, credited as the father of the modern disease theory, rejected a specific genetic origin for alcoholism and saw the disease as socially transmitted. Lester, "The Heritability of Alcoholism: Science and Social Policy."

41. Willett, "Balancing Life-Style and Genomics Research for Disease Prevention"; Merikangas and Risch, "Genomic Priorities and Public Health."

42. Arthur Allen, "The Disappointment Gene: Why Genetics Is So Far a Boondoggle," Slate, October 18, 2005, http://www.slate.com/id/2128292.

43. Douglas C. Jones and Gary W. Miller, "The Effects of Environmental Neurotoxicants on the Dopaminergic System: A Possible Role in Drug Addiction," Biochemical Pharmacology (May 20, 2008), doi: S0006-2952(08)00304-3.

44. Lin and Anthenelli, "Genetic Factors in the Risk for Substance Use Disorders."

45. Ball, "Addiction Science and Its Genetics."

46. World Health Organization, Neuroscience of Psychoactive Substance Use and Dependence, p. 135; T. L. Wall et al., "A Genetic Association with the Development of Alcohol and Other Substance Use Behavior in Asian Americans," Journal of Abnormal Psychology 110, no. 1 (February 2001): 173-178, doi: 11261392; G. C. Tu and Y. Israel, "Alcohol Consumption by Orientals in North America Is Predicted Largely by a Single Gene," Behavior Genetics 25, no. 1 (January 1995): 59-65, doi: 7755519.

47. Mimy Y. Eng, Susan E. Luczak, and Tamara L. Wall, "ALDH2, ADH1B, and ADH1C Genotypes in Asians: A Literature Review," Alcohol Research & Health: Journal of the National Institute on Alcohol Abuse and Alcoholism 30, no. 1 (2007): 22-27, doi: 17718397.

48. Tamara L. Wall, Lucinda G. Carr, and Cindy L. Ehlers, "Protective Association of Genetic Variation in Alcohol Dehydrogenase with Alcohol Dependence in Native American Mission Indians," American Journal of Psychiatry 160, no. 1 (January 2003): 41-46, doi: 12505800; Gill disputes this point, K. Gill et al., "An Examination of ALDH2 Genotypes, Alcohol

Metabolism and the Flushing Response in Native Americans," Journal of Studies on Alcohol 60, no. 2 (March 1999): 149-158, doi: 10091951. See also, H. W. Goedde et al., "Aldehyde Dehydrogenase Polymorphism in North American, South American, and Mexican Indian Populations," American Journal of Human Genetics 38, no. 3 (March 1986): 395-399, doi: 3953578.

49. Y. D. Neumark et al., "Association of the ADH2*2 Allele with Reduced Ethanol Consumption in Jewish Men in Israel: A Pilot Study," Journal of Studies on Alcohol 59, no. 2 (March 1998): 133-139, doi: 9500299; Monika Fischer et al., "Association of the Aldehyde Dehydrogenase 2 Promoter Polymorphism with Alcohol Consumption and Reactions in an American Jewish population," Alcoholism, Clinical and Experimental Research 31, no. 10 (October 2007): 1654-1659, doi: ACER471.

50. Goedde et al., "Aldehyde Dehydrogenase Polymorphism in North American, South American, and Mexican Indian Populations."

51. Ru-Band Lu et al., "No Alcoholism-Protection Effects of ADH1B*2 Allele in Antisocial Alcoholics Among Han Chinese in Taiwan," Alcoholism, Clinical and Experimental Research 29, no. 12 (December 2005): 2101-2107, doi: 00000374-200512000-00003; Cheng-Yi Hahn et al., "Acetaldehyde Involvement in Positive and Negative Alcohol Expectancies in Han Chinese Persons with Alcoholism," Archives of General Psychiatry 63, no. 7 (July 2006): 817-823, doi: 63/7/817.

52. Neal Doran et al., "Stability of Heavy Episodic Drinking in Chinese-and Korean-American College Students: Effects of ALDH2 Gene Status and Behavioral Undercontrol," Journal of Studies on Alcohol and Drugs 68, no. 6 (November 2007): 789-97, doi: 17960296.

53. Tatsuya Takeshita, "Gene-Environmental Interactions in Alcohol-Related Health Problems: Contributions of Molecular Biology to Behavior Modifications," Nippon Eiseigaku Zasshi. Japanese Journal of Hygiene 58, no. 2 (May 2003): 254-259, doi: 12806963.

54. Ibid. 5

5. Akira Yokoyama and Tai Omori, "Genetic Polymorphisms of Alcohol and Aldehyde Dehydrogenases and Risk for Esophageal and Head and Neck Cancers," Japanese Journal of Clinical Oncology 33, no. 3 (March 2003): 111-121, doi: 12672787.

56. For example, Goedde et al., "Aldehyde Dehydrogenase Polymorphism in North American, South American, and Mexican Indian Populations."

57. Schuckit, "Reactions to Alcohol in Sons of Alcoholics and Controls." No molecular referent for Schuckit's findings has been identified. Although Schuckit's thesis appears solid at its core, it is soft at the margins. Schuckit properly eliminated from his sample young men who already met the DSM criteria for alcoholism. Inexplicably, he also eliminated young men who did not drink at all. He assumed that his twenty-year-old drinkers who were not yet alcoholics could not already have acquired tolerance. More recent work has undermined this assumption, showing that significant numbers of men in this age group displayed tolerance without meeting other criteria for dependence. Marc Schuckit et al., "Clinical Implications of Tolerance to Alcohol in Nondependent Young Drinkers," American Journal of Drug and

Alcohol Abuse 34, no. 2 (2008): 133-149, doi: 790777524. It follows that at least some of the supposedly genetic low responsiveness trait identified in Schuckit's twenty-year-olds might have been acquired tolerance. How significant the required downward adjustment in the already modest claimed genetic ratio will be remains to be seen.

58. Schuckit, "Reactions to Alcohol in Sons of Alcoholics and Controls."

59. Marc Schuckit et al., "Response to Alcohol in Daughters of Alcoholics: A Pilot Study and a Comparison with Sons of Alcoholics," Alcohol and Alcoholism (Oxford, Oxfordshire) 35, no. 3 (June 2000): 242-248, doi: 10869242; Mimy Y. Eng, Marc A. Schuckit, and Tom L. Smith, "The Level of Response to Alcohol in Daughters of Alcoholics and Controls," Drug and Alcohol Dependence 79, no. 1 (July 1, 2005): 83-93, doi: 10.1016/j.drugalcdep.2005.01.002; McGue, "A Behavioral-Genetic Perspective on Children of Alcoholics"; Suzette M. Evans and Frances R. Levin, "Response to Alcohol in Females with a Paternal History of Alcoholism," Psychopharmacology 169, no. 1 (August 2003): 10-20, doi: 12721780.

60. Marc Schuckit and Tom L. Smith, "The Clinical Course of Alcohol Dependence Associated with a Low Level of Response to Alcohol," Addiction 96, no. 6 (June 15, 2001): 903-910.

61. Ibid.

62. G. S. Alford, E. N. Jouriles, and S. C. Jackson, "Differences and Similarities in Development of Drinking Behavior Between Alcoholic Offspring of Alcoholics and Alcoholic Offspring of Non-alcoholics," Addictive Behaviors 16, no. 5 (1991): 341-347.

63. A patent granted to Kenneth Blum in 1993 for such a device has not reached market. See also Barrett and Hall, "Dubious Genetic Testing"; Ball, "Addiction Science and Its Genetics."

64. Jeffrey Helm, "Myth of an 'Addict Gene'," The Tyee, July 28, 2006, http://thetyee.ca/News/2006/07/28/AddictGene/.

65. "Take Kids Away from Alcoholic Parents," Daily Record (UK), February 19, 2007.

66. White, Slaying the Dragon, pp. 88-90.

67. Emrick, "Alcoholics Anonymous: Emerging Concepts. Overview."

68. On this point, see also Roizen, The American Discovery of Alcoholism, 1933-1939; Mercadante, Victims and Sinners.

69. Lobdell, This Strange Illness, p. 368.

70. Bill W. and Alcoholics Anonymous, Alcoholics Anonymous: The Story of How Many Thousands Of Men and Women Have Recovered from Alcoholism, 3rd ed. (New York: Alcoholics Anonymous World Services, 1976), p. 30.

71. Granfield and Cloud, Coming Clean, p. 33.

72. E. Sober and D. Wilson, Unto Others: The Evolution and Psychology of Unselfish Behavior (Cambridge Mass.: Harvard University Press, 1998).

CONCLUSION

In Chapter One, I gave three illustrations of individuals who were transformed. First, we saw them in the grip of their addiction – angry, depressed, isolated, alone, self-destructive. Then they were warm, sociable, cheerful, positive, happy, and sober human beings. I posed the following questions:

- What happened to bring about this transformation?

- How is it possible that these are the same people?

- Where did these bright, warm, lively, sober folks come from?

- Where had they been hiding during their active addiction?

- How can we make this miracle happen more often?

That's the great mystery of recovery from chemical dependency.

Recovery as Liberation

The principal argument of this book has been that these bright, warm, lively, sober folks were locked up inside the nasty, self-destructive, addicted people all along. Substance addiction is an overlay that covers up the original sober person. It is a shell that encapsulates the original sober self. It is a prison cell. Recovery means to empower the inner sober self and set it free. With this vision, much of the baffling mystery of recovery can be solved.

Our eyes will make no progress against the mystery of recovery so long as we look at the addicted person through 12-step lenses. To say that such a person is powerless – and insane, morally deficient, filled with wrongs, a menace to others, disoriented, beyond human assistance, afflicted with a progressive fatal disease, and genetically different from normal humans – is to declare that the person's inner nature is a vile and empty wasteland. It is to deny that there is a better self inside. If that is true, recovery is inexplicable, a random act of God, an inscrutable mystery.

The central task in constructing a workable and credible paradigm of recovery is to regain warmth and respect for the character of the person who suffers from addiction. Perhaps a voice from another era can jolt us toward a clearer perspective:

> In my judgment, such of us as have never fallen victims, have been spared more from the absence of appetite, than from any mental or moral superiority over those who have. Indeed, I believe, if we take habitual drunkards as a class, their heads and their hearts will bear an advantageous comparison with those of any other class. There seems ever to have been a proneness in the brilliant, and the warm-blooded, to fall into this vice. The demon of intemperance ever seems to have delighted in sucking the blood of genius and of generosity. What one of us but can call to mind some dear relative, more promising in youth than all his fellows, who has fallen a sacrifice to his rapacity? He ever seems to have gone forth, like the Egyptian angel of death, commissioned to slay if not the first, the fairest born of every family.

This is the voice of Abraham Lincoln, speaking to the Washingtonian Temperance Society in Springfield, Illinois, in 1842.[1]

In describing the class of "habitual drunkards" as having heads and hearts no worse than the average and as including persons of brilliance and passion, genius and generosity, the future president surely was not romanticizing inebriety or minimizing the wreckage it caused. He was affirming that persons who fall prey to addiction are in no way inferior to the rest and that addiction can happen to the best. He was seeing the warm, worthwhile human being inside the addict, the S inside the A.

Modern science, far from undermining Lincoln's compassionate and egalitarian vision, has amply sustained it. As I have shown in earlier chapters:

- Addiction is not an indictment of character, is not a personality trait, and is not the product of psychological defects.

- Addiction is a product of the action of addictive substances on the brain, and it can happen to any organism into which these chemicals enter – even monkeys, rats, mice, fruit flies, and nematodes.

- Genetics, where it plays a role at all, is not a fate but at most an expediting predisposition, speeding the path of an otherwise indistinguishable minority among the addicted populace.

In sum, there is no rational cause to set addicted persons apart by their nature, character, or constitution from the rest of humanity; to view them as inferior; or to accord them less empathy and respect.

To put it more personally, there is no reason for us, who know addiction from the inside, to view ourselves as different, inferior, or less worthy of empathy and respect. To see the sober person inside the addict is not to flip from one absolute to its opposite, from contempt to admiration, but rather to see the person as a living contradiction, a person living two lives and balancing two personalities.

To see addicted persons as living contradictions is to understand why liberation is the fitting metaphor for recovery. Liberation as a metaphor points to the sober self imprisoned within the addicted brain and affirms its inherent dignity and value. Liberation conceives recovery as the empowerment of the sober self, bursting the shackles of chemical dependency, and emerging as the original sober person, newly freed and reborn.

Although this may sound revolutionary, it is in reality a restoration. Addiction has hijacked the person's original self; it has stolen its energies, feelings, thoughts, and dreams, its very identity. Recovery gives them back. What we recover when we recover is our original self, the authentic us, the sober person we were meant to be and really are.

An Invitation to LifeRing

Allow me, in conclusion, to invite you to LifeRing. The LifeRing approach is thoroughly positive. We know very well that the addictive substances may have warped your life and taken you to places that are not pretty to contemplate. We have been there ourselves. No one in LifeRing will judge you for what addiction has done to you. No one will demand that you stand up and relive your drinking and drug-using history. No one will demand that you make a confession. No one will try to label you, to diagnose you, or to convert you. Our only purpose is to support you in getting free of substances and to win your support in return.

In our meetings, we put the focus on our sober today and tomorrow. We throw light on the stream of decisions we make every day, knowing that if we get the small choices right, the big changes will take care of themselves. If you can remember something of what you did in the past week, you can join the conversation. We value books, but no book learning is necessary to take part in our meetings.

We will always speak to you from our sober selves. We address our words to your sober self. We listen to your sober self in reply. If you are unsure whether you have a sober self or where it is and what it looks like, we will help you see it by reflecting it back to you. We have learned from personal experience that when we connect on a sober-to-sober basis, then synergy happens and the sober person in everyone who participates in the connection becomes more empowered. At the end of the meeting, we celebrate one another's achievements with a round of applause.

We know that our recovery work is not done when the meeting ends. Depending on the individual, the use of addictive substances may have left its mark on the person's health, activities, emotional life, relationships, lifestyle, and other areas. Some people work on these issues as they happen to come up. For those who prefer to work in a structured way, Life-Ring offers a workbook, *Recovery by Choice*, that organizes the rebuilding project into nine domains. By either approach, you put together a personal recovery program – a program that will work for you because it fits who you are.

LifeRing is not easy and it is not for everyone. Learning to relate confidently from your sober self may require unlearning ideas that paralyze you and shame you – ideas of powerlessness, moral deficiency, and the like. In our meetings, we do not speak ill of other recovery approaches, but we also leave their disempowering ideas at the door. Learning to build a personal recovery program is harder work than adopting a ready-made program built by someone else, but you can do it. Compared with the work required to maintain a functioning life while supporting an addiction, charting your personal recovery path is no big deal. And the rewards are amply worth the effort.

LifeRing is still young and relatively small. You can always find LifeRing meetings online, at *www.lifering.org*. LifeRing books are at *www.lifering.com*. If you prefer face-to-face meetings, and there isn't one yet in your community, you may have to step forward and organize one yourself. The LifeRing Service Center in Oakland, California – *service@lifering.org* or 1-800-811-4142 – stands ready to assist you and provide you with the necessary information and supplies. Becoming a LifeRing pioneer may become a life-transforming experience; it may give you not only a stronger recovery but also a new meaning and sense of purpose.

Notes

1. Abraham Lincoln, Temperance Address," Sangamo Journal, March 25, 1842, http://www.druglibrary.org/schaffer/History/ancient/TemoAddr.htm.

SUPPLEMENT
FOR THE SECOND EDITION

This Supplement addresses some recent publications on the topic of addiction treatment, discussed in Chapter 6, and reviews highlights of recent research into the genetics of alcoholism, the topic of Chapter 7.

Publications of Interest
About Addiction Treatment

Addiction Medicine: Closing the Gap Between Science and Practice is a research report published in 2012 by CASA Columbia. After a five-year review, the researchers found that about 90 per cent of people who have an addiction issue do not go into treatment for it. This ratio is far out of line with diseases such as diabetes or high blood pressure, where 70 – 80 per cent do get treatment. The small minority who enter addiction treatment find that "most medical professionals who should be providing addiction treatment are not sufficiently trained to diagnose or treat the disease, and most of those providing addiction care are not medical professionals and are not equipped with the knowledge, skills or credentials necessary to provide the full range of effective treatment."

The CASA report strongly underlines the need for individualized treatment:

> Treatment must be tailored to the particular stage and severity of the disease, a patient's overall health status, past treatments and any other personal characteristics and life circumstances that might affect patient outcomes... The research evidence clearly demonstrates that a one-size-fits-all approach to addiction treatment typically is a recipe for failure.

The CASA report is a helpful reference guide for anyone concerned with the state of the addiction rehab industry today.

Anne Fletcher's *Inside Rehab: The Surprising Truth About Addiction Treatment – and How to Get Help That Works* (2013) presents a vivid portrait, told largely through first person accounts, of the unscientific goings-on that CASA found at the core of the traditional rehab model.

Like CASA, Fletcher emphasizes that effective treatment is tailored to the patient; this is standard practice in real medicine. But while addiction rehabs may advertise individualized treatment, once inside the door the rule is "one size fits all." If it doesn't work, the client may be run through the same assembly line over and over again.

Programs tended to focus on the past and not enough on moving forward. "They made me concentrate so much on all the negatives," one client told Fletcher, "that I was starting to get insecure and wanted to use more. They were not focusing on our strengths at all; they were just magnifying our weaknesses." One client in a traditional program said his counselor made him feel "like a lowly worm."

Acknowledging that the 12-step doctrine of powerlessness undermines recovery, particularly for some women, one counselor in an alternative program for women told Fletcher, "Our clients come in so down and discouraged that they don't need to hear that they're powerless over anything. They need to hear that they can change things."

Fletcher interweaves client testimonials with expert opinion and research in a readable book that should be useful for anyone contemplating the rehab route. She provides a helpful checklist for investigating potential rehabs and finding the relatively few that do quality, science-based work.

Addiction rehab also troubles Harvard psychiatrist Lance Dodes MD in *The Sober Truth: Debunking the Bad Science Behind 12-Step Programs and the Rehab Industry* (2014). While the CASA report tiptoes around the elephant in the room, and Fletcher points at it, Dr. Dodes gores it in the gut: the central problem with most rehab is the 12-step model it's based on.

Dodes asks, "Does AA Work?" He critically reviews the various studies that have been done, and concludes emphatically that there are no credible (controlled, randomized) studies to prove that AA is effective at all. Dodes calculates AA's success rate by an entirely different route than I used in my first edition, but comes up with the same number: AA works for about five to eight per cent of those who approach it. That number, Dodes adds, is approximately the same rate as spontaneous remission.

Augusten Burroughs, the New York Times bestselling author of *Running with Scissors* and *Dry*, includes a critique of AA and AA-based rehab in his latest, *This is How* (2012). He writes that attending AA was "interesting and comforting, but not of any particular use." Worse, certain features of the AA experience, he felt, "undermine sobriety."

At the top of the list is the demand to admit powerlessness. Not only is this not true, he writes, but it gives the alcoholic implied permission to drink. Much like Dr. Dodes, Burroughs sees the first step of the 12-step program as a classic trigger for drinking. "The myth that alcoholics are powerless and unable in any way to shape the outcome of their addiction is a fatal, deeply untruthful message," Burroughs writes. "No alcoholic should ever feel powerless over alcohol."

Burroughs also picks up on the crazy contradiction between the disease model of alcoholism and the 12-step treatment paradigm: "That there exists a medically recognized disease that is typically treated through 12-step programs that are based on vague supernatural components is shocking to me. If breast cancer or leukemia were treated in such a medieval fashion, there would be riots."

One might well ask why a system that is shunned by 90 per cent of those who need help, and whose lack of a scientific basis is by now notorious, manages to survive at all. Part of the answer is that it is highly profitable. The disease label qualifies the programs for public and private insurance funding. The one-size-fits-all 12-step protocol lends itself to assembly line processing. It also supplies the industry with an abundant pool of cheap labor: recovering alcoholics recruited from AA meetings who may be grateful to be paid at all for "carrying the message."

The resulting high cash flows have attracted major investors. Bain Capital (the firm Mitt Romney once headed) began in 2006 by buying CRC Health Group, the largest operator of drug rehabs (it runs the celeb rehab Sierra Tucson), and then went on a spree of buying out other formerly independent programs. In 2012, Bain's CRC treated 30,000 patients a day at 140 facilities, employed more than 150 salespeople and reported a 2010 profit margin of 25 per cent (McDonald 2012).

The addiction rehab industry in 2014 is a $34 billion business, of which 80 per cent is money from the government. In recent years, a number of federal courts of appeals have ruled that forcing prisoners into 12-step programs against their religious beliefs is a violation of the Establishment Clause of the Constitution (Nicolaus 2013, 2009). These decisions, although important, don't begin to address the billions of taxpayer money that subsidize 12-step treatment and purchase 12-step literature – a flagrant and massive violation of the Establishment Clause.

The CASA report and the books by Fletcher, Dodes, and Burroughs amplify the point made in my first edition that the addiction rehab system needs a paradigm shift. What should happen? The long-awaited second edition of William L. White's *Slaying the Dragon: The History of Addiction Treatment and Recovery in America* (2014) suggests that, to begin with, the rehab industry should abandon the slogan "Treatment Works."

> Treatment Works, the central promotional slogan of the addiction treatment industry, misrepresents the nature of addiction treatment and its probable outcomes and misplaces the responsibility for such outcomes. The slogan should be abandoned and replaced by a cluster of messages that shift the emphasis from the intervention (treatment) to the desired outcome (recovery), extol the importance of *personal choice and responsibility in the recovery process*, accurately portray the highly variable outcomes of addiction treatment, *celebrate multiple pathways of recovery*, affirm the roles of family and community support in addiction recovery, invite participation in professional treatment and recovery support services, and incorporate catalytic metaphors drawn from

diverse medical, religious, spiritual, political, and cultural traditions. (White 2014 p. 522)

I've emphasized the elements of personal choice and responsibility and multiple pathways of recovery because these are core elements of the LifeRing approach. The LifeRing model of recovery by choice, with each client working up a personal recovery program, needs to become standard practice in addiction treatment and support.

The Genomics Revolution

"What, there's no gene for alcoholism?" The senior member of the psychology faculty at a university in the Pacific Northwest, who heard the gist of my chapter on genetics (Chapter 7) was indignant. In her mind, belief in the "alcoholism gene" formed the cornerstone of a much larger structure, all of which threatened to crumble if "the gene" did not exist.

The five years since I wrote the first edition have not been kind to belief in the "alcoholism gene." The technology now available to researchers allows scanning actual genetic variations of large samples of alcoholics and comparing them with normal people.

According to traditional twin studies, which estimated the genetic role in alcoholism as somewhere between 30 and 80 per cent – many writers diplomatically average it out at 50 per cent – the "alcoholism gene" should have stood out on the genomic profile like the Eiffel Tower. Instead, the most powerful of the studies found that the DNA of alcoholics varied from that of normal people by less than one tenth of one percent (Heath 2011).

In the first edition I mentioned the study by Kenneth Blum, who announced with great fanfare in 1996 that "the alcoholism gene" was found, only to be squelched when replication studies proved that it was a false positive.

A longer and more tortuous replay of this drama came with the "Bingo!" announcement by COGA, the multi-billion dollar chain of laboratories dedicated to pinpointing the genetic basis of alcoholism (Edenberg 2004, 2006). The showpiece gene was called *GABRA2*. Some initial replications were reported.

Problems began almost immediately. It was pointed out that *GABRA2* did not interact with alcohol, so that *GABRA2* probably related not to alcoholism per se, but to a fuzzy-bordered externalizing personality characteristic dubbed "impulsivity" or "conduct disorder" that was associated with getting in trouble with the law and with the use of a wide range of other drugs. Numerous studies supported this view (Dick 2007, 2009, 2010, Lind 2008, Philibert 2009, Villafuerte 2012, 2013, Trucco 2014). Other recent analyses showed that the association between *GABRA2*, impulsivity, and alcohol use disorders is more indirect, indeterminate, and nebulous than earlier studies had suggested (Dick 2013).

Still other studies found *GABRA2* linked instead with anxiety, an internalizing disorder at the other end of the emotional scale from impulsivity (Enoch 2006). *GABRA2* was also found associated with childhood trauma (Enoch 2010), and/or with adult PTSD (Nelson 2009), and/or with a wide spectrum of other psychiatric disorders (Dick 2007, Carmiol 2014). The initial claim that *GABRA2* was specific to alcoholism quickly lost traction (Lind 2008a). Moreover, numerous studies found that the presumed effects of *GABRA2* were strongly modified by age and gender and by environmental factors such as regional subculture, parenting styles, marital status, peer group, and stress, among others (Dick 2013, Perry 2013).

Attempted replication studies in populations other than the 2004 COGA sample came up negative. One study found no association between alcoholism and *GABRA2* in in Finnish and U.S. Plains Indian populations (Enoch 2009). Another found no significant linkage in Australians (Lind 2008). Two separate studies found no evidence that *GABRA2* was linked with alcoholism in Italians (Buscemi 2009, Onori 2010). No linkage between *GABRA2* and alcoholism turned up in a study of white people in the UK (Lydall 2011). No *GABRA2* linkage turned up in a study of U.S. college students in substance abuse treatment (Sakai 2010). It did not help the case for *GABRA2* that mice whose *GABRA2* gene was knocked out showed no change in their alcohol drinking patterns (Walker 2012).

In 2010, a genome-wide association study of nearly 4,000 individuals, signed by an all-star cast of researchers, found neither *GABRA2* nor any other genes with significant and replicable links to alcoholism (Bierut 2010).

A genome-wide association study of families in the original 2004 COGA sample, performed by a number of the same researchers, found no statistically significant gene variant for alcoholism (Edenberg 2010).

An even larger study (11,700 families) that aimed to replicate COGA's positive finding and the studies that supported it came up empty (Heath 2011). The "contribution of individual genetic variants to the heaviness of alcohol consumption and alcoholism risk are small, perhaps accounting for as little as one tenth of 1% of the variance... In no case do we have confidence that a true positive association has been identified." (Heath 2011).

Further replication studies also came up blank (Agrawal 2010, Olfson 2012, Terranova 2014, Melroy 2014, Irons 2012). Two genomic studies of twins – the population sample that underlies high "heritability" claims – found no individual genes significant for alcoholism (Hansell 2010, Salvatore 2014). A study which sought to break down the mixed bag of criteria for alcohol problems in the DSM-IV to see whether there was a genetic signal for any of the sorted subgroups also came up with nothing significant and replicable (Wetherill 2014). As of the end of 2013, nine large genome-wide association studies fishing for gene variants significantly linked to alcoholism had been completed, and none had come up with replicable results (Demers 2014).

Interestingly, the same genomic studies that don't show a gene for alcoholism have no trouble picking up the so-called "protective gene" (*ALDH2*) frequently found in East Asian populations. I discussed this in the first edition; this gene causes people who have it to experience uncomfortable physical reactions if they drink, similar to the effects of disulfiram (Antabuse®). This gene shows up plainly in the genome-wide association studies when the sample includes populations where it occurs (Quillen 2013). It is considered one of the strongest signals in genomic research (Monte 2014).

If the protective gene doesn't show up in a genomic study, researchers quite sensibly conclude that it simply doesn't exist in that population (Edenberg 2012). But when the hypothetical "alcoholism gene" doesn't show up in a population of thousands of diagnosed and certified falling-down-drunk alcoholics, researchers tap the dial as if the needle were stuck and wonder where the "missing heritability" went (Manolio 2009). The sober and logical conclusion is that the "alcoholism gene" doesn't exist (Chaufan 2013).

Why the twin studies consistently come up with grandiose genetic power estimates that don't pan out once we look at the actual genome is a large topic that would take us too far afield here. A good short recent exposition is Joseph (2013). Some leading researchers now recognize that twin studies of genetic influences on behavior are meaningless, have no scientific content, and should be stopped (Johnson 2009, Turkheimer 2011). Others appear to be in classic denial, repeating the twin-based numbers as if we had no way of actually looking at people's genetic makeup (Agrawal 2008). Or they acknowledge the DNA findings but proceed as if twin studies yielded more reliable evidence (Plomin 2014).

The "missing heritability" discussion also goes on outside of addiction studies. Twin studies have generated astronomical "heritability" numbers for practically everything, but the genomic studies have found significant single genes only for a very small handful of diseases (e.g. cystic fibrosis, sickle cell anemia, Huntington's disease, and for some types of Alzheimer's and breast cancer). For the vast majority of topics, particularly behavioral, cognitive, and psychiatric issues, genomic studies looking for single genes linked to single traits "have failed miserably" (Monte 2014).

So, for example, contrary to twin studies claiming elevated genetic factors, a recent genome-wide association study of a very large population found zero genetic variations significantly associated with differences in measures of childhood intelligence or school achievement (Benyamin 2014, Rietveld 2013). A large meta-analysis of genetic studies of personality traits found no evidence that any particular gene variant modulated personality traits (Balestri 2014). Another study found no significant genetic influence on childhood behavior problems (Trzaskowski 2013). A series of studies found nothing resembling clinically significant genes for common psychiatric disorders (Maughan 2014, Vinkhuyzen 2012, Alliey-Rodriguez 2011, Ng 2009).

It is now obvious to genomic researchers and widely understood in the profession that complex traits like alcoholism and other cognitive, behavioral and psychiatric disorders are associated with a large number of genes, each with a very small effect. In the words of the veteran genetics researcher Robert Plomin, "Genome-wide association studies throughout the life sciences have shown that there are no DNA associations of large effect size. The largest effect sizes are less than 1% and the smallest effect sizes are likely to be infinitesimal" (Plomin 2014, see also Morozova 2014, Salvatore 2014, Trzaskoski 2013, Enoch 2013, Wang 2012, Heath 2011, Bierut 2011, Manolio 2009).

This means that the genetic difference between people with and without the trait is clinically meaningless (Maughan 2014, Yan 2014). The likelihood of developing drugs that affect the trait by modifying one or a small number of genes having a very small effect is vanishingly low. The prospect of inventing a DNA test to detect whether an individual is likely to develop a given behavioral or psychiatric trait is nil, and test kits marketed with this claim are frauds (Mathews 2012, Foroud 2010). Since the genetic risk for alcoholism is distributed evenly across the population, and there is no distinct subset of people genetically more susceptible than the average, it makes policy sense to devote resources to wide-ranging prevention and other public health measures (Cunningham 2013).

Bottom line: the problem is simply not in the DNA. A number of scholars have been saying this for a long time, even before the genomics revolution (e.g. Rose 1984, Schönemann 1997, Conrad 1999, Joseph 2004). The genomics revolution has proved them correct.

Schuckit's Low Responsiveness Hypothesis

Trouble has also brewed in the past five years for one of the genetic hypotheses that is not dependent on twin studies. In the first edition, I summarized the findings of Prof. Marc Schuckit in San Diego, who found that the sons of alcoholic fathers were on the average less responsive to alcohol than sons of non-alcoholic fathers, and this was probably a genetically transmitted trait. This pattern supports the plausible theory that the less responsive sons have to drink more to get the same effect, and so end up becoming alcoholics sooner than others. In the first edition I generally endorsed this theory, but expressed some reservations in footnote 57. Those reservations are now fortified.

A paper published shortly after the first edition of my book went to press squarely challenged Schuckit's theory (Newlin 2009). The author pointed to a considerable number of studies that not only failed to replicate Schuckit's findings, but found that sons of alcoholic fathers were more responsive to alcohol, rather than less. These contrary findings support the also plausible theory that because these sons found alcohol more stimulating they drank more of it, speeding them on the road to alcoholism (Söderpalm Gordh 2011). As I write this, a consensus position on this issue does not seem to have been reached (Quinn 2011).

I wonder if these studies have adequately controlled for the amount and type of drinking that the young people did before they were tested for responsiveness. The participants in all of the responsiveness studies had done some drinking before being tested, some more, some less. No study participant was alcohol-naïve. It has been plausibly suggested by others, and in some instances documented (e.g. Schuckit 2011), that some of the study participants had acquired tolerance (Newlin 1990). Tolerance is a poorly researched trait in humans (Crabbe 2012), but its defining trait is lowered responsiveness. The initial efforts to distinguish acquired tolerance from the hypothesized inherited low responsiveness, and to relate the difference (if any) to family drinking history, have not produced consistent or compelling results (Corbin 2013, Morean 2008).

Scientists successfully tested for the presence of the "protective gene" (*ALDH2*) in the 1980s by dosing infants with a small amount of alcohol and watching for skin flushing (Hartz 2010). According to Schuckit, the low responsiveness trait reveals itself in part through measurable physiological markers such as alterations in hormones, electrophysiology, and motor performance patterns (Schuckit 2013). If so, the trait should be observable in alcohol-naïve subjects, even quite young ones. Apparently this has not been attempted. Until Schuckit's hypothesis is vindicated with alcohol-naïve subjects, the whole inherited responsiveness topic remains murky.

Epigenetics

One of the most interesting areas that has emerged into the spotlight in the past five years is epigenetics. It has long been known that genes can turn other genes on or off (*epistasis*). What is now becoming much more widely appreciated is that the power to manage what genes do also resides in the members of the epigenome: histones and several different kinds of RNA and other factors not yet well understood. These are wound into and around the DNA nucleus; hence the name epigenome (epi = around).

It is well known that DNA by itself has no influence on the functioning of the body. Genes affect cells only by expressing themselves, which they do by manufacturing proteins. It is the proteins that do the actual biological work. To produce a protein, however, a gene must go through the epigenome, and in this process the epigenome can and does amend, swap, redirect, turn on or turn off the protein production process. Under epigenetic direction, a single gene can produce a great variety of different proteins. In this way, the epigenome orchestrates a broad range of bodily functions and behaviors without any changes in the sequence of the genetic nucleus (the DNA).

While the DNA does not normally change significantly in response to the environment, the epigenome is highly sensitive to environmental factors. Environmental influences –

not only physical factors such as nutrition and chemicals, but also psychological stress, parenting styles, social interactions – can bring about epigenetic changes, some of which endure for the individual's life (Feil 2012, Starkman 2012).

What does this have to do with alcohol and alcoholism? In the past five years there has been a lot of research on the pharmacological effects of alcohol on the body (e.g. Gass 2012, George 2014). One of the most consistent findings is that alcohol has strong and widespread effects on the epigenome. These impacts occur not only on the fetus in the womb (Resendiz 2014) but in adults. Alcohol consumption changes gene expression in brain reward regions (Nieratschker 2013). It has been proposed that alcohol-induced epigenetic changes are responsible for key markers of alcoholism such as tolerance and dependence (Krishnan 2014, Zhang 2013, Starkman 2012).

Probably the hottest area in genetic research today concerns the heritability of epigenetic changes. It's long been dogma in genetics that acquired characteristics are not transmitted to offspring. It now appears that there are exceptions. Human studies have demonstrated epigenetic transmission for as long as three generations stemming from stress, diet, and toxic exposure (Saab 2014, Carey 2012). At the leading edge of addiction research today are studies exploring whether and to what extent the epigenetic impact of alcohol and other drugs of addiction in men and in non-pregnant women can impact the following generations (Finegersh 2014, Vassoler 2014, Rachdaoui 2014). New technology that tracks changes in the epigenome has been developed, and the first large scale epigenomic studies have been published (Zhang 2013). Epigenetics is well on the way to replacing genetics as the mother lode where the big discoveries and prizes of tomorrow will be won.

Conclusion

What does all this mean for a person in recovery? Well, for a person of the old school, like the senior psychologist who hated my chapter on genetics in the first edition, it may mean a wrenching reorientation. She is not alone, of course, in the belief that each disease is caused by one gene, and that if we only look hard enough we will find it. That's basically what I and millions of other people learned in high school biology, and what much of the media still purveys as popular gospel. Today, this kind of belief is a mark of genetic illiteracy. The genomic revolution of 2001-2003, when the human genome was decoded, has made practically everything everyone learned in school about genetics obsolete.

Today we can say with confidence that the genetic make-up of people who develop alcoholism and other drug addictions is not significantly different from people we call normal. There's not a penny's worth of genetic difference. Put another way, alcoholism is something that happens to normal people when they put too much alcohol into their bodies.

The science as we know it today fundamentally contradicts the central historical thesis of the alcoholic beverage industry, framed in the 1930s. The industry's party line says that there is nothing harmful about alcohol, but some people have a bad gene that gives rise, or makes them susceptible, to the disease of alcoholism. In the industry's credo, the problem is not in the bottle, it is in the man (White 2014).

We know today, thanks to the genomic revolution, that the problem is not in the man or in the woman. It is in the bottle and in the environment.

Modern genomics has toppled the central geneticist credo of the alcoholic beverage industry. Good riddance. It has also disappointed the initial expectations of the pharmaceutical industry, which hoped to find key single genes for complex disorders (Hendershot 2014). Drugs targeted at those genes could work miracle cures. That's dead. But the new frontier of epigenetics has given new energy to the pharmaceutical treasure hunt. The impact of alcohol and other drugs on the epigenome might very well be reversible with novel pharmaceuticals (Krishnan 2014). I, for one, would welcome such developments. The pharmaceutical industry has already produced lifesaving tools for addiction medicine, such as naloxone as an antidote to opiate overdose. Anything that helps to relieve the enormous harm that alcohol and other addictive drugs are causing is worthy of support.

However, there is no need for the person suffering today to wait for the pharmaceutical industry to develop an effective palliative for alcoholism. That might take years and it will be expensive. There is a cure available today, right now, that costs practically nothing. In fact, it will save you money. You might need some routine medical help at the outset. You may need to attend support groups like LifeRing or whatever else works for you. Those things are helpful auxiliaries, but they are not the cure itself. The cure that can restore you to health and possibly happiness is, of course, to stop putting alcohol into your body. There is nothing wrong with your basic character. There is nothing wrong with your genes. If and when you make the decision to get free, you can do it.

References for this Supplement

Agrawal, Arpana, and Michael T. Lynskey. 2008. "Are There Genetic Influences on Addiction: Evidence from Family, Adoption and Twin Studies." *Addiction* 103 (7): 1069–81. doi:10.1111/j.1360-0443.2008.02213.x.

Agrawal, Arpana, Michael T. Lynskey, Alexandre A. Todorov, Andrew J. Schrage, Andrew K. Littlefield, Julia D. Grant, Qin Zhu, et al. 2011. "A Candidate Gene Association Study of Alcohol Consumption in Young Women." *Alcoholism: Clinical and Experimental Research* 35 (3): 550–58. doi:10.1111/j.1530-0277.2010.01372.x.

Alliey-Rodriguez, Ney, Dandan Zhang, Judith A. Badner, Benjamin B. Lahey, Xiaotong Zhang, Stephen Dinwiddie, Benjamin Romanos, Natalie Plenys, Chunyu Liu, and Elliot S. Gershon. 2011. "Genome-Wide Association Study of Personality Traits in Bipolar Patients." *Psychiatric Genetics* 21 (4): 190–94. doi:10.1097/YPG.0b013e3283457a31.

Balestri, Martina, Raffaella Calati, Alessandro Serretti, and Diana De Ronchi. 2014. "Genetic Modulation of Personality Traits: A Systematic Review of the Literature." *International Clinical Psychopharmacology* 29 (1): 1–15. doi:10.1097/YIC.0b013e328364590b.

Benyamin, B, Bst Pourcain, O S Davis, G Davies, N K Hansell, M-Ja Brion, R M Kirkpatrick, et al. 2014. "Childhood Intelligence Is Heritable, Highly Polygenic and Associated with FNBP1L." *Molecular Psychiatry* 19 (2): 253–58. doi:10.1038/mp.2012.184.

Bierut, L. J., A. Agrawal, K. K. Bucholz, K. F. Doheny, C. Laurie, E. Pugh, S. Fisher, et al. 2010. "A Genome-Wide Association Study of Alcohol Dependence." *Proceedings of the National Academy of Sciences* 107 (11): 5082–87. doi:10.1073/pnas.0911109107.

Burroughs, Augusten. 2012. *This Is How.* St Martin's Press.

Buscemi, Loredana, Nicoletta Onori, Chiara Turchi, Giovanni Solito, and Adriano Tagliabracci. 2009. "Genetic Susceptibility for Addiction: Searching of Risk Loci for the Widespread Drugs of Abuse." *Forensic Science International: Genetics Supplement Series* 2 (1): 487–88. doi:10.1016/j.fsigss.2009.08.065.

Carey, Nessa. 2012. *The Epigenetics Revolution: How Modern Biology Is Rewriting Our Understanding of Genetics, Disease, and Inheritance.* New York: Columbia University Press.

Carmiol, N., J.M. Peralta, L. Almasy, J. Contreras, A. Pacheco, M.A. Escamilla, E.E.M. Knowles, H. Raventós, and D.C. Glahn. 2014. "Shared Genetic Factors Influence Risk for Bipolar Disorder and Alcohol Use Disorders." *European Psychiatry* 29 (5): 282–87. doi:10.1016/j.eurpsy.2013.10.001.

CASA Columbia. 2012. *Addiction Medicine: Closing the Gap between Science and Practice.*

Chaufan, Claudia, and Jay Joseph. 2013. "The 'Missing Heritability' of Common Disorders: Should Health Researchers Care?" *International Journal of Health Services* 43 (2): 281–303. doi:10.2190/HS.43.2.f.

Conrad, Peter. 1999. "A Mirage of Genes." *Sociology of Health and Illness* 21 (2): 228–41. doi:10.1111/1467-9566.00151.

Corbin, William R., Caitlin Scott, Robert F. Leeman, Lisa M. Fucito, Benjamin A. Toll, and Stephanie S. O'Malley. 2013. "Early Subjective Response and Acquired Tolerance as Predictors of Alcohol Use and Related Problems in a Clinical Sample." *Alcoholism: Clinical and Experimental Research* 37 (3): 490–97. doi:10.1111/j.1530-0277.2012.01956.x.

Crabbe, J. C. 2012. "Translational Behaviour-Genetic Studies of Alcohol: Are We There Yet?" *Genes, Brain and Behavior* 11 (4): 375–86. doi:10.1111/j.1601-183X.2012.00798.x.

Demers, Catherine H., Ryan Bogdan, and Arpana Agrawal. 2014. "The Genetics, Neurogenetics and Pharmacogenetics of Addiction." *Current Behavioral Neuroscience Reports* 1 (1): 33–44. doi:10.1007/s40473-013-0004-8.

Dick, Danielle M. 2007. "Identification of Genes Influencing a Spectrum of Externalizing Psychopathology." *Current Directions in Psychological Science* 16 (6): 331–35. doi:10.1111/j.1467-8721.2007.00530.x.

Dick, Danielle M., Fazil Aliev, Shawn Latendresse, Bernice Porjesz, Marc Schuckit, Madhavi Rangaswamy, Victor Hesselbrock, et al. 2013. "How Phenotype and Developmental Stage Affect the Genes We Find: GABRA2 and Impulsivity." *Twin Research and Human Genetics* 16 (03): 661–69. doi:10.1017/thg.2013.20.

Dick, Danielle M., Shawn J. Latendresse, Jennifer E. Lansford, John P. Budde, Alison Goate, Kenneth A. Dodge, Gregory S. Pettit, and John E. Bates. 2009. "Role of GABRA2 in Trajectories of Externalizing Behavior Across Development and Evidence of Moderation by Parental Monitoring." *Archives of General Psychiatry* 66 (6): 649. doi:10.1001/archgenpsychiatry.2009.48.

Dick, Danielle M., Gregory Smith, Peter Olausson, Suzanne H. Mitchell, Robert F. Leeman, Stephanie S. O'Malley, and Kenneth Sher. 2010. "Understanding the Construct of Impulsivity and Its Relationship to Alcohol Use Disorders." *Addiction Biology* 15 (2): 217–26. doi:10.1111/j.1369-1600.2009.00190.x.

Dixon, Claire I., Sophie E. Walker, Sarah L. King, and David N. Stephens. 2012. "Deletion of the gabra2 Gene Results in Hypersensitivity to the Acute Effects of Ethanol but Does Not Alter Ethanol Self Administration." Edited by Rudolph Uwe. *PLoS ONE* 7 (10): e47135. doi:10.1371/journal.pone.0047135.

Dodes, Lance, and Zachary Dodes. 2014. *The Sober Truth: Debunking the Bad Science behind Twelve-Step Programs and the Rehab Industry.* Beacon Press.

Edenberg, Howard. 2012. "Genes Contributing to the Development of Alcoholism: An Overview." *Alcohol Res* 34 (3): 336–38.

Edenberg, Howard, and Danielle Dick. 2004. "Variations in GABRA2, Encoding the ⊠2 Subunit of the GABAAReceptor, Are Associated with Alcohol Dependence and with Brain Oscillations." *The American Journal of Human Genetics* 74 (4): 705–14. doi:10.1086/383283.

Edenberg, Howard J., and Tatiana Foroud. 2006. "The Genetics of Alcoholism: Identifying Specific Genes through Family Studies." *Addiction Biology* 11 (3-4): 386–96. doi:10.1111/j.1369-1600.2006.00035.x.

Edenberg, Howard J., Daniel L. Koller, Xiaoling Xuei, Leah Wetherill, Jeanette N. McClintick, Laura Almasy, Laura J. Bierut, et al. 2010. "Genome-Wide Association Study of Alcohol Dependence Implicates a Region on Chromosome 11: GENOME-WIDE ASSOCIATION STUDY OF ALCOHOL DEPENDENCE." *Alcoholism: Clinical and Experimental Research* 34 (5): 840–52. doi:10.1111/j.1530-0277.2010.01156.x.

Enoch, Mary-Anne. 2013. "Genetic Influences on the Development of Alcoholism." *Current Psychiatry Reports* 15 (11). doi:10.1007/s11920-013-0412-1.

Enoch, Mary-Anne, Colin A Hodgkinson, Qiaoping Yuan, Bernard Albaugh, Matti Virkkunen, and David Goldman. 2009. "GABRG1 and GABRA2 as Independent Predictors for Alcoholism in Two Populations." *Neuropsychopharmacology* 34 (5): 1245–54. doi:10.1038/npp.2008.171.

Enoch, Mary-Anne, Lori Schwartz, Bernard Albaugh, Matti Virkkunen, and David Goldman. 2006. "Dimensional Anxiety Mediates Linkage ofGABRA2 Haplotypes with Alcoholism." *American Journal of Medical Genetics Part B: Neuropsychiatric Genetics* 141B (6): 599–607. doi:10.1002/ajmg.b.30336.

Feil, Robert, and Mario F. Fraga. 2012. "Epigenetics and the Environment: Emerging Patterns and Implications." *Nature Reviews Genetics*, January. doi:10.1038/nrg3142.

Finegersh, Andrey, and Gregg E. Homanics. 2014. "Paternal Alcohol Exposure Reduces Alcohol Drinking and Increases Behavioral Sensitivity to Alcohol Selectively in Male Offspring." Edited by Thomas H. J. Burne. *PLoS ONE* 9 (6): e99078. doi:10.1371/journal.pone.0099078.

Fletcher, Anne. 2012. *Inside Rehab: The Surprising Truth About Addiction Treatment – And How to Get Help That Works.* Viking.

Foroud, Tatiana, and Howard Edenberg. 2010. "Foroud T, Edenberg HJ, Crabbe JC. Genetic Research: Who Is at Risk for Alcoholism. Alcohol Res Heal J Natl Inst Alcohol Abuse Alcohol. 2010;33:64–75." *Alcohol Res Heal J* 33: 64–75.

Gass, Justin T., and M. Foster Olive. 2012. "Neurochemical and Neurostructural Plasticity in Alcoholism." *ACS Chemical Neuroscience* 3 (7): 494–504. doi:10.1021/cn300013p.

George, Olivier, George F. Koob, and Leandro F. Vendruscolo. 2014. "Negative Reinforcement via Motivational Withdrawal Is the Driving Force behind the Transition to Addiction." *Psychopharmacology* 231 (19): 3911–17. doi:10.1007/s00213-014-3623-1.

Hansell, Narelle K., Arpana Agrawal, John B. Whitfield, Katherine I. Morley, Scott D. Gordon, Penelope A. Lind, Michele L. Pergadia, et al. 2010. "Linkage Analysis of Alcohol Dependence Symptoms in the Community." *Alcoholism: Clinical and Experimental Research* 34 (1): 158–63. doi:10.1111/j.1530-0277.2009.01077.x.

Hartz, Sarah M., and Laura J. Bierut. 2010. "Genetics of Addictions." *Clinics in Laboratory Medicine* 30 (4): 847–64. doi:10.1016/j.cll.2010.07.005.

Heath, Andrew C., John B. Whitfield, Nicholas G. Martin, Michele L. Pergadia, Alison M. Goate, Penelope A. Lind, Brian P. McEvoy, et al. 2011. "A Quantitative-Trait Genome-Wide Association Study of Alcoholism Risk in the Community: Findings and Implications." *Biological Psychiatry* 70 (6): 513–18. doi:10.1016/j.biopsych.2011.02.028.

Hendershot, Christian S. 2014. "Pharmacogenetic Approaches in the Treatment of Alcohol Use Disorders: Addressing Clinical Utility and Implementation Thresholds." *Addiction Science & Clinical Practice* 9 (1): 20. doi:10.1186/1940-0640-9-20.

Irons, Daniel E. 2012. "Characterizing Specific Genetic and Environmental Influences on Alcohol Use". Twin Cities: Univ of Minnesota. http://purl. umn.edu/142504.

Johnson, Wendy, Eric Turkheimer, Irving I. Gottesman, and Thomas J. Bouchard Jr. 2009. "Beyond Heritability: Twin Studies in Behavioral Research." *Current Directions in Psychological Science* 18 (4): 217–20. doi:10.1111/j.1467-8721.2009.01639.x.

Joseph, Jay. 2004. *The Gene Illusion: Genetic Research in Psychiatry and Psychology under the Microscope.* New York: Algora Pub.

– – –. 2013. "The Use of the Classical Twin Method in the Social and Behavioral Sciences: The Fallacy Continues." *Journal of Mind & Behavior* 34 (1).

Krishnan, Harish R., Amul J. Sakharkar, Tara L. Teppen, Tiffani D.M. Berkel, and Subhash C. Pandey. 2014. "The Epigenetic Landscape of Alcoholism." In *International Review of Neurobiology*, 115:75–116. Elsevier. http://linkinghub.elsevier.com/retrieve/pii/B9780128013113000032.

Lind, Penelope A., Stuart Macgregor, Arpana Agrawal, Grant W. Montgomery, Andrew C. Heath, Nicholas G. Martin, and John B. Whitfield. 2008. "The Role of *GABRA2* in Alcohol Dependence, Smoking, and Illicit Drug Use in an Australian Population Sample." *Alcoholism: Clinical and Experimental Research* 32 (10): 1721–31. doi:10.1111/j.1530-0277.2008.00768.x.

Lind, Penelope A., Stuart MacGregor, Grant W. Montgomery, Andrew C. Heath, Nicholas G. Martin, and John B. Whitfield. 2008. "Effects of GABRA2 Variation on Physiological, Psychomotor and Subjective Responses in the Alcohol Challenge Twin Study." *Twin Research and Human Genetics* 11 (02): 174–82. doi:10.1375/twin.11.2.174.

Lydall, G.J., J. Saini, K. Ruparelia, S. Montagnese, A. McQuillin, I. Guerrini, H. Rao, et al. 2011. "Genetic Association Study of GABRA2 Single Nucleotide Polymorphisms and Electroencephalography in Alcohol Dependence." *Neuroscience Letters* 500 (3): 162–66. doi:10.1016/j.neulet.2011.05.240.

Manolio, Teri A., Francis S. Collins, Nancy J. Cox, David B. Goldstein, Lucia A. Hindorff, David J. Hunter, Mark I. McCarthy, et al. 2009. "Finding the Missing Heritability of Complex Diseases." *Nature* 461 (7265): 747–53. doi:10.1038/nature08494.

Mathews, Rebecca, Wayne Hall, and Adrian Carter. 2012. "Direct-to-Consumer Genetic Testing for Addiction Susceptibility: A Premature Commercialisation of Doubtful Validity and Value: Direct-to-Consumer Genetic Testing for Addiction Liability." *Addiction* 107 (12): 2069–74. doi:10.1111/j.1360-0443.2012.03836.x.

Maughan, Barbara, and Edmund J.S. Sonuga-Barke. 2014. "Editorial: Translational Genetics of Child Psychopathology: A Distant Dream?" *Journal of Child Psychology and Psychiatry* 55 (10): 1065–67. doi:10.1111/jcpp.12323.

McDonald, Duff. 2012. "Private Equity's Rehab Roll-Up." *Fortune*, April 30.

Melroy, Whitney E., Sarah H. Stephens, Joseph T. Sakai, Helen M. Kamens, Matthew B. McQueen, Robin P. Corley, Michael C. Stallings, et al. 2014. "Examination of Genetic Variation in GABRA2 with Conduct Disorder and Alcohol Abuse and Dependence in a Longitudinal Study." *Behavior Genetics* 44 (4): 356–67. doi:10.1007/s10519-014-9653-y.

"Molecular Psychiatry - Genetics and Intelligence Differences: Five Special Findings." 2014. Accessed September 22. http://www.nature.com/mp/journal/vaop/ncurrent/full/mp2014105a.html.

Monte, Andrew A, Chad Brocker, Daniel W Nebert, Frank J Gonzalez, David C Thompson, and Vasilis Vasiliou. 2014. "Improved Drug Therapy: Triangulating Phenomics with Genomics and Metabolomics." *Human Genomics* 8 (1): 16. doi:10.1186/s40246-014-0016-9.

Morean, Meghan E., and William R. Corbin. 2008. "Subjective Alcohol Effects and Drinking Behavior: The Relative Influence of Early Response and Acquired Tolerance." *Addictive Behaviors* 33 (10): 1306–13. doi:10.1016/j.addbeh.2008.06.007.

Morozova, Tatiana V., Trudy F. C. Mackay, and Robert R. H. Anholt. 2014. "Genetics and Genomics of Alcohol Sensitivity." *Molecular Genetics and Genomics* 289 (3): 253–69. doi:10.1007/s00438-013-0808-y.

Nelson, E C, A Agrawal, M L Pergadia, M T Lynskey, A A Todorov, J C Wang, R D Todd, et al. 2009. "Association of Childhood Trauma Exposure and GABRA2 Polymorphisms with Risk of Posttraumatic Stress Disorder in Adults." *Molecular Psychiatry* 14 (3): 234–35. doi:10.1038/mp.2008.81.

Newlin, David B., and Rachael M. Renton. 2010. "High Risk Groups Often Have Higher Levels of Alcohol Response Than Low Risk: The Other Side of the Coin." *Alcoholism: Clinical and Experimental Research* 34 (2): 199–202. doi:10.1111/j.1530-0277.2009.01081.x.

Newlin, David B., and James B. Thomson. 1990. "Alcohol Challenge with Sons of Alcoholics: A Critical Review and Analysis." *Psychological Bulletin* 108 (3): 383–402. doi:10.1037/0033-2909.108.3.383.

Ng, M Y M, D F Levinson, S V Faraone, B K Suarez, L E DeLisi, T Arinami, B Riley, et al. 2009. "Meta-Analysis of 32 Genome-Wide Linkage Studies of Schizophrenia." *Molecular Psychiatry* 14 (8): 774–85. doi:10.1038/mp.2008.135.

Nicolaus, Martin. 2009. "Choice of Support Groups - It's the Law." *Counselor*, October.

– – – . 2013. "Federal Court: Provide a Secular Option, or Else." *Counselor Connection*, November. http://www.counselormagazine.com/Counselor-Connection/Federal-Court/.

Nieratschker, Vanessa, Anil Batra, and Andreas J Fallgatter. 2013. "Genetics and Epigenetics of Alcohol Dependence." *Journal of Molecular Psychiatry* 1 (1): 11. doi:10.1186/2049-9256-1-11.

Olfson, Emily, and Laura Jean Bierut. 2012. "Convergence of Genome-Wide Association and Candidate Gene Studies for Alcoholism." *Alcoholism: Clinical and Experimental Research* 36 (12): 2086–94. doi:10.1111/j.1530-0277.2012.01843.x.

Onori, Nicoletta, Chiara Turchi, Giovanni Solito, Rosaria Gesuita, Loredana Buscemi, and Adriano Tagliabracci. 2010. "GABRA2 and Alcohol Use Disorders: No Evidence of an Association in an Italian Case-Control Study." *Alcoholism: Clinical and Experimental Research* 34 (4): 659–68. doi:10.1111/j.1530-0277.2009.01135.x.

Perry, Brea L., Bernice A. Pescosolido, Kathleen Bucholz, Howard Edenberg, John Kramer, Samuel Kuperman, Marc Alan Schuckit, and John I. Nurnberger. 2013. "Gender-Specific Gene–Environment Interaction in Alcohol Dependence: The Impact of Daily Life Events and GABRA2." *Behavior Genetics* 43 (5): 402–14. doi:10.1007/s10519-013-9607-9.

Philibert, Robert A., Tracy D. Gunter, Steven R.H. Beach, Gene H. Brody, Nancy Hollenbeck, Allan Andersen, and William Adams. 2009. "Role of GABRA2 on Risk for Alcohol, Nicotine, and Cannabis Dependence in the Iowa Adoption Studies." *Psychiatric Genetics* 19 (2): 91–98. doi:10.1097/YPG.0b013e3283208026.

Plomin, R, and I J Deary. 2014. "Genetics and Intelligence Differences: Five Special Findings." *Molecular Psychiatry*, September. doi:10.1038/mp.2014.105.

Plomin, Robert. 2014. "Genotype-Environment Correlation in the Era of DNA." *Behavior Genetics*, September. doi:10.1007/s10519-014-9673-7.

Quillen, Ellen E., Xiang-Ding Chen, Laura Almasy, Fang Yang, Hao He, Xi Li, Xu-Yi Wang, et al. 2014. "*ALDH2* Is Associated to Alcohol Dependence and Is the Major Genetic Determinant of 'daily Maximum Drinks' in a GWAS Study of an Isolated Rural Chinese Sample." *American Journal of Medical Genetics Part B: Neuropsychiatric Genetics* 165 (2): 103–10. doi:10.1002/ajmg.b.32213.

Quinn, Patrick D., and Kim Fromme. 2011. "Subjective Response to Alcohol Challenge: A Quantitative Review." *Alcoholism: Clinical and Experimental Research* 35 (10): 1759–70. doi:10.1111/j.1530-0277.2011.01521.x.

Rachdaoui, Nadia, and Dipak K. Sarkar. 2014. "Transgenerational Epigenetics and Brain Disorders." In *International Review of Neurobiology*, 115:51–73. Elsevier. http://linkinghub.elsevier.com/retrieve/pii/B9780128013113000020.

Resendiz, Marisol, Stephen Mason, Chiao-Ling Lo, and Feng C. Zhou. 2014. "Epigenetic Regulation of the Neural Transcriptome and Alcohol Interference during Development." *Frontiers in Genetics* 5 (August). doi:10.3389/fgene.2014.00285.

Rietveld, C. A., S. E. Medland, J. Derringer, J. Yang, T. Esko, N. W. Martin, H.-J. Westra, et al. 2013. "GWAS of 126,559 Individuals Identifies Genetic Variants Associated with Educational Attainment." *Science* 340 (6139): 1467–71. doi:10.1126/science.1235488.

Rose, Steven P. R, Leon J Kamin, and Lewontin. 1984. *Not in Our Genes: Biology, Ideology and Human Nature*. Harmondsworth: Penguin Books.

Saab, B. J., and I. M. Mansuy. 2014. "Neurobiological Disease Etiology and Inheritance: An Epigenetic Perspective." *Journal of Experimental Biology* 217 (1): 94–101. doi:10.1242/jeb.089995.

Sakai, Joseph T., Michael C. Stallings, Thomas J. Crowley, Heather L. Gelhorn, Matthew B. McQueen, and Marissa A. Ehringer. 2010. "Test of Association between GABRA2 (SNP rs279871) and Adolescent Conduct/alcohol Use Disorders Utilizing a Sample of Clinic Referred Youth with Serious Substance and Conduct Problems, Controls and Available First Degree Relatives." *Drug and Alcohol Dependence* 106 (2-3): 199–203. doi:10.1016/j. drugalcdep.2009.08.015.

Salvatore, Jessica, Fazil Aliev, Alexis Edwards, David Evans, John Macleod, Matthew Hickman, Glyn Lewis, et al. 2014. "Polygenic Scores Predict Alcohol Problems in an Independent Sample and Show Moderation by the Environment." *Genes* 5 (2): 330–46. doi:10.3390/genes5020330.

Schönemann, Peter. 1997. "On Models and Muddles of Heritability." *Genetica* 99 (2-3): 97–108.

Schuckit, Marc A., and Tom L. Smith. 2013. "Stability of Scores and Correlations with Drinking Behaviors over 15 Years for the Self-Report of the Effects of Alcohol Questionnaire." *Drug and Alcohol Dependence* 128 (3): 194–99. doi:10.1016/j.drugalcdep.2012.08.022.

Schuckit, Marc A., Tom L. Smith, Jon Heron, Matthew Hickman, John Macleod, Glyn Lewis, John M. Davis, et al. 2011. "Testing a Level of Response to Alcohol-Based Model of Heavy Drinking and Alcohol Problems in 1,905 17-Year-Olds." *Alcoholism: Clinical and Experimental Research* 35 (10): 1897–1904. doi:10.1111/j.1530-0277.2011.01536.x.

Söderpalm Gordh, Anna H. V., and Bo Söderpalm. 2011. "Healthy Subjects with a Family History of Alcoholism Show Increased Stimulative Subjective Effects of Alcohol." *Alcoholism: Clinical and Experimental Research*, May, no–no. doi:10.1111/j.1530-0277.2011.01478.x.

Starkman, Bela, Amul Sakharkar, and Subhash Pandey. 2012. "Epigenetics – Beyond the Genome in Alcoholism." *Alcohol Research: Current Reviews* 34 (3). http://pubs.niaaa.nih.gov/publications/arcr343/293-305.htm.

Terranova, Claudio, Marianna Tucci, Laura Di Pietra, and Santo Davide Ferrara. 2014. "GABA Receptors Genes Polymorphisms and Alcohol Dependence: No Evidence of an Association in an Italian Male Population." *Clinical Psychopharmacology and Neuroscience* 12 (2): 142. doi:10.9758/cpn.2014.12.2.142.

Trucco, Elisa M., Sandra Villafuerte, Mary M. Heitzeg, Margit Burmeister, and Robert A. Zucker. 2014. "Rule Breaking Mediates the Developmental Association between *GABRA2* and Adolescent Substance Abuse." *Journal of Child Psychology and Psychiatry*, May, n/a–n/a. doi:10.1111/jcpp.12244.

Trzaskowski, Maciej, Philip S. Dale, and Robert Plomin. 2013. "No Genetic Influence for Childhood Behavior Problems From DNA Analysis." *Journal of the American Academy of Child & Adolescent Psychiatry* 52 (10): 1048–1056.e3. doi:10.1016/j.jaac.2013.07.016.

Turkheimer, E. 2011. "Commentary: Variation and Causation in the Environment and Genome." *International Journal of Epidemiology* 40 (3): 598–601. doi:10.1093/ije/dyq147.

Vassoler, F.M., and G. Sadri-Vakili. 2014. "Mechanisms of Transgenerational Inheritance of Addictive-like Behaviors." *Neuroscience* 264 (April): 198–206. doi:10.1016/j.neuroscience.2013.07.064.

Villafuerte, S, M M Heitzeg, S Foley, W-Y Wendy Yau, K Majczenko, J-K Zubieta, R A Zucker, and M Burmeister. 2012. "Impulsiveness and Insula Activation during Reward Anticipation Are Associated with Genetic Variants in GABRA2 in a Family Sample Enriched for Alcoholism." *Molecular Psychiatry* 17 (5): 511–19. doi:10.1038/mp.2011.33.

Villafuerte, S., V. Strumba, S. F. Stoltenberg, R. A. Zucker, and M. Burmeister. 2013. "Impulsiveness Mediates the Association between *GABRA2* SNPs and Lifetime Alcohol Problems: Impulsiveness Mediates the Association of GABRA2 and Alcohol Problems." *Genes, Brain and Behavior* 12 (5): 525–31. doi:10.1111/gbb.12039.

Wang, Jen-Chyong, Manav Kapoor, and Alison M. Goate. 2012. "The Genetics of Substance Dependence." *Annual Review of Genomics and Human Genetics* 13 (1): 241–61. doi:10.1146/annurev-genom-090711-163844.

Wetherill, Leah, Manav Kapoor, Arpana Agrawal, Kathleen Bucholz, Daniel Koller, Sarah E. Bertelsen, Nhung Le, et al. 2014. "Family-Based Association Analysis of Alcohol Dependence Criteria and Severity." *Alcoholism: Clinical and Experimental Research* 38 (2): 354–66. doi:10.1111/acer.12251.

White, William L. 2014. *Slaying the Dragon: The History of Addiction Treatment and Recovery in America*. Second Edition. Chestnut Health Systems.

Yan, Jia, Fazil Aliev, Bradley T. Webb, Kenneth S. Kendler, Vernell S. Williamson, Howard J. Edenberg, Arpana Agrawal, et al. 2014. "Using Genetic Information from Candidate Gene and Genome-Wide Association Studies in Risk Prediction for Alcohol Dependence: Genetic Risk Prediction for AD." *Addiction Biology* 19 (4): 708–21. doi:10.1111/adb.12035.

Zhang, Ruiling, Qin Miao, Chuansheng Wang, Rongrong Zhao, Wenqiang Li, Colin N. Haile, Wei Hao, and Xiang Yang Zhang. 2013. "Genome-Wide DNA Methylation Analysis in Alcohol Dependence: Alcohol Abuse and Methylation." *Addiction Biology* 18 (2): 392–403. doi:10.1111/adb.12037.

REFERENCES
FOR THE FIRST EDITION

Ader, R., and N. Cohen. "Conditioning of the Immune Response." *Netherlands Journal of Medicine* 39, no. 3/4 (October 1991): 263–73.

Alford, G. S., E. N. Jouriles, and S. C. Jackson. "Differences and Similarities in Development of Drinking Behavior Between Alcoholic Offspring of Alcoholics and Alcoholic Offspring of Non-alcoholics." *Addictive Behaviors* 16, no. 5 (1991): 341–347.

Allen, Arthur. "The Disappointment Gene: Why Genetics Is so Far a Boondoggle." *Slate*, October 18, 2005. http://www.slate.com/id/2128292.

American Psychiatric Association. *American Psychiatric Association: Diagnostic and Statistical Manual of Mental Disorders.* (4th ed.) Washington, D.C.: American Psychiatric Press, 1994.

Anthony, James C. "Epidemiology of Drug Dependency." In Marc Galanter and Herbert D. Kleber (eds.), *The American Psychiatric Publishing Textbook of Substance Abuse Treatment* (2nd ed.), 52, Arlington, Va.: American Psychiatric Publishing, 1999.

Ashcraft, Lori H., and William A. Anthony. "Breaking Down Barriers." *Behavioral Healthcare* (April 2008).

Asyyed, Asma, Daniel Storm, and Ivan Diamond. "Ethanol Activates cAMP Response Element-Mediated Gene Expression in Select Regions of the Mouse Brain." *Brain Research* 1106, no. 1 (August 23, 2006): 63–71.

"Atherosclerosis Risk Factors, Prevention and Wellness Tips." *Wellness Tips.* http://www.recoverymedicine.com/atherosclerosis_wellness_tips.htm.

Augustine of Hippo. *Confessions.* Vol. 10. Pusey Translation. http://ccat.sas.upenn.edu/jod/augustine/Pusey/book10.

Ball, David. "Addiction Science and Its Genetics." *Addiction (Abingdon, England)* 103, no. 3 (March 2008): 360–367.

Bandura, Albert. *Self-Efficacy: The Exercise of Control.* New York: Freeman, 1997.

Barrett, Stephen, and Harriett Hall. "Dubious Genetic Testing." *Quackwatch*, 2002. http://www.quackwatch.com/01QuackeryRelatedTopics/Tests/genomics.html.

Beeder, Ann B., and Robert Millman. "Patients with Psychopathology." In Joyce H. Lowinson (ed.), *Substance Abuse: A Comprehensive Textbook*, Philadelphia: Lippincott, 1997.

Begleiter, Henri. "What Is Inherited in The Predisposition Toward Alcoholism? A Proposed Model." *Alcoholism: Clinical and Experimental Research* 23, no. 7 (1999): 1125–1135.

Bischof, Gallus, Hans-Jürgen Rumpf, Christian Meyer, Ulfert Hapke, and Ulrich John. "Stability of Subtypes of Natural Recovery from Alcohol Dependence After Two Years." *Addiction (Abingdon, England)* 102, no. 6 (June 2007): 904–908.

Blum, Kenneth G., John R. Cull, Eric E. Braverman, and David Comings. "Reward Deficiency Syndrome." *American Scientist* 84 (March 1, 1996): 132–145.

Boettinger, Charlotte. "UCSF News Office – Brain Imaging and Genetic Studies Link Thinking Patterns to Addiction." http://pub.ucsf.edu/newsservices/releases/200712262.

"Book Review." *Journal of the American Medical Association* 113, no. 16 (October 14, 1939). http://www.silkworth.net/bbreviews/01007.html.

Brown, Sally, and David Brown. "Marty Mann and the Evolution of Alcoholics Anonymous [Excerpts]," 2001. http://www.barefootsworld.net/aamarty-mann.html.

Brown, Sally, and David Brown. *A Biography of Mrs. Marty Mann: The First Lady of Alcoholics Anonymous*. Center City, Minn.: Hazelden, 2005.

Burnham, John C. *Bad Habits: Drinking, Smoking, Taking Drugs, Gambling, Sexual Misbehavior*. New York: New York University Press, 1994.

Carr, Allen. *The Easy Way to Stop Smoking*. [Rev. and updated]. New York: Sterling, 2004.

Cherpitel, Cheryl J. "Injury and the Role of Alcohol: County-Wide Emergency Room Data." *Alcoholism: Clinical and Experimental Research* 18, no. 3 (June 1994): 679–684.

Ciccocioppo, Roberto, and Petri Hyytia. "The Genetic of Alcoholism: Learning from 50 Years of Research." *Addiction Biology* 11, no. 3/4 (2006): 193–194.

Clarke, Toni-Kim, Jens Treutlein, Ulrich S. Zimmermann, Falk Kiefer, Markus H. Skowronek, Marcella Rietschel, et al. "HPA-Axis Activity in Alcoholism: Examples for a Gene-Environment Interaction." *Addiction Biology* 13, no. 1 (March 2008): 1–14.

Cohen, N., J. A. Moynihan, and R. Ader. "Pavlovian Conditioning of the Immune System." *International Archives of Allergy and Immunology* 105, no. 2 (October 1994): 101–106.

Cohen, Peter D. A. "Is the Addiction Doctor the Voodoo Priest of Western Man?" *Addiction Research & Theory* 8, no. 6 (2000): 589.

Comings, D. E., and K. Blum. "Reward Deficiency Syndrome: Genetic Aspects of Behavioral Disorders." *Progress in Brain Research* 126 (2000): 325–341.

Conrad, Peter. *The Medicalization of Society: On the Transformation of Human Conditions.* Baltimore: Johns Hopkins University Press, 2007

Crabbe, John C. "Genetic Contributions to Addiction." *Annual Review of Psychology* 53 (2002): 435–462.

Crabbe, John C., J. C. Crabbe, Jr., and R. Adron Harris. *The Genetic Basis of Alcohol and Drug Actions.* New York: Springer, 1991.

Crabbe, John C., Tamara J. Phillips, R. Adron Harris, Michael A. Arends, and George F. Koob. "Alcohol-Related Genes: Contributions from Studies with Genetically Engineered Mice." *Addiction Biology* 11, no. 3/4 (2006): 195–269.

Dawson, Deborah A. "Correlates of Past-Year Status Among Treated and Untreated Persons with Former Alcohol Dependence: United States, 1992." *Alcoholism: Clinical and Experimental Research* 20, no. 4 (1996): 771–779.

Deroche-Gamonet, Veronique, David Belin, and Pier Vincenzo Piazza. "Evidence for Addiction-Like Behavior in the Rat." *Science* 305, no. 5686 (August 13, 2004): 1014–1017.

"Diabetic Diet (Diabetes Diet) Information on Medicinenet.com." *Diabetic Diet (cont'd).* http://www.medicinenet.com/diabetic_diet/page4.htm#toce.

Dick, Danielle M. "Identification of Genes Influencing a Spectrum of Externalizing Psychopathology." *Current Directions in Psychological Science* 16, no. 6 (December 2007): 331–335.

"Diet and Hypertension." http://www.ext.colostate.edu/pubs/foodnut/09318.html.

DiFranza, Joseph R. "Hooked from the First Cigarette: New Findings Reveal That Cigarette Addiction Can Arise Astonishingly Fast. But the Research Could Lead to Therapies That Make Quitting Easier." *Scientific American* (May 2008): 82–87.

Dimeff, Linda, and Alan Marlatt. "Relapse Prevention." In *Handbook of Alcoholism Treatment Approaches: Effective Alternatives* (2nd ed.), 176, Boston: Allyn & Bacon, 1995.

Dodes, Lance M. *The Heart of Addiction.* New York: HarperCollins, 2002.

Doran, Neal, Mark G. Myers, Susan E. Luczak, Lucinda G. Carr, and Tamara L. Wall. "Stability of Heavy Episodic Drinking in Chinese- and Korean-American College Students: Effects of ALDH2 Gene Status and Behavioral Undercontrol." *Journal of Studies on Alcohol and Drugs* 68, no. 6 (November 2007): 789–797

Doumas, Diana M., Christine M. Blasey, and Cory L. Thacker. "Attrition from Alcohol and Drug Outpatient Treatment Psychological Distress and Interpersonal Problems as Indicators." *Alcoholism Treatment Quarterly* 23, no. 4 (June 9, 2005): 55–67.

Edenberg, Howard J. "The Collaborative Study on the Genetics of Alcoholism: An update," September 22, 2002. http://findarticles.com/p/articles/mi_m0CXH/is_/ai_106731236.

Edenberg, Howard J., and Tatiana Foroud. "The Genetics of Alcoholism: Identifying Specific Genes Through Family Studies." *Addiction Biology* 11, no. 3/4 (2006): 386–396.

Elliott, Victoria. "Addictive Cocktail: Alcoholism and Genetics." *American Medical News*, February 5, 2001. http://www.ama-assn.org/amednews/2001/02/05/hlsa0205.htm.

Emrick, Chad. "Alcoholics Anonymous: Emerging Concepts. Overview." In Marc Galanter (ed.), *Recent Developments in Alcoholism: Treatment Research,* 7, New York: Springer, 1989.

Emrick, Chad, and J. Scott Tonigan. "Alcoholics Anonymous and Other 12-Step Groups." In Marc Galanter (ed.), *Recent Developments in Alcoholism: Treatment Research.* New York: Springer, 433, 2004.

Eng, Mimy Y., Marc A. Schuckit, and Tom L. Smith. "The Level of Response to Alcohol in Daughters of Alcoholics and Controls." *Drug and Alcohol Dependence* 79, no. 1 (July 1, 2005): 83–93.

Eng, Mimy Y., Susan E. Luczak, and Tamara L. Wall. "ALDH2, ADH1B, and ADH1C Genotypes in Asians: A Literature Review." *Alcohol Research & Health: Journal of the National Institute on Alcohol Abuse and Alcoholism* 30, no. 1 (2007): 22–27.

Evans, Suzette M., and Frances R. Levin. "Response to Alcohol in Females with a Paternal History of Alcoholism." *Psychopharmacology* 169, no. 1 (August 2003): 10–20.

Fan, Li, Frederick Bellinger, Yong-Liang Ge, and Peter Wilce. "Genetic Study of Alcoholism and Novel Gene Expression in the Alcoholic Brain." *Addiction Biology* 9, no. 1 (March 2004): 11–18.

Farnsworth, Dorothy. "Quality Assurance Report." *CAADAC*, November 6, 2007. http://www.capwiz.com/caadac/attachments/qa_final_report_12_07__fin.pdf.

Farren, Conor K., and Keith F. Tipton. "Trait Markers for Alcoholism: Clinical Utility." *Alcohol Alcohol.* 34, no. 5 (September 1, 1999): 649–665.

Ferri, M., L. Amato, and M. Davoli. "Alcoholics Anonymous and Other 12-Step Programmes for Alcohol Dependence." *Cochrane Database of Systematic Reviews (Online)* 2006, no. 3. http://www.mrw.interscience.wiley.com/cochrane/clsysrev/articles/CD005032/frame.html.

Fields, Howard. "Alcoholism: Vice or Disease? A Conversation with Howard Fields, Part 3 of 3 – UCSF Science Café" http://www.ucsf.edu/science-cafe/conversations/fields3/.

Finn, Deborah A., and John C. Crabbe. "Exploring Alcohol Withdrawal Syndrome." *Alcohol Health and Research World* 21, no. 2 (1997): 149.

Fischer, Monika, Leah Flury Wetherill, Lucinda G. Carr, Min You, and David W. Crabb. "Association of the Aldehyde Dehydrogenase 2 Promoter Polymorphism with Alcohol Consumption and Reactions in an American

Jewish Population." *Alcoholism, Clinical and Experimental Research* 31, no. 10 (October 2007): 1654–1659.

Flatscher-Bader, Traute, Marcel Van Der Brug, John W. Hwang, Peter A. Gochee, Izuru Matsumoto, Shin-Ichi Niwa, et al. "Alcohol-Responsive Genes in the Frontal Cortex and Nucleus Accumbens of Human Alcoholics." *Journal of Neurochemistry* 93, no. 2 (April 2005): 359–370.

Fletcher, Anne M. *Sober for Good: New Solutions for Drinking Problems: Advice from Those Who Have Succeeded.* Boston: Houghton Mifflin Cookbooks, 2002.

Flynn, William R. "A Biography of Mrs. Marty Mann: The First Lady of Alcoholics Anonymous [Book Review]." *American Journal of Psychiatry* 159 (November 2002): 1950–1951

Fuchs, Rita A., R. Kyle Branham, and Ronald E. See. "Different Neural Substrates Mediate Cocaine Seeking After Abstinence Versus Extinction Training: A Critical Role for the Dorsolateral Caudate-Putamen." *Journal of Neuroscience,* 26, no. 13 (March 29, 2006): 3584–3588

Gardner, Eliot. "Brain-Reward Mechanisms." In Joyce H. Lowinson (ed.), *Substance Abuse: A Comprehensive Textbook,* Philadelphia: Lippincott, 1997.

Geller, Anne. "Comprehensive Treatment Programs." In Joyce H. Lowinson (ed.), *Substance Abuse: A Comprehensive Textbook,* 425–429, Philadelphia: Lippincott, 1997.

Gill, K., M. Eagle Elk, Y. Liu, and R. A. Deitrich. "An Examination of ALDH2 Genotypes, Alcohol Metabolism and the Flushing Response in Native Americans." *Journal of Studies on Alcohol* 60, no. 2 (March 1999): 149–158.

Gladwell, Malcolm. *The Tipping Point: How Little Things Can Make a Big Difference.* Boston: Back Bay, 2002.

Glantz, Stanton A. (ed.). *The Cigarette Papers.* Berkeley: University of California Press, 1998

Goedde, H. W., D. P. Agarwal, S. Harada, F. Rothhammer, J. O. Whittaker, and R. Lisker. "Aldehyde Dehydrogenase Polymorphism in North American, South American, and Mexican Indian Populations." *American Journal of Human Genetics* 38, no. 3 (March 1986): 395–399.

Goldstein, Avram. *Addiction: From Biology to Drug Policy.* (2nd ed.) New York: Oxford University Press, 2001.

Gordis, E. "Accessible and Affordable Health Care for Alcoholism and Related Problems: Strategy for Cost Containment." *Journal of Studies on Alcohol* 48, no. 6 (November 1987): 579–585.

Granfield, Robert, and William Cloud. *Coming Clean: Overcoming Addiction Without Treatment.* New York: New York University Press, 1999.

Hahn, Cheng-Yi, San-Yuan Huang, Huei-Chen Ko, Chau-Hsiang Hsieh, I-Hui Lee, Tzung-Lieh Yeh, et al. "Acetaldehyde Involvement in Positive and Negative Alcohol Expectancies in Han Chinese Persons with Alcoholism." *Archives of General Psychiatry* 63, no. 7 (July 2006): 817–823.

Hall, Carl T. "Smokers, your addiction is all in your head, study finds." *San Francisco Chronicle*, January 25, 2007. http://www.sfgate.com/cgi-bin/article.cgi?f=/c/a/2007/01/25/BAG89NOCVN9.DTL&feed=rss.news.

Hartigan, Francis. *Bill W.: A Biography of Alcoholics Anonymous Cofounder Bill Wilson*. Old Tappan, N.J.: Macmillan, 2000.

Heberlein, Ulrike. "Research." *Ernest and Julio Gallo Research Center*. http://www.galloresearch.org/site/HeberleinLab/section.php?id=187.

Heilig, Markus. "Imagen: Implications for Addiction Science and Science Policy." *Addiction (Abingdon, England)* 102, no. 11 (November 2007): 1699–1700.

Helm, Jeffrey. "Myth of an 'Addict Gene.'" *The Tyee*, July 28, 2006. http://thetyee.ca/News/2006/07/28/AddictGene/.

Herman, Judith Lewis. *Trauma and Recovery: The Aftermath of Violence – From Domestic Abuse to Political Terror*. New York: Basic Books, 1997

Hester, Reid K., and William R. Miller. *Handbook of Alcoholism Treatment Approaches: Effective Alternatives* (2nd ed.) Boston: Allyn & Bacon, 1995.

Higgins, Stephen T. "Principles of Learning in the Study and Treatment of Substance Abuse." In Marc Galanter and Herbert D. Kleber (eds.), *The American Psychiatric Publishing Textbook of Substance Abuse Treatment* (3rd ed.), 65, Arlington, Va.: American Psychiatric Publishing, 2004.

Hiroi, N., and S. Agatsuma. "Genetic Susceptibility to Substance Dependence." *Molecular Psychiatry* 10, no. 4 (December 7, 2004): 336–344

Holden, Constance. "Behavioral Genetics : New Clues to Alcoholism Risk." *Science* 280, no. 5368 (May 29, 1998): 1348b–1349.

Horgan, Constance. *Substance Abuse: A Comprehensive Factbook*. Princeton, N.J.: Robert Wood Johnson Foundation, 2001.

Jellinek, Elvin Morton. *The Disease Concept of Alcoholism*. Ossining, N.Y.: Hill House Press, 1960.

Jones, Douglas C., and Gary W. Miller. "The Effects of Environmental Neurotoxicants on the Dopaminergic System: A Possible Role in Drug Addiction." *Biochemical Pharmacology* (May 20, 2008).

Joseph, Jay. "Twin Studies in Psychiatry and Psychology: Science or Pseudoscience?" *Psychiatric Quarterly* 73, no. 1 (March 1, 2002): 71–82.

Kalivas, Peter W., Jamie Peters, and Lori Knackstedt. "Animal Models and Brain Circuits in Drug Addiction." *Mol. Interv.* 6, no. 6 (December 1, 2006): 339–344

Kasl, Charlotte Davis, and Charlotte S. Kasl. *Many Roads, One Journey: Moving Beyond the Twelve Steps*. New York: HarperCollins, 1992.

Kelly, John F. "Toward an Addiction-ary: A Proposal for More Precise Terminology." *Alcoholism Treatment Quarterly* 22, no. 2 (June 21, 2004): 79–87.

Kessler, R. C., K. A. Mcgonagle, S. Zhao, C. B. Nelson, M. Hughes, S. Eshleman, et al. "Lifetime and 12-Month Prevalence of DSM-III-R Psychiatric Disorders in the United States. Results from the National Comorbidity Survey." *Archives of General Psychiatry* 51, no. 1 (January 1994): 8–19.

Ketcham, Katherine, and William Asbury. *Beyond the Influence: Understanding and Defeating Alcoholism*. New York: Bantam Books, 2000.

Khazaal, Y., E. Frésard, and D. Zullino. "[Exposure to addictogenic substances, conditioned response and treatment of the exposure with response prevention]." *L'Encéphale* 33, no. 3 Pt. 1: 346–351.

Kiberstis, Paula, and Leslie Roberts. "It's Not Just The Genes." *Science* 296, no. 5568 (April 26, 2002): 685.

Kliesthernes, Christopher, and John Crabbe. "Genetic Independence of Mouse Measures of Some Aspects of Novelty Seeking." *PNAS* 103, no. 13 (March 28, 2006): 5–18

Koob, G. F., and F. E. Bloom. "Cellular and Molecular Mechanisms of Drug Dependence." *Science* 242, no. 4879 (November 4, 1988): 715–723.

Koob, George, and Michel Le Moal. *Neurobiology of Addiction*. Orlando: Academic Press, 2006.

Kurtz, Ernest. *Not-God: A History of Alcoholics Anonymous*. Center City, Minn.: Hazelden, 1991.

Kurtz, Ernest. "Alcoholics Anonymous and the Disease Concept of Alcoholism." *Alcoholism Treatment Quarterly* 20, no. 3/4 (2002): 5–40.

Layman with a Notebook, A. *What Is the Oxford Group?* Oxford University Press, 1933. http://www.stepstudy.org/downloads/what_is.pdf

Le, Christine, Erik P. Ingvarson, and Richard C. Page. "Alcoholics Anonymous and the counseling profession: Philosophies in conflict." *Journal of Counseling and Development; http://unhooked.com/sep/aacouns.htm* (July 1, 1995): 603.

Lester, David. "The Heritability of Alcoholism: Science and Social Policy." In Edith Gomberg, *Current Issues in Alcohol/Drug Studies* (New York: Routledge, 1990).

Lin, Show W., and Robert Anthenelli. "Genetic Factors in the Risk for Substance Use Disorders." In Joyce H. Lowinson (ed.), *Substance Abuse: A Comprehensive Textbook*, Philadelphia: Lippincott, 2004.

Lincoln, Abraham. "Temperance Address." *Sangamo Journal*, March 25, 1842. http://www.druglibrary.org/schaffer/History/ancient/TempAddr.htm.

Lobdell, Jared. *This Strange Illness: Alcoholism and Bill W.* Piscataway, N.J.: Aldine Transaction, 2004.

Lovinger, David M., and John C. Crabbe. "Laboratory Models of Alcoholism: Treatment Target Identification and Insight into Mechanisms." *Nature Neuroscience* 8, no. 11 (November 2005): 1471.

Lowinson, Joyce H. *Substance Abuse: A Comprehensive Textbook*. (3rd ed.) Philadelphia: Lippincott, 1997.

Lu, Ru-Band, Huei-Chen Ko, Jia-Fu Lee, Wei-Wen Lin, San-Yuan Huang, Tso-Jen Wang, et al. "No Alcoholism-Protection Effects of ADH1B*2 Allele in Antisocial Alcoholics Among Han Chinese in Taiwan." *Alcoholism, Clinical and Experimental Research* 29, no. 12 (December 2005): 2101–2107.

MacDonald, E. B., and A. R. Patel. "Attitudes Towards Alcoholism." *British Medical Journal* 2, no. 5968 (May 24, 1975): 430–431.

Malone, Stephen M., William G. Iacono, and Matt McGue. "Drinks of the Father: Father's Maximum Number of Drinks Consumed Predicts Externalizing Disorders, Substance Use, and Substance Use Disorders in Preadolescent and Adolescent Offspring." *Alcoholism: Clinical and Experimental Research* 26, no. 12 (December 2002): 1823–1832.

Marlatt, Alan, Kimberly Barrett, and Dennis Daley. "Relapse Prevention." In Marc Galanter and Herbert D. Kleber (eds.), *The American Psychiatric Publishing Textbook of Substance Abuse Treatment* (3rd ed.), 357, Arlington, Va.: American Psychiatric Publishing, 2004.

Matsushita, Sachio, and Susumu Higuchi. "[A Review of the Neuroimaging Studies of Alcoholism]." *Nihon Arukoru Yakubutsu Igakkai Zasshi = Japanese Journal of Alcohol Studies & Drug Dependence* 42, no. 6 (December 2007): 615–621.

McGue, Matt. "A Behavioral-Genetic Perspective on Children of Alcoholics." *Alcohol Health and Research World* 21, no. 3 (1997): 210–217.

McIntire, Don. "How Well Does A.A. Work? An Analysis of Published A.A. Surveys (1968–1996) and Related Analyses/Comments." *Alcoholism Treatment Quarterly* 18, no. 4 (2000): 1–18.

McIntire, Steve. "Welcome to the McIntire Lab." *Ernest and Julio Gallo Research Center*. http://www.galloresearch.org/site/McIntireLab/.

McLellan, A. T., Deni Carise, and H. D. Kleber. "Can the National Addiction Treatment Infrastructure Support the Public's Demand for Quality Care?" *Journal of Substance Abuse Treatment* 25 (2003): 117–121.

McLellan, A. T., D. C. Lewis, C. P. O'Brien, and H. D. Kleber. "Drug dependence, a Chronic Medical Illness: Implications for Treatment, Insurance, and Outcomes Evaluation." *Journal of the American Medical Association* 284, no. 13 (October 4, 2000): 1689–1695.

Mercadante, Linda A. *Victims and Sinners: Spiritual Roots of Addiction and Recovery*. Louisville, Ky.: Westminster John Knox Press, 1996.

Merikangas, Kathleen Ries, and Neil Risch. "Genomic Priorities and Public Health." *Science* 302, no. 5645 (October 24, 2003): 599–601.

Midanik, Lorraine T. *Biomedicalization of Alcohol Studies: Ideological Shifts and Institutional Challenges*. Piscataway, N.J.: Aldine Transaction, 2006.

Midanik, Lorraine T. "What's in a Name? Proposed Name Changes of the U.S. National Institute on Drug Abuse and the U.S. National Institute on Alcohol Abuse and Alcoholism." *Addiction* 103, no. 1 (January 1, 2008): 1–3.

Milam, James R. "The Alcoholism Revolution." *Professional Counselor*, August 1992. http://www.lakesidemilam.com/TheAlcoholismRevolution.htm.

Milam, James R., and Katherine Ketcham. *Under the Influence: A Guide to the Myths and Realities of Alcoholism*. New York: Bantam Books, 1983.

Milgram, Gail Gleason. "the Need for Clarity of Terminology." *Alcoholism Treatment Quarterly* 22, no. 2 (June 12, 2004): 89–95.

Miller, William R., and William White. "Confrontation in Addiction Treatment." *Counselor* (October 4, 2007). http://www.counselormagazine.com/content/view/608/63.

Moos, Rudolf H. "Iatrogenic Effects of Psychosocial Interventions for Substance Use Disorders: Prevalence, Predictors, Prevention." *Addiction* 100, no. 5 (May 12, 2005): 595–604.

National Institute on Alcohol Abuse and Alcoholism. "Alcohol Alert #60," July 2003. http://pubs.niaaa.nih.gov/publications/aa60.htm.

National Institute on Drug Abuse. *Principles of Drug Abuse Treatment: A Research-Based Guide*. National Institute on Drug Abuse, 1999.

Neumark, Y. D., Y. Friedlander, H. R. Thomasson, and T. K. Li. "Association of the ADH2*2 Allele with Reduced Ethanol Consumption in Jewish Men in Israel: A Pilot Study." *Journal of Studies on Alcohol* 59, no. 2 (March 1998): 133–139.

Nicolaus, Martin. *How Was Your Week? Bringing People Together in Recovery the LifeRing Way*. Oakland, Calif.: LifeRing Press, 2003.

Nicolaus, Martin. *Recovery by Choice: Living and Enjoying Life Free of Alcohol and Drugs, a Workbook*. (3rd ed.) Oakland, Calif.: LifeRing Press, 2006.

Nicolaus, Martin. "The Role of Mirror Neurons in Addiction and Recovery." Denver; Nashville, 2007. http://www.unhooked.com/discussion/index.htm#mirror.

Oakes, Edward T. "Original Sin: A Disputation." *First Things: The Journal of Religion, Culture, and Public Life* (November 1998): 16–24.

Paz Filho, G. J., L. J. Sato, M. J. Tuleski, S. Y. Takata, C. C. Ranzi, S. Y. Saruhashi, et al. "[Use of the CAGE Questionnaire for Detecting Alcohol Use Disorders in the Emergency Room]." *Revista Da Associação Médica Brasileira* (1992) 47, no. 1: 65–69.

Pert, Candace B. *Molecules of Emotion: The Science Behind Mind-Body Medicine*. (1st ed.) New York: Simon & Schuster, 1999.

Pfaff, Donald W., Wade H. Berrettini, and Tong H. Joh. *Genetic Influences on Neural and Behavioral Functions* (Boca Raton, Fla.: CRC Press, 1999).

Powell v. Texas, 392 U. S. 514 (1968). http://supreme.justia.com/us/392/514/case.html.

Powell, David J. "It's Time for a National Approach on Staff Development." *Behavioral Healthcare* (March 2006). http://www.behavioral.net/.

Rhodes, Justin S., and John C. Crabbe. "Progress Towards Finding Genes for Alcoholism in Mice." *Clinical Neuroscience Research* 3, no. 4/5 (December 2003): 315–323.

Rhodes, Justin S., and John C. Crabbe. "Gene Expression Induced by Drugs of Abuse." *Current Opinion in Pharmacology* 5, no. 1 (February 2005): 26–33.

Robins, Lee N. "The Sixth Thomas James Okey Memorial Lecture. Vietnam Veterans' Rapid Recovery from Heroin Addiction: A Fluke or Normal Expectation?" *Addiction* (Abingdon, England) 88, no. 8 (August 1993): 1041–1054.

Robins, Lee N., J. E. Helzer, and D. H. Davis. "Narcotic Use in Southeast Asia and Afterward: An Interview Study of 898 Vietnam Returnees." *Archives of General Psychiatry* 32, no. 8 (August 1975): 955–961.

Robins, Lee N., and Sergey Slobodyan. "Post-Vietnam Heroin Use and Injection by Returning U.S. Veterans: Clues to Preventing Injection Today." *Addiction* (Abingdon, England) 98, no. 8 (August 2003): 1053–1060.

Roeber, Jim. "Excessive Drinking, Not Alcoholism, May Lead To Most Alcohol-Related Problems." Eureka Alerts, January 25, 2007. http://www. eurekalert.org/pub_releases/2007-01/ace-edn011807.php.

Roizen, R. "The Great Controlled Drinking Controversy." *Alcohol Sociology Home Page*, 1987. http://www.roizen.com/ron/cont-dri.htm.

Roizen, R. "The American Discovery of Alcoholism, 1933–1939." Doctoral dissertation, sociology, University of California, Berkeley, 1991. http:// www.roizen.com/ron/dissch8.htm.

Roizen, R. "Jellinek's Phantom Doctorate," 1997. http://www.roizen.com/ron/ index.htm.

Roizen, R. "Marty Mann: An Experiment That failed." *Alcohol Sociology Home Page*, 1997. http://www.roizen.com/ron/mann.htm.

Room, Robin. "Sociology and the Disease Concept of Alcoholism." In *Research Advances in Alcohol and Drug Problems*, 747–791. New York and London: Plenum Press, 1983. http://www.robinroom.net/sociolog.pdf.

Room, Robin. "Alcohol." In *Detels: Oxford Textbook of Public Health*. Oxford University Press, 2002. http://www.robinroom.net/alcohol.htm.

Room, Robin. "What If We Found The Magic Bullet? Ideological and Ethical Constraints on Biological Alcohol Research and Its Application." *Robin Room*, 2004. http://www.robinroom.net/magic.doc.

Rush, B., M. Bass, M. Stewart, E. McCracken, M. Labreque, and S. Bondy. "Detecting, Preventing, and Managing Patients' Alcohol Problems." *Canadian Family Physician Médecin de Famille Canadien* 40 (September 1994): 1557–1566.

Schermer, Michael. "Adam's Maxim and Spinoza's Conjecture." *Scientific American*, March 2008.

Schneekloth, T. D., R. M. Morse, L. M. Herrick, V. J. Suman, K. P. Offord, and L. J. Davis. "Point Prevalence of Alcoholism in Hospitalized Patients: Continuing Challenges of Detection, Assessment, and Diagnosis." *Mayo Clinic Proceedings. Mayo Clinic* 76, no. 5 (May 2001): 460–466.

Schuckit, Marc. "Reactions to Alcohol in Sons of Alcoholics and Controls." *Alcoholism: Clinical and Experimental Research* 12, no. 4 (1988): 465–470.

Schuckit, Marc. *Drug and Alcohol Abuse: A Clinical Guide to Diagnosis and Treatment*. New York: Springer, 2000.

Schuckit, Marc. "Vulnerability Factors for Alcoholism." In *Neuropsychopharmacology: The Fifth Generation of Progress*, 1399–1411. American College of Neuropsychopharmacology, 2002. http://www.acnp.org/Docs/G5/ CH98_1399-1412.pdf

Schuckit, Marc, and Tom L. Smith. "The Clinical Course of Alcohol Dependence Associated with a Low Level of Response to Alcohol." *Addiction* 96, no. 6 (June 15, 2001): 903–910.

Schuckit, Marc, Tom L. Smith, J. Kalmijn, J. Tsuang, V. Hesselbrock, and K. Bucholz. "Response to Alcohol in Daughters of Alcoholics: A Pilot Study and a Comparison with Sons of Alcoholics." *Alcohol and Alcoholism* (Oxford, Oxfordshire) 35, no. 3 (June 2000): 242–248.

Schuckit, Marc, Tom L. Smith, Victor Hesselbrock, Kathleen K. Bucholz, Laura Bierut, Howard Edenberg, et al. "Clinical Implications of Tolerance to Alcohol in Nondependent Young Drinkers." *American Journal of Drug and Alcohol Abuse* 34, no. 2 (2008): 133–149.

Schumann, Gunter. "Okey Lecture 2006: Identifying the Neurobiological Mechanisms of Addictive Behaviour." *Addiction* (Abingdon, England) 102, no. 11 (November 2007): 1689–1695.

Senay, Edward C. "Diagnostic Interview and Mental Status Examination." In Joyce H. Lowinson (ed.), *Substance Abuse: A Comprehensive Textbook*, Philadelphia: Lippincott, 1997.

Shavelson, Lonny. *Hooked: Five Addicts Challenge Our Misguided Drug Rehab System.* (New York: New Press, 2001).

Siegel, Daniel J. *The Developing Mind: Toward a Neurobiology of Interpersonal Experience.* New York: Guilford Press, 1999.

Singer, Emily. "Technology Review: More Effective Alcoholism Treatment." *Technology Review Published by MIT*, October 27, 2006. http://www.technologyreview.com/read_article.aspx?id=17669&ch=biotech.

Sober, E., and D. Wilson. *Unto Others: The Evolution and Psychology of Unselfish Behavior.* Cambridge Mass.: Harvard University Press, 1998.

Sontag, Susan. *Illness as Metaphor and AIDS and Its Metaphors.* Old Tappan, N.J.: Macmillan, 2001. http://susansontag.com/SusanSontag/books/illnessAsMetaphorExcerpt.shtml

Sparks, Robert D. "Watch Your Language!" *Alcoholism Treatment Quarterly* 22, no. 2 (June 21, 2004): 97–100.

Stoltenberg, Scott F., and Margit Burmeister. "Recent Progress in Psychiatric Genetics: Some Hope but No Hype." *Human Molecular Genetics,* 9, no. 6 (April 1, 2000): 927–935

Straus, R. "Medical Practice and the Alcoholic." *Annals of the American Academy of Political and Social Science,* 315, no. 1 (1958): 117–124 .

Substance Abuse and Mental Health Administration. "Overarching Principles to Address the Needs of Persons with Co-occurring disorders." Substance Abuse and Mental Health Administration, 2006. http://www.coce.samhsa.gov/cod_resources/PDF/OverarchingPrinciples(OP3).PDF.

"Take Kids Away from Alcoholic Parents." *Daily Record* (United Kingdom), February 19, 2007.

Takeshita, Tatsuya. "Gene-Environmental Interactions in Alcohol-Related Health Problems: Contributions of Molecular Biology to Behavior Modifications." *Nippon Eiseigaku Zasshi. Japanese Journal of Hygiene* 58, no. 2 (May 2003): 254–259.

Tarter, R. E. "What Is Inherited in the Predisposition to Alcoholism: New Model or More Muddle?" *Alcoholism, Clinical and Experimental Research* 24, no. 2 (February 2000): 246–250.

Traynor v. Turnage, 485 U. S. 535 (1988). http://supreme.justia.com/us/485/535/.

Trimpey, Jack. *Rational Recovery: The New Cure for Substance Addiction.* New York: Pocket Books, 1996.

Tu, G. C., and Y. Israel. "Alcohol Consumption by Orientals in North America Is Predicted Largely by a Single Gene." *Behavior Genetics* 25, no. 1 (January 1995): 59–65.

Vaillant, George E. *The Natural History of Alcoholism Revisited.* Cambridge, Mass.: Harvard University Press, 1995.

Vaillant, George E. "Interview: A Doctor Speaks." *AA Grapevine,* May 2001.

Vogel, Friedrich, and Arno G. Motulsky. *Human Genetics: Problems and Approaches.* New York: Springer, 1996.

Volkow, Nora D., Gene-Jack Wang, Henri Begleiter, Bernice Porjesz, Joanna S. Fowler, Frank Telang, et al. "High Levels of Dopamine D2 Receptors in Unaffected Members of Alcoholic Families: Possible Protective Factors." *Archives of General Psychiatry* 63, no. 9 (September 1, 2006): 999–1008

Volpicelli, Joseph, and Maia Szalavitz. *Recovery Options: The Complete Guide.* New York: Wiley, 2000.

W., Bill, and Alcoholics Anonymous. *Alcoholics Anonymous: The Story of How Many Thousands of Men and Women Have Recovered from Alcoholism.* (3rd ed.) New York: Alcoholics Anonymous World Services, 1976

Wall, T. L., S. H. Shea, K. K. Chan, and L. G. Carr. "A Genetic Association with the Development of Alcohol and Other Substance Use Behavior in Asian Americans." *Journal of Abnormal Psychology* 110, no. 1 (February 2001): 173–178.

Wall, Tamara L., Lucinda G. Carr, and Cindy L. Ehlers. "Protective Association of Genetic Variation in Alcohol Dehydrogenase with Alcohol Dependence in Native American Mission Indians." *American Journal of Psychiatry* 160, no. 1 (January 2003): 41–46.

Walters, Glenn D. "The Heritability of Alcohol Abuse and Dependence: A Meta-Analysis of Behavior Genetic Research." *American Journal of Drug and Alcohol Abuse* 28, no. 3 (2002): 557.

Warren, Jazmin I., Judith A. Stein, and Christine E. Grella. "Role of Social Support and Self-Efficacy in Treatment Outcomes Among Clients with Co-occurring Disorders." *Drug and Alcohol Dependence* 89, no. 2/3 (July 10, 2007): 267–274.

Washton, Arnold, and Richard Rawson. "Substance Abuse Treatment under Managed Care: A Provider Perspective." In Marc Galanter and Herbert D. Kleber (eds.), *The American Psychiatric Publishing Textbook of Substance*

Abuse Treatment (3rd ed.) Arlington, Va.: American Psychiatric Publishing, 2004.

"Wave-Particle Duality – Wikipedia, The Free Encyclopedia." http://en.wikipedia.org/wiki/Wave%E2%80%93particle_duality.

White, William. *Slaying the Dragon: The History of Addiction Treatment and Recovery in America.* Chicago: Chestnut Health Systems, 1998.

White, William. "The Rebirth of the Disease Concept of Alcoholism in the 20th Century." *Counselor* 1, no. 2 (2000): 62–66.

White, William. "Addiction as a Disease: Birth of a Concept." *Counselor* 1, no. 1 (2000). http://www.bhrm.org/papers/Counselor1.pdf.

White, William. "Addiction Disease Concept: Advocates and Critics." *Counselor* 2, no. 2 (February 2001). http://www.bhrm.org/papers/Counselor3.pdf.

White, William. "A Disease Concept for the 21st Century." *Counselor* 2, no. 4 (April 2001). http://www.bhrm.org/papers/Counselor4.pdf.

White, William. "It's Time to Stop Kicking People Out of Addiction Treatment." *Counselor* (April 2005). http://www.bhrm.org/papers/AD-PDF.pdf.

Wilbourne, Paula, and Ken Weingardt. "Therapeutic Outcome Research and Dissemination of Empirically Based Treatment for Alcohol Use Disorders." *Translation of Addictions Science into Practice* (2007): 259–276.

Willett, Walter C. "Balancing Life-Style and Genomics Research for Disease Prevention." *Science* 296, no. 5568 (April 26, 2002): 695–698.

Williams, Cecil, and Rebecca Laird. *No Hiding Place: Empowerment and Recovery for Our Troubled Communities.* Harper San Francisco, 1992.

Wilson, Bill. "Why Alcoholics Anonymous Is Anonymous." *AA Grapevine*, January 1955. http://silkworth.net/grapevine/whyaaanonymous.html.

Wilson, Bill. "What Happened to Those Who Left?" 1965. http://www.silkworth.net/aahistory/billw2/gsc1965.html.

Wilson, Bill. "Statement Before the U.S. Senate," July 24, 1969. http://www.hopenetworks.org/bill_w.htm.

Wing, Nell. *Grateful to Have Been There: My 42 Years with Bill and Lois, and the Evolution of Alcoholics Anonymous.* Center City, Minn.: Hazelden, 1998.

Winick, Charles. "Epidemiology." In Joyce H. Lowinson (ed.), *Substance Abuse: A Comprehensive Textbook*, 10–16, Philadelphia: Lippincott, 1997.

Wise, Roy A. "Addiction Becomes a Brain Disease." *Neuron* 26, no. 1 (April 2000): 27–33.

Wise, Roy A. "Addiction." In Hal Pashler and Douglas Medin (eds.), *Stevens' Handbook of Experimental Psychology, Memory and Cognitive Processes*, 801–839, New York: Wiley, 2002.

Woerle, Sandra, Jim Roeber, and Michael G. Landen. "Prevalence of Alcohol Dependence Among Excessive Drinkers in New Mexico." *Alcoholism, Clinical and Experimental Research* 31, no. 2 (February 2007): 293–298.

World Health Organization. *Neuroscience of Psychoactive Substance Use and Dependence.* World Health Organization, 2004.

Wu, Da-Yu. "Decoding Drug Abuse in Noncoding RNA?." *Scientific World Journal* 7, no. S2 (2007): 142–145.

Yokoyama, Akira, and Tai Omori. "Genetic Polymorphisms of Alcohol and Aldehyde Dehydrogenases and Risk for Esophageal and Head and Neck Cancers." *Japanese Journal of Clinical Oncology* 33, no. 3 (March 2003): 111–121.

ABOUT THE AUTHOR

Martin Nicolaus is a founder of LifeRing Secular Recovery and served as its first CEO for fourteen years until his retirement in 2011. He is the author of *Recovery by Choice: Living and Enjoying Life Free of Alcohol and Drugs, A Workbook* and *How Was Your Week: Bringing People Together in Recovery the LifeRing Way*. Until his retirement, he wrote the New Recovery blog (*http://newrecovery.blogspot.com/*). He was and remains a speaker to audiences of recovering people and treatment professionals.

By profession a lawyer, he holds a J.D. from Boalt Hall School of Law (University of California at Berkeley); a master's in sociology from Brandeis University, where he was a Woodrow Wilson Fellow; and a bachelor's in letters from Wesleyan University. In a previous life, he taught sociology, translated Marx's *Grundrisse* from German to English, was an alternative press journalist, and participated in the civil rights and anti-Vietnam war movements. He is married, with two grown-up sons, and lives in Berkeley, California. His personal and professional website is *http://nicolaus.com*.

INDEX

A

Abstinence
> and higher power 135
> and self-efficacy 108
> basic LifeRing philosophy 14
> common element of all LifeRing PRPs 107
> easier 108
> in LifeRing Bylaws 13
> LifeRing "prime directive" 100
> most popular option 107
> no divine assistance needed 108
> safer 107
> same as AA 16
> satisfying 108
> sustainable 108
> v. moderation 108, 134

Addiction
> addictogenic substances 38
> and genetics 219
> balancing act 2, 43
> caused by 65
> definition 38
>> debated 41
> dormancy 142
> etiology 219
> hijacks brain 40
> in animals 4, 64, 68, 110
> many roads into 66
> not a character defect 219
> not a sin 83
> paraphernalia 71

R

Also from LIFERING PRESS:

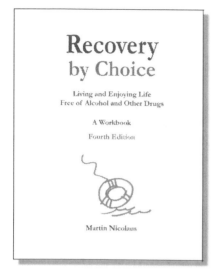

Recovery by Choice is a how-to book for achieving lifelong freedom from alcohol and other drugs. Using this book, you can construct an effective abstinence-based recovery program tailored to your individual reality. You will learn to act with confidence as your own therapist. You will empower your sober self.

Now in its fourth edition, **Recovery by Choice** works by working the 'choice muscles' in your brain. You will master a simple but powerful tool for making the right choice in every life situation. You will make many hundreds of concrete decisions related to your personal recovery, and in the process you will gain in independence and self-efficacy.

Recovery by Choice guides you through the nine key domains where people getting free of alcohol and other drugs may want to make changes:

(1) My Body (2) My Exposure (3) My Activities
(4) My People (5) My Feelings (6) My Life Style
(7) My History (8) My Culture (9) My Treatment

Thousands of people have used **Recovery by Choice** to close the drinking/drugging chapter of their lives. They have made new choices that give them a healthier body, cleaner environment, engaging activities, fulfilling relationships, intelligent emotions, satisfying life style, authentic identity, positive cultural role, and the power to get help and take care of themselves in any situation.

Recovery by Choice is a workbook, with the accent on work. If you roll up your sleeves and get into it, you can change your life forever.

Recovery by Choice: Living and Enjoying Life Free of Alcohol and Other Drugs, A Workbook. By Martin Nicolaus.
ISBN 978-9659429-3-5

www.lifering.com
LIFERING PRESS
1440 Broadway Suite 400
Oakland CA 94612
1-800-811-4142
publisher@lifering.com